Smart Cards

THE GLOBAL INFORMATION PASSPORT

Managing A Successful Smart Card Program

Smart Cards

THE GLOBAL INFORMATION PASSPORT

Managing A Successful Smart Card Program

JACK M. KAPLAN

Stern School of Business—New York University
DATAMARK Software Inc.

INTERNATIONAL THOMSON COMPUTER PRESS

I(T)P ™   An International Thomson Publishing Company

London • Bonn • Boston • Johannesburg • Madrid • Melbourne • Mexico City • New York • Paris
Singapore • Tokyo • Toronto • Albany, NY • Belmont, CA • Cincinnati, OH • Detroit, MI

For more information, contact:

International Thomson Computer Press
20 Park Plaza, Suite 1001
Boston, MA 02116
USA

International Thomson Publishing GmbH
Königswinterer Strasse 418
53227 Bonn
Germany

International Thomson Publishing Europe
Berkshire House 168-173
High Holborn
London WCIV 7AA
England

International Thomson Publishing Asia
221 Henderson Road #05-10
Henderson Building
Singapore 0315

Thomas Nelson Australia
102 Dodds Street
South Melbourne, 3205
Victoria, Australia

International Thomson Publishing Japan
Hirakawacho Kyowa Building, 3F
2-2-1 Hirakawacho
Chiyoda-ku, 102 Tokyo
Japan

Nelson Canada
1120 Birchmount Road
Scarborough, Ontario
Canada M1K 5G4

International Thomson Editores
Campos Eliseos 385, Piso 7
Col. Polanco
11560 Mexico D.F. Mexico

International Thomson Publishing Southern Africa
Bldg. 19, Constantia Park
239 Old Pretoria Road, P.O. Box 2459
Halfway House, 1685 South Africa

International Thomson Publishing France
1, rue st. Georges
75 009 Paris France

1 2 3 4 5 6 7 8 9 10 QEBFF 01 00 99 98 97 96 95
Library of Congress Cataloging-in-Publication Data
(available upon request)

ISBN: 1850 322 120

Publisher/Vice President: Jim DeWolf, ITCP/Boston
Project Director: Chris Grisonich, ITCP/Boston
Marketing Manager: Kathleen Raftery, ITCP/Boston
Art Director: Jo-Ann Campbell • Production: mle design • 562 Milford Point Rd. • Milford, CT 06460 • 203-878-3793

To my wife Eileen for her inspiration, support, and entrepreneurial perspective.

Contents

Preface

Today, the smart card is poised on the threshold of an even greater revolution in the United States and throughout the world. As the flagship of what is referred to as "interactive card technology," the smart card will soon replace the use of cash, credit cards, personal checks, and other payment methods in worldwide consumer transactions.

Its impact can already be felt. Eighty million Germans carry smart cards with their health-insurance data. Health care smart cards can even accommodate medical histories and records of life-sustaining procedures. In France smart cards are revolutionizing the way people bank, pay their bills, and keep financial records. In fact, by the end of 1992, 21 million banking cards have a chip in the card that allows cash withdrawal and payments. Between 1992 and 1994, nationwide smart card programs and pilots for stored value programs were launched in a variety of countries around the world. The first and perhaps most influential of these is the Danmønt program in Denmark. Piloted in late 1992 and now fully operational, this Danish payment system represents more than 200 banks in launching a stored value program throughout the country.

Following on this success, other stored value programs have been launched in South Africa, Australia, Singapore, the U.K., and the United States.

In the early 1990s, however, several developments converged to give new urgency to the smart card movement. First, new and more efficient technologies offered the prospect of much less costly infrastructure development. Second, card fraud was on the rise, and smart cards, with their unique security capabilities, were increasingly seen as a highly effective way to combat it. Third, concern was growing over the limitations of magnetic stripe technology. Finally, interest in new revenue-producing chip card applications by financial institutions began to grow.

In 1994 an estimated 420 million smart cards were sold for use in all industries worldwide. Some believe that by the year 2000 one-half of all payment cards issued in the world will be smart cards.

As most of us know, a smart card business is characterized by rapid innovation. As quickly as one technology begins to unfold, the next one comes along to make it obsolete.

You may ask, why now. Smart cards have been around since the mid-seventies. There are some compelling reasons for you to examine building a smart card business, as well as participate in its development.

- The cost of smart cards is continuing to decrease rapidly.

- Fraud issues are increasing as firms search for more secure technologies.

- Due to technological advances, new companies are entering the business of financial services, telecommunications and information data services.

- Consumers are demanding convenience, security, and specialized services that smart cards can provide.

Starting or managing a smart card business does not require a large staff or extensive capital. For every large smart card company such as AT&T Smart Card Division, there are hundreds of smaller companies that offer their smart card services within a defined market.

To start or manage a smart card business, you need to address five key areas: application and opportunity development; marketing and sales plan analysis; operations; financial options; intellectual properties for protection. This book addresses all of these topics that most of you tend to overlook or do not fully understand. My goal is to provide managers with a better understanding of the process of managing a smart card business and to help them make better decisions in a business so characterized by rapid innovation. In doing so, I point out weaknesses in many of the present applications used today and examples of actual companies that appear to be doing poorly or succeeding within the smart card arena. In a race to develop a global view of smart cards and understanding consumer interests, we have included the special chapter, "World Tour of Smart Card Applications," written by Robin Townend, senior vice president of MasterCard, who has extensive global experience in smart cards.

Audience

This book is intended for executives, managers, and entrepreneurs who are considering expanding their business into smart cards or who wish to start a company using smart card technology. This book also contains valuable guidelines to executives and managers to select a consultant in assisting you in this business and how to choose a vendor to obtain products and services. For those who are initially starting a smart card business, a special section has been added to guide you through the process of setting up the corporation, assistance in obtaining financing, and legal issues to be addressed.

- You will find out what the market is all about and how to succeed if you are considering starting a smart card business.

- You will value the special information for both start-ups and ongoing companies to limit your risks and increase profits.

- You will be able to identify a smart card idea opportunity and what you will need to succeed.

- You will learn about the industry—all the key ingredients for success from a business perspective—making you extremely valuable to your company.

Additionally, you will use the Appendix to locate sources of trade associations and smart card guidelines to follow for success.

Focus

This book is an indispensable guide for building a successful smart card businesses. It is directed at both a marketing and business perspective. If you are an executive or business manager, you will benefit from each chapter.

I have divided this book into three parts. The first three chapters offer a model for understanding smart cards, building an opportunity, and becoming competitive for a successful enterprise. It explores how to build your smart card application and how to analyze an industry and competitors, and how to identify an application for a specific market. Part 2, "Managing for Success," analyzes the smart card skills and resources required for a successful business. Part 3 focuses on starting a smart card business, and the types of financing available for your business venture.

- Start with chapter 1 and read the whole book if you are new to the industry.

- To create an opportunity and to understand the application of marketing, read chapter 2 through 7.

- If you need to write a smart card business plan, read chapter 7 and review the sample business plan.

- To protect your idea and application by filing a patent, copyright, or trademark, you must read chapter 9.

- For preparing a major business opportunity in a global perspective, read chapters 6 and 8.

- If you are planning to start a smart card business, read chapters 11, and 12.

Contacts

Please contact me for comments at my office number, (212) 736-2838, or to be listed on our mailing list, my Internet e-mail address is kaplanj0@stern.nyu.edu If you know of others who can benefit from this book, it can only be to your advantage to share the information contained in this book. The more marketing people, executives, and entrepreneurs who know about this industry, the more likely it will succeed.

Acknowledgments

I relied on the contributions of many people in the preparation of this book. A tremendous amount of assistance was provided by colleagues and practicing executives in the smart card industry. I would like to acknowledge all those who took on active roles in preparing materials and making editorial contributions.

I owe a special thanks to the Center For Entrepreneurial Studies, Stern School of Business, New York University; Vice Dean Avijit Ghosh who provided me with resources to pursue research essential to writing this manuscript; Loretta Poole, and Patricia Miller for their assistance and research assistant Stacy Asher. I especially wish to thank Robin Townend for his chapter on World Tour of Smart Card Applications and for his willingness to share ideas concerning smart card business opportunities. My gratitude is also due to Robert Katz, Esq. Cooper & Dunham, and Douglas Taylor, executive vice president of Datamark, who provided valuable assistance on the "Intellectual Properties" part of the book and my son Andrew Kaplan who made a number of thoughtful editorial suggestions.

A number of reviewers provided invaluable feedback on the early draft and on the final version. Their insights helped me to mold the book and organize my efforts. I am equally grateful from colleagues who helped prepare the cases. My thanks to the following: Mark Landis, Health Information Technologies; Arlen Lessin, Smart Card International; Jean McKenna, Visa International; Jerry Smith, IBM; Andrew Tarbox,

MasterCard International; and Robert Wesley, American Express. Finally, ITCP editor Jim DeWolf, who led the editorial team.

While I can't recognize all of them here, a few others who went beyond the call of duty include:

Kurt Brunner	SOLAIC Smart Cards
Dan Cunningham	Gemplus International
Nancy Elder	MasterCard
William Elliott	AT&T Ventures
Kevin E. Fenning	IBM
Alexis Giakoumis	SOLAIC Smart Cards
Bill Keenan	US West
Michael Mathews	Westgate Capital
Benjamin Miller	PIN News
Gerald Pulver	Amerivend
Joseph Schuler	Stored Value Systems, Division of National City Processing Co.
Dr. Steven Schulman	Faraday
Stephen Seidman	Smart Card Monthly
Michael P. Weekes	IBM

Part 1

Prepare the Opportunity, Manage the Technology

1

Smart Cards: A New Way of Life

There is no security on this earth, only opportunity.

—General Douglas MacArthur

THE REVOLUTION

Throughout this book, I'll be using the phrase "smart card revolution" to describe the tremendous changes occurring in the financial, communications, retail, and health care industries. While this phrase may seem heavy-handed to those unfamiliar with this burgeoning technology, it is my hope that this book will convince you that smart cards are here to stay, and that this business opportunity of the future cannot do without them.

In 1789, the French Revolution was partially inspired by the American Revolution of 1776. Now, in the 1990s, a new French/American revolution is brewing, but this time in reverse order. Originating in France in the 1980s, a "smart card revolution" has quickly spread throughout Europe. This revolution overthrew the formerly impenetrable bastion of "cash purchases" in many areas of the European consumer marketplace. Typical of this has been the extensive use of smart cards for telephone calling.

Today, the smart card is poised on the threshold of an even greater revolution in the United States and throughout the world. As the flagship of what is referred to as "interactive card technology," the smart card will soon replace the use of cash, credit cards, personal checks, and other payment methods in worldwide consumer transactions.

Its impact can already be felt. Eighty million Germans carry smart cards with their health-insurance data. Health-care smart cards can even accommodate medical histories and records of life-sustaining procedures. Standardized software in French dialysis centers now makes it possible for French patients with kidney disease to travel for work or pleasure. In the same country the Carte Bancaire organization coordinates the usage of smart cards, which are revolutionizing the way people bank, pay their bills, and keep financial records, and in doing so has established the world's most advanced and flexible payment system.

In 1994 an estimated 420 million smart cards were sold for use in all industries worldwide. Some believe that by the year 2000 one-half of all payment cards issued in the world will be smart cards.[1]

In France alone, 22 million smart cards are used for bank cards and 100 million are used in pay phones. Before the smart card introduction, France faced the world's highest fraud rate, three times higher than the U.S. In the last few years, the smart card has cut this figure to about half the American average. Experts estimate that the total card fraud in the U.S. reached $500 million in 1994 and $1.7 billion as increasingly sophisticated scamsters come up with a variety of ways to rip off card holders and issuers.[2] In the U.S. one smart card company is allying with Chemical Banking Cooperation to conduct trials of a smart card banking and stored cash debit card program in the New York area

Drivers in Orange, California are using smart card as an electronic toll collection device. A driver inserts card into a personal radio transponder on the car's dashboard and the toll is deducted automatically from the cash deposited on the card. The driver does not have to stop or slow down to pay the toll.

Why then is smart card technology not yet prevalent in the United States? Resistance to the adoption of interactive smart card technology in the United States is rooted in the dominance of existing magnetic stripe cards as well as in companies' failure to recognize the immense potential of the smart card. Evidence is now mounting, however, that impediments to a smart card explosion are rapidly crumbling. In fact, smart cards are rapidly finding acceptance worldwide. At present, some 200 applications are utilized by 39 countries, mostly in the field of telecommunications. Here prepaid telephone smart cards have resulted in more frequent use of pay telephones as the instruments, no longer broken into by thieves, are reliable; numbers can't be pirated as access codes are eliminated; and callers talk longer when freed from anxiety about exact and sufficient change.

The financial services industry is already catching on. Recognizing capabilities like point-of-sale approval or rejection, customer retention via instant incentives and rewards, not to mention the elimination of fraud, bad-debt losses, and data-entry errors, the smart card revolution is beginning to spread worldwide.

Yet in order for the smart card to become a universal product, global standards must be developed and used in the marketplace. Standardization, is the key to economic viability as smart cards exchange and communicate information with computers, networks, and readers.

WHAT ARE SMART CARDS?

In most basic terms, a smart card, or what is now called a "chip card" by industry professionals, is a plastic card which is an intelligent device containing a microprocessor and which is capable of calculations. Chip cards that do not contain a microprocessor are not considered a smart card by industry professionals. The type of chip-card is distinguished by the kind of the integrated circuit (IC) used in the card. One would classify these cards into two categories; the ones that use *memory ICs* and the others that use microcomputer ICs, which are more commonly known as *smart cards*. Also known as an integrated circuit card, ICC, it can be used both within and outside of the payment systems world—as a purchasing device to exchange value or as an information card to access or exchange information. The complexity of the chip varies according to the application (or applications) for which a particular card is designed. Types of chips currently employed range from fairly simple memory devices to sophisticated microprocessors.

Microprocessor cards can be used for applications that require security, multiple applications and also on emerging products such as stored value cards, also known as "electronic purse" or "prepaid" cards. These are cards on which consumers "load" a certain amount of value and then typically use in small transaction environments such as telephones and public transportation.

Soon people will be carrying these very personal computers in their wallets. Smart cards have an enormous range of use. (See chapter 2 for specific details on applications and chapter 6 for global applications.) Some of the uses of smart cards include:

- National health care cards that maintain coverage, deductibles, and even medical history

- Multi-function cards that replace several separate credit cards in your wallet or purse

- Retail debit cards used instead of cash

- The key to retail "customer loyalty" promotional programs that attract and retain customers with on-the-spot rewards

- Toll-coupon cards that enable tolls to be paid as you drive (without stopping) through electronic "toll booths"

- As a substitute for money in telephones, casino slot-machines, or vending machines of all types and kinds

- Unbreakable security-identification cards holding a fingerprint or voice print, precluding use by any other person than the one that the card biologically matches

- Very secure bank cards

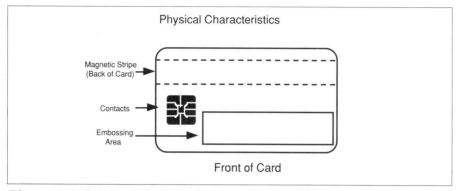

Figure 1-1. Smart card physical characteristics.

The gold rectangle or oval on the left-hand side of the card is the contact point for the card and card terminal. The International Standards Organization (ISO) has set the standard for the position of the contact points. Contact smart cards have contacts and contactless cards have points encased within the card and are read by induction. This visibly distinguishes the two types of card technologies.

There are six contact points, shown in Figure 1-2, which are different in shape depending on the card manufacturer, but which all serve the same function. In the past we used eight contacts with EPROM chips since there was a need for a external 24V power supply. Today, this is not required, so only six contacts are used.

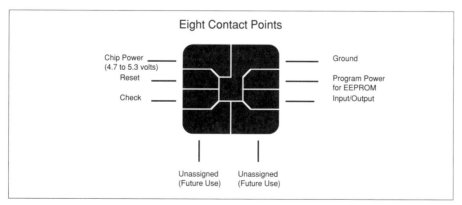

Figure 1-2. Six contact points.

Typically the chip is placed under the six contact points and is connected by wires to the contact points.

The memory chip contains only memory but a microprocessor chip will contain random-access memory (RAM), read-only memory (ROM), and nonvolatile memory.

Types of smart cards range in intelligence from those that use only their memory storage to cards with interactive computer logic and to optical cards that contain your medical records, or X-rays. There are cards that are read by means of contact with a reader device, cards that don't require any contact, and cards that can even be read at a distance by radio beams. Some even have tiny keypads and displays. There's a smart cart for every purpose! But bear in mind, a chip card without a microprocessor is not a smart card since it has no intelligence for calculations and processing.

Most importantly, smart cards are much more secure and have far more powerful, multi-functional capabilities than cards having the existing magnetic stripe or bar codes. Because they can both store and process large amounts of information (unlike magnetic stripe and bar code cards, which hold only limited amounts of information and cannot actually perform any processing), smart cards represent the principal technological weapon in the coming of the "smart card revolution."

ADVANTAGES OF CHIP TECHNOLOGY

One reason why worldwide interest in chip cards is growing is the chip's advantages over today's existing card technology, the magnetic stripe. The "mag" stripe is a one-quarter-inch-wide strip that runs across the back of each card and can carry about 130 bits of proprietary information about the type of card used, the cardholder, and so forth.

Compared to the mag stripe, the chip card is a much more intelligent access and security device. Currently it can store significantly greater amounts of data, typically about 80 times more than a magnetic stripe.

In addition, the chip card is more "self-sufficient." Incorporating internal processing capabilities, the chip can follow its own programs and organize its own memory independent from an on-line payment systems network. This allows a consumer to have free rein to myriad functions and applications, e.g., personal health and identification information, and communication access.[3]

Finally, the chip itself is more durable compared to the vulnerable magnetic stripe. Unlike the mag stripe, the chip is significantly less susceptible to damage and can endure greater use and abuse.

HISTORY

Microprocessor chips were first manufactured in 1966 by Fairchild Instruments and Texas Instruments. The idea of using plastic cards as the carrier for microchips was developed by Jergen Dethloff In 1968. The concept of using a personal identification number to secure information in the chip was the idea of Roland Moreno, founder of Innovatron, who filed his first patent in 1974. Motorola produced the first plastic card with a single chip in 1979 which was demonstrated in Monaco in 1980. Cards with microchips were first field-tested in Lyon, France, in 1982 using chip cards made by the CP8 subsidiary of Bull, one of Europe's leading computer firms. Gie Carte Bancaire, the French association of bank card issuers, was first to adopt microchips on Visa debit cards in Blois, France, in 1984. MasterCard and Visa both began researching chip cards in 1984 when Visa conducted as study with Groupment Carte Bleue, Bank of America, and The Royal Bank of Canada. MasterCard was first to test smart cards in the U.S. in Columbia, Maryland, and Palm Beach, Florida, in 1986 using cards made by Casio of Japan and Bull. Visa tested a "SuperSmart" calculator-type version of a smart card made by Toshiba in Japan in 1988. The first Visa card with microchips in the U.S. appeared on Central Trust of Cincinnati credit cards called Vision Value for a supermarket (APT) test in Iowa in 1989. A Visa International Integrated Circuit Card Users Group was formed in 1990. France was the first country to mandate microchips on all bank cards in 1993, and PIN verification on all 22 million will be completed in 1995.[4] The smart card milestones that have impacted both the technology and application are shown in Figure 1-3.

1970 Dr. Kunitaka Arimura files first basic smart card patent in
      Tokyo (Japan only).

1974 Smart Card invented by Roland Moreno of France.

1979 French Government founds international organization to
      promote smart card technologies.

1980's Smart cards successfully implemented in telephone, banking,
        and other commercial systems throughout Europe and Asia.

1981 First smart card pilot launched in the U.S. for home
      banking application.

1986 Non-contact smart cards introduced for telephone and
      highway toll systems.

1993 Smart Card Forum established by leading U.S. firms
      to accelerate widespread, multi-industry use of smart cards in
      the U.S.

1994 MasterCard International and Visa announce the completion
      of integrated circuit card specification for payment system.

1995 Projected number of stored value smart cards to reach $1.25
      billion.
      EMV Group releases Version 2.0 for IC Card Specifications
      and Version 1.0 for Terminal Specifications.

2000 Estimated volume of smart-card-related transactions projected
      to exceed $20 billion annually.

Figure 1-3. Smart card milestones.

OPPORTUNITY ANALYSIS

"Those firms that seize early advantage of the benefits and profits that smart cards promise will assume dominant positions in the new smart economy," says Kevin Fenning, product manager of Financial and Security Applications at IBM. "We are constantly examining opportunities that fit the IBM strategy. The role of smart cards will have an impact on uses we have not even imagined today. The business applications are still in their infancy but smart cards will play a role in most Americans' personal finances. It will be a new means of tendering cash and will primarily address security issues that are becoming extremely important in the financial industry."[5]

In building a smart card business, the first step is to prepare an opportunity analysis. Why is opportunity analysis so important? Opportunity analysis helps you find out where you are now, where you intend to go, what options are available, and above all what the milestones, goals, and time frames are along the way. With this information you can now formulate a plan and commit to a schedule. In opportunity analysis, there are four distinct phases:

1. Seize the opportunity.

2. Develop the action plan.

3. Determine the technical and business resources required.

4. Manage the attributes that set the business apart.

While these phases proceed progressively, they often overlap and none is dealt with in isolation.

Seize the Opportunity

To evaluate potential opportunities, you will want to consider how this valuable and capable technology can impact the following features and functions.

- A wide range of payment functions that now rely on checks and cash.

- Improved performance in current payment card environments.

- Non-financial applications, such as personal ID.

- Increased security for both cardholder and merchant.

- Reduced telecommunications costs because it allows chip card transactions to be authorized off-line, or without the need to communicate on-line with a cardholder's bank to authorize a transaction.

- New value-added features for the cardholder, such as multiple accounts and/or the ability to keep a running tally of expenditures on the card.

- Differentiating features for service providers, such as the ability to accommodate loyalty programs or other sales incentive programs.

Questions you should ask while keeping in mind your own personal and company experiences are as follows:

Opportunity Review

- Why do you believe there is an opportunity?

- What are the ideal conditions for this opportunity to occur?

- How is the rapidly changing smart card technology going to affect your idea?

- How long in time is your window of opportunity?

Customer Need

- Describe the unique features of the product or service.

- Will customers feel the need to buy this service?

- How will you exploit this need?

- Who are your potential competitors?

Follow-up

- Describe and analyze your competition.

- Are there other opportunities that could arise from this idea?

- What are the profit margins?

- What are the investments required?

- How will the management team you plan to use strengthen the opportunity?

For a summary of factors that create opportunity, see Figure 1-4.

Discovering a smart card opportunity can happen in many ways but it usually occurs in a specific format, according to *Inc.* magazine. In a recent survey of 500 growing companies, 47 percent of the business application opportunities came from the present work activity environment, 15 percent came from showing improvement on present activities, and 11 percent came from seeing opportunities in an unfitted niche. The balance came from planning, brainstorming, and events that led to an opportunity.[6]

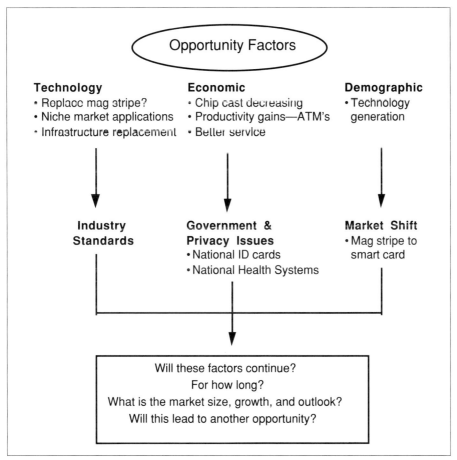

Figure 1-4. What factors create opportunity?

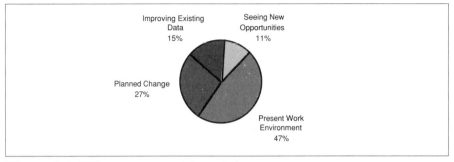

Figure 1-5. Where opportunities originate.

Examples of Smart Card Opportunities

Figure 1-6 shows just a few examples of new and improved applications both within and outside of the payments world.

PRE-PAYMENT	NON-PREPAYMENT
Pay phone card	Electronic Cash
Public transport season ticket	Electronic Check
Pay TV	Road tolls
Food vending	Pension payment
Electricity/gas payments	Trading of stocks and shares
Road tolls	Social Security and welfare payments

Some of the financial applications in which the IC cards are used

PROTECTION OF ITEMS	PHYSICAL ACCESS
Computer terminals	Secure sites
Software	Sports stadium
Corporate cash management	Hotel facilities
Sealed orders	Holiday complexes
Weapons firing authority	Car parks
Control desks	Sports centres

A short list of applications where IC cards are used for protection and physical access

ITEM DATA STORAGE	PERSONAL DATA STORAGE
Car maintenance records	Military records
Car fleet record	Student records
Telephone call logger	General medical records
Parameter loading card	Driving license
Equipment maintenance	Electronic note pad
Inspection recording	Maternity card

A short list of applications where IC cards are used for item and personal data storage

Figure 1-6. Examples of opportunities.

Payment Applications

With chip-driven cards, consumers will soon be able to load "electronic cash" on a card and use it to perform any number of the seemingly limitless small-value payment transactions, avoiding the need to carry exact change or rely upon change machines. They will be used, for example, at such places as laundromats, vending machines, parking meters, bridge and road toll crossings and fast food establishments. Service providers, too, will benefit from reduced operating costs and increased business.

With chip cards, cost-conscious shoppers may soon receive discounts and/or bonus points by using their cards frequently at their favorite stores. Service providers, too, will benefit by being able to access a customer's shopping preferences and then letting the customer know of special offers that might be of particular interest.

With chip cards, business travelers or vacationers may someday eliminate many of the nuisances and annoyances they have come to expect as part of traveling. These cards can help people avoid long lines for ticketing and seat assignment. They may even be used to unlock rental cars and hotel rooms without first having to check in at rental car agencies or hotel desks.

With chip cards, it will also be faster, easier, and more secure for consumers to perform many of the kinds of transactions they perform today. With the aid of "card-compatible" PCs and interactive TVs, for example, chip cards will make tasks such as home banking and home shopping many times more attractive.

Non-Payment Applications

With chip cards, people will be able to receive additional value in many arenas outside the financial payments world. These cards may someday be used, for example, to store important health care information, function as a personal ID card with onboard passport to reduce the wait in customs lines at airports, store driver's licenses and other information, access a library or a health club; control a company's inventory, or even— as has been suggested—be a person's key to the information superhighway.

Successful companies find and exploit markets that others have missed or explore new markets that recent technologies have created. Many other companies, however, tend to unconsciously hinder this force. They adapt a set of assumptions and traditional practices that leave their blinders on. Most believe that they are too big to pursue an ill-defined market for smart card technology. That's why so few large companies have spotted an opportunity for this technology.

Another problem that companies face is a climate that punishes failure rather than encouraging calculated risk taking. Even so, some large companies are beginning to make a difference. IBM has remade itself into becoming more entrepreneurial and its culture is beginning to create smart card innovation. "It's my job to find financial smart card opportunities," says Kevin Fenning of IBM. "I am constantly meeting with companies and discussing the future direction of smart cards and how we can be a player in the marketplace."[7]

Is the Opportunity Viable?

An opportunity is deemed viable when the advantages outweigh the present activity and can show a profit between benefits and costs. This is obviously important to demonstrate, for only then can the opportunity be conceived as a successful business operation.

Frank Gruppuso, for instance, senior vice president of technology for Smart Card International (see chapter 4, "Successes and Failures: Smart Card International"), a start-up smart card company formed in 1984, was responsible for developing a smart card transaction terminal for a health care information and payment systems market. The management team concluded that they could build and manufacture a transaction terminal that could use both mag stripe and smart cards for electronic processing of medical insurance claims by major health carriers. The company was successful in securing a contract in June, 1991, from Princeton-based Health Information Technologies for the production and delivery of more than 20,000 terminals. The transaction terminals to be delivered under this agreement were to be installed in doctors' offices and medical testing laboratories to capture medical insurance claims by the health carriers.

Figure 1-7. Evaluating the opportunity.

What at first seemed like a great opportunity for Smart Card International turned out to be riddled by flaws that may have been corrected had the company adequately assessed its opportunity analysis. Factors and clues that determined the eventual outcome of the situation are as follows:

- **Technology and Timing**

    The health care markets were beginning to use PCs as a vehicle for processing and claim information. Why would they use a terminal?

- **Marketability and Price**

    The price of PCs was dropping dramatically and the price differential between the PC and the terminal was minimal. Since PCs could be used for far more purposes than the terminal, the PC was the clear winner.

- **Demographic Changes**

  Medical and physician's organizations were adjusting to PCs and did not want two types of hardware and two different systems to process data.

- **Resources Required**

  Most offices were cutting back on personnel and lacked the time to be trained on a new terminal.

Analyzing the information about the marketability of this new business was vital in judging its potential success. Three major areas for this analysis include:

1. Carefully investigating market potential and identifying customers

2. Analyzing the extent to which the company might exploit this potential market

3. Using market analysis to determine the risks involved with this opportunity

Examples are:

- General economic trends—indicators such as the use of PC's in health care and doctor's offices

- Pricing data—prices for the same complementary or substitute products

Develop the Plan for your Smart Card Operation

Once an opportunity is identified, decisions must be made regarding performance and staffing. How will a given business be realized and by whom? Operations may have to be reconfigured to extend assets. Of course, any agenda must be expansive enough to assure long-range profitability.

One of the difficult chores you face is the preparation and writing of a business plan. Whatever difficulties the preparation of a business plan may present, a plan is an absolute necessity for any business. The exercise of writing a business plan will force you to examine each element of the prospective venture closely. It is anticipated that many flaws will be identified and addressed in this process.

In some cases where problems cannot be answered and where there are serious issues that cannot be properly addressed, it can offer you the chance to reexamine the smart card business venture before resources of time and money have been committed.

The business plan is a written document usually about 30 to 40 pages that describes all of the key elements and tasks for a business opportunity venture. Some refer to it as a game plan or road map that guides you through the process of "where are you now, where are you going, and how you are going to get there."[8]

The plan is valuable to you because it serves three main purposes:

- Determines the viability of the business and application in selected markets

- Provides guidance to you in planning and organizing your activities and goals

- Serves as a vehicle to obtain financing and personnel for the business

Though a good business plan is essential to opportunity development, resource determination/acquisition, and effective management, newcomers to the field rarely prepare one and lack the skills to do so. Business-plan preparation is detailed later in this book (see chapter 8), but the basic components deserve mention here. They include market segment characteristics and size; marketing, strategy, sales planning, organizational, and financial plans; and production and fiscal requirements

Preparing the Technical Resources Needed

To determine the specific industry in which your smart card business will operate, prepare a list of industry leaders who would consider using your services. Join professional organizations, attend their meetings, and subscribe to their newsletters. Read available studies or publications.

Study the annual reports of publicly held firms, visit trade associations to learn about technologies and trends, and by all means consider hiring a smart card consultant to identify market niches and help you to avoid costly mistakes.

Case analysis is somewhat analogous to role playing as you follow a real or fictional character along the path. Niche focus helps you brainstorm ideas within a specific industrial framework. And a needs-aimed search, possibly accomplished with experts in selected fields, uncovers problems best recognized and addressed in advance. All are part of opportunity analysis and the information search which must precede the business plan itself.

As we tend to merge fresh knowledge with stale preconceptions, opportunity-analysis methodology allows us to travel an uphill route that actually brings us closer to reality. Strewn with obstacles and limitations, it originates at supposition, winds through exploration (a vertiginous plateau where beliefs are qualified and refined while goals are modified), and ultimately attains its highest elevation: informed understanding. Only when we arrive at this summit, can we make intelligent decisions. Our grandest dreams *must* be grounded in reality if they are to be realized.

If the new business involves smart cards, then technical skills specific to the competitive implementation and marketing of a smart-card opportunity must be yours. At some point, your organization will have to match or outperform others offering the same product or services. Weak start-up companies are often vanquished when better-prepared and more highly skilled contenders enter the fray. This is exactly what happened to Smart Card International, who tried to manufacture smart cards and terminals. Weak technical capacity, failure to focus on core business opportunities, and inadequate assets were ultimately responsible for its demise only four years later.

To prepare the resources needed for your business opportunity you will need to attract the following capabilities and answer these questions:

- **Business and Financial Support**

Can the business operate in a cost-effective manner? Who will the management team be?

- **Personal Contacts and Networking**

  Who will introduce you and get you into the right companies? How should your network be set up?

- **Financing Requirements**

  Given that your enterprise will require capital to sustain the company over a one-to-two-year period, does the company have enough resources to make it?

Manage the Attributes that Set the Business Apart

Once the business plan is executed, operational problems common to any growing enterprise must be handled. To accomplish this, a management structure and style must be instituted and principal variables for success determined.

I can't overemphasize that the most successful businesses invest heavily in their people, the business processes and the information technology that empowers them to move ahead. Here are key attributes that will set your business apart from others in the smart card business.

Spend the Time on Planning

The most successful companies know where they fit in the market and where they want to be. Planning should be used to assist your organization in the designing, testing, and marketing about your business opportunity. The focus should be on:

- Testing the business concept and determine the go-ahead or rejection of the opportunity

- Determining the improvement needed for the product or service to become more effective

- Anticipating what time frame is needed

- Defining problems and anticipating any barriers

- Aligning strategic partners for the process

- Assisting in preparation of pricing for the strategies, and anticipating future direction

Be Competitive at All Times

It used to be that most small companies operated in unchallenged territories and had special sales channels in which their projects were usually sold. Today, on the other hand, all companies—both large and small—are playing in the same markets. Delivering smart card solutions, therefore, is one way of staying competitive.

Resource Control

Corporate refugees are applying their business skills and experiences to start-ups that are creating small companies with better links to major companies, access to partners and capital, and knowledge about selected markets. Hiring an executive to market and grow your business may require you to concede some control, but the results may be worth the emotional and financial discomfort.

BARRIERS TO SMART CARD SUCCESS

Having a favorable window of opportunity is attractive, such as exclusive rights to a market or with a leading distributor. If a company cannot keep others out or it faces existing entry barriers, it is unattractive. An easily overlooked issue is a company's capacity to gain distribution of its smart card services. SmartCard International assembled all the licensing rights to sell smart cards in the United States, but was unable to secure sufficient distribution for its products. Even though the company had both United States and worldwide licensing rights to sell smart cards, it had no strategic alliances with other companies to assist in the selling and distribution of its products.

A company should be aware of several entry barriers when beginning its marketing assessment of the smart card business opportunity.

"Technology Looking for a Solution"

Upon presenting the smart card to potential clients, management are never slow to describe the many wonderful possibilities that come with this technology but often ask "isn't this a case of technology looking for a solution?" Management must recognize there is something special about a chip in a card and at once acknowledge its vast potential, but all too often the Management focuses on the card's technology and not on the solutions it offers.

Obstacles Remain but Coming Down

When smart cards first came on the scene, the technology faced many barriers before being accepted by major companies. While obstacles remain, however, the outlook is far brighter. Carmody and Bloom Inc., for example, a New Jersey-based consulting firm, shows that senior financial industry executives' perceptions of smart card obstacles are changing. In 1987, 60 percent cited smart card costs as the most significant barrier. Today this is no longer the case, as smart cards now only cost from $2 and $8 (with volume discounts the cost can be as low as $1), rather than the initial cost of $10–$12. For those cards intended for prepaid applications where limited memory is required, costs dip below $2. In addition, terminal-reader costs are coming down in price. Initially priced at $200, these readers now cost the same as mag stripe readers—in the $100 range.

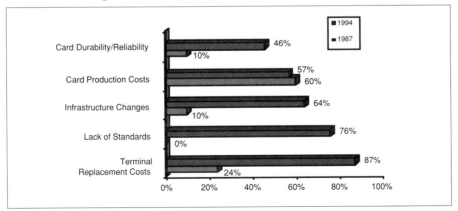

Figure 1-8. Barriers to smart card entry.

No one knows how much the industry will spend to make the smart card transmission possible. MasterCard estimates that there are 4500 terminals using magnetic stripe systems today with a customer base of 300 million.

The major payment card associations, such as Visa, MasterCard and Europay International, now are publishing specifications for smart card payment systems. The final specifications will be delivered by 1996 and will play a vital role in reducing the entry barriers that exist because of the lack of standards and also terminal replacement costs.

PASSPORT TO THE INFORMATION HIGHWAY

The key topic that dominates the news is the celebrated "information highway." Hardly a week or a day goes by without the media announcing that a better future lies just down the road.

Rarely has the emergence of a new technology been so closely linked to a profound shift in society. Today is the dawn of the information civilization, and the way we work, communicate, and, ultimately, think will be forever changed by this new environment.

Smart cards represent an incredible transformation in our industries. Not only the telecommunications industry, but also banking, retailing, and television will see radical changes in the way they do business.

Today, television is considered a form of entertainment or communication, and those industries see it as a delivery technology. Tomorrow, with TV-set top boxes capable of interactive communications and which use a smart card as a token or a key, a vast new set of options emerge. A personalized banking card provides the capability to load cash, make a credit purchase, apply for a loan, review transactions, or simply check an account balance. Where one of multiple bank cards today would be required, all accounts desired will reside on a single smart card for selection at the time and point of contact. A health card will provide emergency medical information, medical history, current medication authorized, diagnosis, and insurance information that can be provided in the event of an emergency or simply when making a scheduled appointment. Even the latest diagnostic information can be recorded by your personal automobile smart card key. Finally, your smart card provides the identification and authentication to place your vote or renew your drivers license, passport, electronic newspaper and magazines, and on and on. The TV, once the domain of entertainment and communications, becomes only one example of the access points through which your miniature personalized smart cards deliver the services you want, when and where you want them.

Whether using a computer terminal, automatic teller machine, kiosk, telephone, point-of-sale terminal, or other such data-capture device, the smart card becomes the common key to the information highway. While we may think in terms of today's application uses, most of the future uses of smart cards are likely not even thought of yet.

FREQUENTLY ASKED QUESTIONS ABOUT SMART CARDS

What Is a Smart Card?

A smart card is defined as being an intelligent device that contain a microprocessor chip to store and/or process information. Unlike magnetic stripe cards, a single smart card can be used for multiple applications. In addition, smart cards are more secure, and contain three kinds of memories (ROM, RAM, and EEPROM).

Where Are Smart Cards Used?

Smart cards have predominantly been used in the public phone systems around the world. More than 50 countries currently use smart cards in the form of a prepaid phone card rather than a credit card. Smart cards are now expanding into other areas such as health care, banking and transportation. In 1994, Germany issued smart cards as its national health card to all of its citizens.

How Many Smart Cards Are in Use and in What Major Areas?

The use of smart cards is expected to skyrocket over the next few years.

Table 1-1. Smart Card Market Forecast

Segment	1994 Million Units	2000 Million Units	Average Yearly Growth
Phone card	310	1400	29%
GSM	9	*50	33%
Health	62	*400	36%
Bank & Loyalty	20	*500	71%
Identity	1	*400	171%
Transportation	1	*200	142%
Pay TV	10	*100	47%
Gaming	1	500	182%
Metering	2	50	71%
Access Control/Vending	4	200	92%
Total	420	3800	44%

Source: Gem Plus, May, 1995   * = Microprocessor Cards

Why Don't We See Smart Card Applications in the U.S.?

There are a number of significant smart card pilot projects under way in the banking, phone, and health care industries. Leaders from the financial smart card and payment industries are planning to form SmartCash a company that will develop and manage a stored value card business. SmartCash will speed the implementation of smart card technology and the stored value application throughout the United States. Initial roll-out will occur next year in multiple locations. The U.S. has been slow to adopt the smart card, since business has already invested heavily in the magnetic stripe technology used for credit cards. In Europe, the French government backed the use of smart cards and made a technology leap over mag stripe cards in the 1980s. Prior to this, the U.S. phone system had always been superior, allowing for a well-dispersed, inexpensive, yet effective verification of credit card transactions. But this is all changing as the U.S. is rushing to introduce smart card technology.

How Quickly Will Smart Cards be Introduced in Larger Scale in the U.S.?

The best estimate is that smart cards will start to be introduced in large scale during 1996. Major institutions like Visa and MasterCard have already announced they will be converting to smart cards and their smart card specifications are now being accepted. Credit card fraud currently exceeds $500 million a year in the U.S. and $1.7 billion worldwide and is expected to help drive the change to the more secure smart card. Fraud alone, however, will not build a case for smart card acceptance, which will grow only through the use of multiple applications.

What Is the Smart Card Forum?

The Smart Card Forum was formed in 1993. Its purpose is "to accelerate the widespread acceptance of multiple application smart card technology by bringing together in an open forum, leading users and technologists from both the public and private sectors." One of the main goals of the forum is to help set specification standards for smart cards.

Where Will Smart Card Usage be in Five Years?

The future of smart cards lies in the ability for a single card to be used for multi-applications. One card will replace several or many "credit cards" or "frequency cards" now carried in one's wallet or purse. The functionality of combining cards plus their added security features will drive consumer demand and dictate a conversion to smart cards.

END NOTES

1. "Chipcards Information." March, 1995. Visa International. pp. 2–4.

2. "Bank Cards." December, 1994. Nilson Report Issue. p. 3.

3. "More Power to the Cardholder." March, 1995. Visa International. pp. 3–6.

4. "Bank Cards." December, 1994. Nilson Report Issue. p. 5.

5. Interview with Kevin Fenning, IBM. June 10, 1995. NYC.

6. "CEO Survival Kit." March, 1994. Inc. Magazine. p. 50.

7. Interview with Kevin Fenning, IBM. June 10, 1995. NYC.

8. Entrepreneurial Strategy. Donal Kuratho. Dryden Press: 1994. pp. 53–55.

2

How Business Can Capitalize on Smart Card Technology

Smart cards will have uses we have not even imagined today.

—Author

INTRODUCTION

Smart card technology has the potential to not only change the future of traditional consumer service, but to introduce the development of new applications and opportunities. From financial services to portable information databases, smart card technology can be utilized to improve existing services and to capitalize on significant new business opportunities. Therefore, for a business considering the implementation of a smart card application, it is extremely important to identify these new business opportunities and develop effective strategies to target profitable market segments.

EXPANDING SMART CARD APPLICATIONS

You may ask, "Why now?" Smart cards have been around since the mid-1970s. There are some compelling reasons to look again at smart card technology today, as well as to participate in development of the infrastructure in the U.S.

Several factors are generally recognized as being responsible for this relatively slow progress.

First, many likely participants, especially in the U.S., have believed that the cost of making the transition to chip cards would be prohibitive, at least for the near-term. One factor has been the cost of individual cards, ranging from $2 to $8 each depending on the kind of chip in it, as opposed to the cost of magnetic stripe cards, typically about 25¢ to 50¢ apiece. Another factor has been the cost of transitioning to new merchant terminals, which can vary in price from $500 to $2000 apiece.

Second, many have not felt sufficiently compelled to change. For many years, the magnetic stripe has served the payments world quite well.

Third, widely accepted global chip card specifications have not been put in place. This has made it impossible to develop the "open" global systems needed to support the use of cards in a wide variety of service provider environments all around the world.

Fourth, there has been a lack of value-added applications to support such a commitment. While there has been talk of such applications for many years, they have been slow to materialize.

There are today close to 200 smart card applications in use scattered across 33 countries.[1] Figure 2-1 displays some of the most common applications.

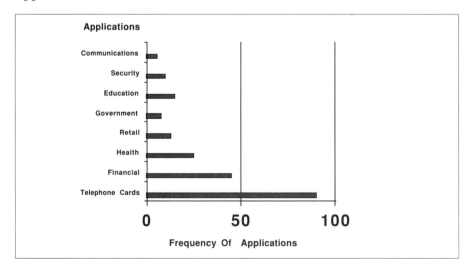

Figure 2-1. Current smart card applications.

GLOBAL APPLICATIONS IN SMART CARD INDUSTRY—AN OVERVIEW—FOR MORE DETAILS SEE CHAPTER 6

Education

Á la Carte Menu in French School

An á la carte food service system has been introduced for the first time in a public school in Metz, France. The new René Cassin High School is offering students, teachers and administrative staff the choice for starters, main courses, desserts, and beverages by paying with the FUNCHIP Education Smart Card. Each card contains the name, account number, access profile, and category of its holder. Users can check the balance on the electronic purse at the entrance to the restaurant and use the card to pay for the meal. The FUNCHIP Card cuts out the handling of cash within the school and is used to control access to the car parking area and the bike shed and to pay for photocopies.[2]

Government

A French smart card manufacturer has signed a letter of intent with China's Golden Card Project. China Hua Xu Golden Card Company, a state-owned entity under the country's Ministry of Electronics Industry, has teamed up with a smart card company to explore the development of smart cards in China. The Golden Card project is a government-backed initiative designed to build up the country's fledgling payments infrastructure. The project, which is estimated to cost $5.8 billion, aims to issue 200 million payment cards to China's 1.2 billion people by the turn of the century.[3]

Spain's Social Security Project

Spain's Ministry of Labor and Social Security has initiated the Spanish Social Security Card (Tarjeta de la Seguridad Social Espanola—TASS) project to substitute for the previous Social Security membership document. Initially, 300,000 Social Security cards will be issued for an EBT pilot project in the province of Cordoba. Within five years it is expected that cards will have been issued to the entire Spanish population of 40 million citizens. More than 3000 self-service information terminals will be installed along with more than 20,000 personal computers for health management information in all health centers. The card will store information about a citizen's work history, pension, general practitioner, and clinical history.[4]

Retailing

AMICA Loyalty Card in Italy

Philips of France and Promoptima of Italy jointly have developed a new smart card program dubbed AMICA. The loyalty program rewards customers with points according to the amount they spend on purchases and exchanging the points in various gift programs. Each retailer subscribing to the program receives a smart card reader with a built-in AMICA application program and smart cards for customers. Promoptima is offering retailers dedicated terminals, customer and retailer cards, gifts distribution, and full management of the system, including statistical data and mailing facilities. Retailer benefits are seen as increasing customer loyalty, building a customer database, and obtaining more information on customer's purchasing habits.[5]

Stored Valued Smart Card System Introduced to the National Footall League

The Jacksonville Jaguars is one of the National Football League's newest teams, and they are playing their games in a new, state-of-the-art stadium in Jacksonville, Florida. Beginning with their inaugural season in 1995, they have implemented stored value card payment using smart cards. Virtually all purchases at the stadium may be made using the cards. Fans attending the game can purchase cards in denominations of $20, $50 and $100 for use at any of the food and beverage concessions.

At each point of sale, the customer has the option of using the smart card for payment via a special terminal. The amount of the purchase is displayed in the terminal, for approval by the customer. The customer inserts the stored value card into the terminal which displays the balance on the card, deducts the purchase amount, and then shows the card's balance.

The customers benefit from fast transactions (less than 5 seconds) and the convenience of not carrying cash. Cards are sold by mail for season ticket holders and at the stadium and at First Union Bank branch offices. The stadium concessionaires benefit from better customer service with faster through-put and lower handling and theft-related costs.

The system was implemented by First Union Bank, Schlumberger, and Diebold, using Schlumberger cards and terminals.[6]

Travel and Entertainment

Ticketless Fly Delta Shuttle

Ticketless travel is under test on hourly flights between New York and Washington, D.C., and between New York and Boston. In the second phase of trials using AT&T Smart Cards, frequent customers of Delta Air Lines have been issued personalized Delta Shuttle Cards. Cardholders can go directly to the Delta shuttle gate—a previous reservation is not necessary—to insert the card into a reader. Within five seconds, a reservation is created, the customer's Frequent Flyer account is credited, his credit card is charged, and a receipt is issued. Delta reports a high level of satisfaction among passengers for ticketless travel. Delta says it will expand the scheme to include approximately 5000 Shuttle customers, including corporate customers, within the next few months.[7]

Of these, the majority of smart card applications are in Europe, with the number of telephone cards ranked first and the number of financial services growing at a rapid rate. Why are smart cards (i.e., telephone cards) accepted more readily in Europe than the U.S. and why have they been predominant outside the U.S. for the last decade. Possible reasons are:

- Foreign governments' early involvement in the underwriting and installation of such projects

- The monopolistic character of most telephone companies in foreign counties, which tend to be government-controlled

- The need for a common payment mechanism among neighboring countries

- The immediate need to quickly replace an outdated phone system

- The lack of a magnetic stripe card infrastructure in most foreign countries

The application of smart cards to solve these problems could be characterized by the "first wave" of smart cards.

The "second wave" is being driven today by consumer demands, lower costs of smart cards, and privacy and security needs (particularly in health care). In other words, government was the initial and necessary driving force behind smart cards, but the second wave is beginning to manifest itself through the broader use of this technology by private industry, which will ultimately dictate its direction.

THE NEXT FRONTIER IN PAYMENT PROCESSING

Since its beginnings, the payment systems industry has focused on developing new electronic-based products to replace older—and usually more inefficient—ways of conducting financial transactions. The credit card emerged, for example, as a more attractive alternative to the small loan. More recently, the deposit access card (also known as the debit or check card) has gained popularity as a more convenient, secure, and cost-effective option to the traditional paper check and cash.

But, while credit and deposit access cards have taken hold in many markets, another enormous worldwide arena for payments of $10 or less—an approximately $1.8 trillion market in the U.S.—remains virtually untapped.

In March, 1994, both Visa and MasterCard announced that it would address this need with a smart card product, the *stored value card*. Also known as the "electronic purse," it offers important new benefits to consumers and merchants. With a stored value card, for example, consumers won't have to search their pockets or purses for the right change when they purchase a candy bar from a vending machine, buy a newspaper from the stand, or pay for parking. Merchants will also be able to reduce theft losses at unintended point-of-sale locations, as well as increase sales dramatically through incremental business.

WHAT IS A STORED VALUE CARD?

A stored value card is a plastic payment card that stores a certain amount of prepaid monetary value in an embedded microchip. Targeted to low-value consumer transactions (usually the equivalent from $2 to $10), it is intended to displace coins and currency. Transactions are fast the cardholder inserts the card, selects and receives the desired goods and services, and the transaction is complete. There is no PIN (personal identification number), no signature, and no identification presented by the cardholder. There is no authorization associated with the transaction, a receipt is not required, and the issuer doesn't provide a periodic statement.[8]

Figure 2-2. Portable credit card terminal using smart card.

A stored value card may be either disposable or reloadable. If the card is disposable, it may be disregarded once the value has been spent. If the card is reloadable, the consumer can replenish the value on the card as often as he or she likes. It can be done at modified ATMs, special terminals, home or office telephones, or cash-to-card terminals. (See chapter 6 for specific trial applications.)

INNOVATIVE SMART CARD APPLICATIONS

Alex Giakoumis, vice president of strategic marketing for SOLAIC, a French smart card manufacturer, believes that "In the U.S., like in some other parts of the world, the smart card technology is not well known. The people who make decisions really don't know enough and they are not informed about the potentials of this technology." Decision makers should begin to do a few things so that they will accept it and consider smart cards.

- Join Smart Card Forum, participate at sessions, and ask a lot of questions.

- Attend Smart Card conferences such as the Card Tech EAST and WEST held in Washington, D.C., and San Francisco; and the International Card Technology shows as the one in London, U.K., and Paris, France in October.

- Possibly hire a consultant to help you understand the smart card issues.

The education market offers the best world of smart card because of its multi-application features. SOLAIC has developed over seventy applications in forty different countries. We feel the education market offers the best world of smart card because its multi-application features. At the University of Lille, Bordeaux, Toulouse, Compiegne in France and the University of Barcelone in Spain, over 100,000 students use a card for access control to buildings, libraries and laboratories with security; payment, as cash purse for the cafeteria, bookstore, photocopy and vending machines; and as data storage, for minimum medical data and the university student records.[9]

US WEST is a Fortune 40 regional Bell Telephone Operating Company (RBOC) servicing 10 million households and 1 million businesses in 14 western and mid-western states. Their primary market consists of over 25 million customers. The company's scope has expanded to be a leader in selected markets worldwide in information, communications, and entertainment. US WEST is a major stakeholder in Time Warner Entertainment and owns several cable properties. US WEST is currently the nation's largest investor in building a truly interactive highway. At the center of its strategy is a commitment to meet consumer needs one customer at a time. Smart card technology is being tested and evaluated as the enabling device or platform by which to deliver multipurpose applications. US WEST is issuing chip cards and installing 16,000 phones with smart card readers in five cities. The program is designed for local calls from public telephones. It features disposable cards, and is geared to reduce the need for repairs and collection of coins.

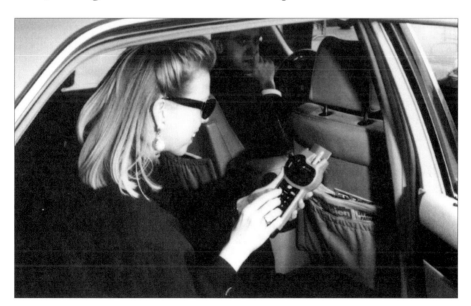

Figure 2-3. Smart card taxi portable payment system.

William F. Keenan, Managing Director, US WEST Card Services, said, "Contact and proximity smart cards may be the simple solution for better wallet or purse management—it addresses needs for control, choices, and security."[10] Keenan is a member of the board of directors of the Smart Card Forum and chairs the US WEST Smart Card Council. US WEST is currently market-testing several smart card applications, mostly focusing on electronic purse or prepaid cards.

Accordingly, many other applications, in industries as diverse as food service, retail, and travel, are beginning to make inroads. These newer applications offer excellent illustrations of companies looking to a new technology to provide additional benefits for their customers as well as efficiencies for the companies themselves.

Loyalty Programs

David Falk, director of Business Development for the author's company, Datamark Software, Inc., New York, a developer of smart card systems says: We selected food service, retail, and oil and gas as the industries we would target first for smart card system opportunities. These industries are similar in that they both include large national and multi-national chains which have the resources to implement a smart card program today. In addition, perhaps most importantly, these chains are what I would call closed environments in which they control all the points of entry by their customers and can dictate the technology of choice to be used.

Beyond these factors, there are significant marketing and financial justifications for smart cards in these industries. Many retail and restaurant chains today are looking for new and potent ways to reach their customers with targeted and even individualized marketing messages. One of our major clients, for example, is utilizing smart cards as part of an overall marketing strategy of building loyalty and increasing its retention rate of existing customers. The cards have enabled them to introduce a sophisticated yet highly cost-efficient electronic frequent shoppers program across a national chain. Ultimately, they view these cards as a means to build a reliable database of their customers' demographics, purchase habits and transaction history. In addition, they provide this retailer a platform upon which to develop other innovative marketing programs, some even involving other retailers and vendors, and the infra-structure necessary to accept the anticipated onslaught of smart cards into the marketplace from financial services companies.[11]

As Mr. Falk suggested, loyalty programs are becoming a growth industry for smart cards. Many companies already using smart cards for financial application are realizing the advantage of combining it with a marketing driven frequency or loyalty program. They are able to do this because of the unique properties of smart cards, most prominently the ability of this technology to handle multiple applications on one card. Figure 2-4 illustrates the advantage of retaining your existing customers through a loyalty program.

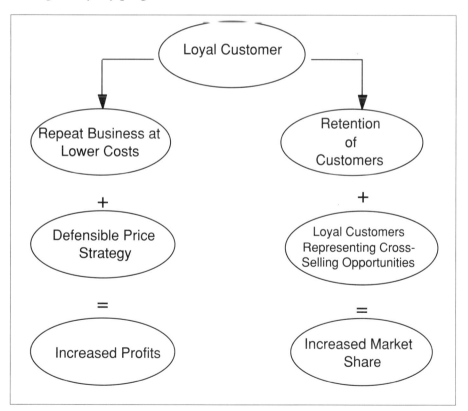

Figure 2-4. Customer loyalty leads to profitability and growth.

Case Study

Gerald Pulver, president of Amerivend Corporation, is using smart cards to replace coin devices on commercial laundry equipment. He says: We are operators of coin laundry equipment in multi-family complexes. We had the smart card device developed because of the following conditions:

1. A large percentage of the machines were vandalized regularly to steal money.

2. The cost of collecting coins from individual machine money boxes was high.

3. There is no practical way to guarantee secure collections.

4. It was often inconvenient for users to obtain the quarters necessary to operate the machinery.

We hired a company that had been in the field for four years doing research and development on smart card devices. They satisfied us on their ability to produce the devices at a cost we felt was vital to the smart card development company in order to successfully develop a design that exactly met our needs.

We would like to believe that Amerivend Corporation has always been in the forefront in the use of new technology that is applicable to our business. Our people are always open to new ideas or new ways to achieve old ideas. Without the complete cooperation of all necessary personnel, the implementation of the smart card system would have been much more difficult.

Our first installation was 18 months ago. As of this writing, we have installed smart card devices in over 350 machines at 12 different demographic types of multi-family complexes. In 11 of these 12 applications, we had sales figures from previous years as a comparison. All 11 accounts have shown increases. We have taken the capital cost of the smart card devices and, using an acceptable formula, have been able to determine whether monies invested in this manner have produced the same, less, or more of a return than an equal investment in coin devices.

The penetration of smart cards is not measurable at this point. We believe the use of smart card devices will increase geometrically between 1995 and the year 2000 at which time our estimate is that 75 to 80 percent of the commercial laundry machines will be equipped with smart card devices.[12]

The most critical success factor for any smart card application developer is a complete and working knowledge of the industry for which the device is being developed. The most ideal scenario would be a joint venture between a leading industry user and a developer with practical, as well as theoretical, knowledge. Both parties must have a driving ambition to complete the project and be prepared to fund as required. It always takes more than originally estimated.

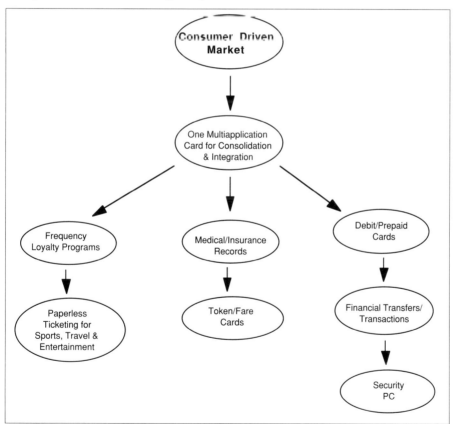

Figure 2-5. Smart card opportunity analysis.

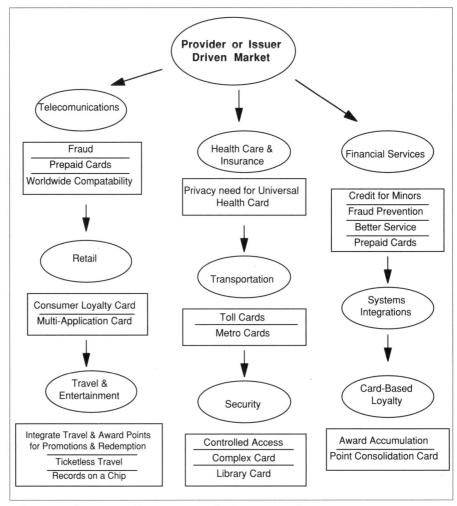

Figure 2-6. Factors driving provider/issuer market.

FIVE STEPS FOR SELECTING YOUR INDUSTRY

There are a number of useful steps that can assist you in examining the industry which you have selected. Following are five of the most helpful:

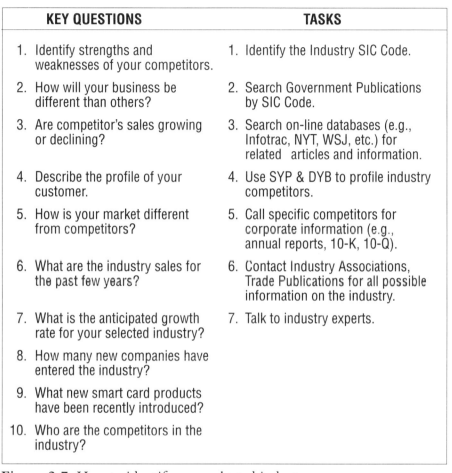

KEY QUESTIONS	TASKS
1. Identify strengths and weaknesses of your competitors.	1. Identify the Industry SIC Code.
2. How will your business be different than others?	2. Search Government Publications by SIC Code.
3. Are competitor's sales growing or declining?	3. Search on-line databases (e.g., Infotrac, NYT, WSJ, etc.) for related articles and information.
4. Describe the profile of your customer.	4. Use SYP & DYB to profile industry competitors.
5. How is your market different from competitors?	5. Call specific competitors for corporate information (e.g., annual reports, 10-K, 10-Q).
6. What are the industry sales for the past few years?	6. Contact Industry Associations, Trade Publications for all possible information on the industry.
7. What is the anticipated growth rate for your selected industry?	7. Talk to industry experts.
8. How many new companies have entered the industry?	
9. What new smart card products have been recently introduced?	
10. Who are the competitors in the industry?	

Figure 2-7. How to identify your selected industry.

1. *Clearly define the industry.* The task here is to develop a definition that describes your smart card product or service. Definitions will vary, of course, depending on the venture and its specific target market. The more clearly you can define the industry for the new business, the better the chance your idea will get started.

2. *Competition Review.* An analysis of the number, relative size, management team, and pricing of direct competitors in the industry can help establish the nature of the competition. Will competition become more or less intense over time? This is answered through

detailed analysis. What factors will affect competition if (a) market growth increases rapidly, (b) one or two direct competitors become larger in size, or (c) smart card products and services are not ready to be accepted in many places?

3. *Determine the strength and weaknesses of vendors*. It is important to establish the relationship to vendors. How will you be treated compared to other more-established firms? Are there choice offerings or must you be prepared to accept limited services from a few?

4. *Establish the "value-added" service of smart cards*. You must measure how much value is being added. You should meet with potential customers, perform some research, and clearly determine your value-added service.

5. *Prepare a cost summary and revenue plan*. Markets are prone to change over time. Therefore, it is important to understand the flow of the market, its present size, and the data to project the growth of the market. This should be accomplished by researching the industry life cycle, consumers, product/service developments, and by competitive analysis.

These five key points are important and represent an initial analysis of the industry environment. This type of analysis is needed to establish the framework for you to start growing and building a business opportunity for a smart card venture.

Finally, the following are some particular characteristics and concerns of companies who are probably good candidates for a smart card program:

- Large fraud problem

- Multiple services or benefits that might be combined on one card

- Large and repetitive transaction volume

- Need for data security

- Interest in prepaid applications (cashless transactions)

- Requirement for speedier transactions

- Potential for customers to carry individual portable database

- Need to lower operating costs

- On-line hook-up not necessary

HOW TO GET CLIENTS COMMITTED—THE IBM VIEW

At IBM, Michael Weekes, manager of food service consulting, said "The first steps in getting our clients involved in smart cards is to develop the vision for this technology and show how it impacts the business.

Food service companies must focus on the strategic implication of this technology. IBM asks its clients questions like:

- What is your vision for smart card?

  - Access the dollars and data that need to be identified.
  - How can your customers benefit from smart cards?
  - How can it work with your internal applications and departments?
  - What are your internal information requirements for installing a smart card project?
  - What are your supply chain advantages for such a program?
  - What strategic alliances can you develop to grow the business?

- Do you know the risks and liabilities?

  - Are you competing with the bank?
  - How does Regulation E affect your business?
  - Can it fit franchise needs for further opportunities?

- What is your strategic plan for this program?

  - Identify your competitive advantages and timing requirements.
  - Identify critical success factors and how it impacts the organization and efficiency.
  - Define security requirements that need to be addressed.

IBM Food Service Consulting has a four-step approach to assist restaurant operators launching smart card programs quickly with low risk and high impact.

Step 1: Prepare Strategic Assessment Methodology

- Top-down approach from the executive level to manager.
- Determine the threats and opportunities for each department involved in the program.
- What benefits will apply to other groups and divisions by implementing the program?
- How should we develop alliance potentials?

Step 2: Conceptual Design

- Operational issues and opportunities.
- Detail the components of the program and sequence the milestones to accomplish.
- Work plan and time table to be completed.
- What other alternative approaches are to be addressed?

Step 3: Feasibility Analysis

- Prepare a cost benefit analysis for implementation.
- Access the risks and barriers to overcome.
- Describe the window of opportunity and timing.
- Final detail design and approval.

Step 4: Implementation Pilots

Other factors affecting this technology may also include:

- Interactive multimedia—CD ROM.
- Voice/speech recognition.
- Integrated POS systems.
- Integrated home PCs.
- ATM network compatibility.
- Multi-function cards.
- On-line or off-line transactions.

Food service and other industries will likely evolve rather than revolutionize with smart card implementation. said Mike Weekes. "From the information systems point of view, the challenge is system integration capability. We believe these key information components will drive the smart card market. How they will function and become important is what we are focusing on today."[13]

CRITICAL FACTORS FOR MANAGING A SMART CARD PROGRAM

A number of critical factors are important for managing a smart card program in your company.

Six important factors can determine your success or failure in managing a smart card operation: Let's examine each factor and see why all play a vital role in the success of the program.

1. The *proprietary application* of your plan

2. The capital *investment* needed to achieve success

3. The *expected growth* of sales and/or profits as the company moves through the different phases

4. The *availability of the smart card service or products*

5. *Customers reactions*

6. The *environment* for smart cards

Proprietary Application

A smart card business application in terms of being proprietary is extremely important to the success of the company. The amount of innovation required during initial operations separates the routine application from others, and creates a distinction for other companies to recognize you as a leader in the field. The proprietary application is further characterized by the length of time it remains non-routine. For instance, will new products or enhanced technology such as adding more memory be required on a continuing basis? Or will your company be able to sustain the smart card service on a constant basis?

Financial Investment

The capital required to grow your smart card business can vary considerably. The type of financing is usually segmented by the stage of development your company is in. Most smart card companies are in the early stages of growth and can be defined in four general categories for capital investment.

Seed Capital

This usually is a small amount of capital, under $50,000, that provides the company with the opportunity to prove the smart card product or service works. In some cases it is used to prepare a smart card demonstration of a particular service the company is intending to offer. This usually excludes the development of a complete service and preparing a marketing analysis plan of the opportunity, as well as getting a management team in place.

Smart Card Research and Development

This usually is a tax-advantage group or partnership set up to initially finance smart card product development for a start-up or companies that are investing opportunities to pursue on a trial-and-error basis. Investors can get a tax write-off for the investment as well as sharing in the profits if successful.

Start-up Capital

This is usually for a company that has demonstrated and completed a smart card application and has prepared a marketing plan to begin operations. In most cases, the business has been operative for at least a year, but has achieved only limited sales. These companies have a solid business plan, have put together a management team and are prepared to implement a marketing strategy to become successful.

First Stage Capital

This is for companies that have spent their initial capital to begin a smart card business and require additional funds to meet the goals of the company. Usually in these cases the company has not met the projected sales volume as described in the marketing plan and the funds are required to gain a competitive advantage in the marketplace and become profitable.

Expected Company Sales Growth

The sales growth of the company is another critical factor for success. Key questions should focus on both the short- and long-term sales growth such as: What is the anticipated growth pattern for sales in year one versus year five? How are sales and profits expected to grow in the first five years—slowly or will they level off? When are large profits expected? At what point will the company become self-sufficient and will not require additional funding for growth? In answering these questions, it is important to remember that most companies fall into one of the following three business classifications.

Lifestyle Company

The primary driving force of a lifestyle business is independence and control. Neither large sales nor profits are important. Key considerations are maintaining a business instead of really growing the business opportunity. These kind of smart card companies are usually composed of individuals who are most interested in maintaining a comfortable standard of living and creating the environment in which to live and work.

Smaller Profitable Businesses

This kind of company emphasizes the financial considerations and this plays a major role in the life of the organization. Autonomy and control are very important in the sense that the owners do not want to give up an ownership position. These companies usually compromise by maintaining control, versus a large growing company, which gives the management team control over the organization.

High-Growth Business

Companies that command the majority of funding in the smart card industry are considered foundation or high-growth businesses. This kind of company has significant sales and profit growth potential and is very attractive to venture-capital firms.

The Availability of the Smart Card Service

Having the defined smart card service available is essential to the success of your business when it begins. Many companies have problems because the product or service is still in development and needs further modification or testing. Other companies find that they bring their services to market too soon so they must be recalled for additional work. A typical example is a smart card software firm that rushes the development of its service and is then besieged by customers who find bugs in the program. Lack of product availability in finished form can affect the company's image and its bottom line.

Customer Reactions

Since no business has the skills and resources to be all things to all people, the company must identify which customer needs can and should be met by introducing a smart card service. Deciding which preferences and potential customers to serve is crucial, given the company's limited resources and competitive strengths. A target market is a group of existing or potential customers within a product market toward which the company directs its marketing efforts. Selectivity in choosing target markets is a key path to test customer reactions and building customer satisfaction for your services.

The Environment for Smart Cards

There are many ways to make an environmental assessment of the company's smart card business application. Generally, the approach is neither highly sophisticated nor does it require a heavy marketing analysis. The average new business application can conduct an assessment in several ways. This often entails contacting trade associations, like Smart Card Forum, trade publications like Pin News, Smart Card Monthly, and political action committees. Key issues for assessment include privacy of information in a smart card chip, who has access to the data, and how to protect the data from others. Also, governmental issues or legislation that would affect your ability to conduct business is highly important.

CASE ANALYSIS: SMART CARD VERSUS MAG STRIPE LOYALTY PROGRAM

A major petroleum company was seeking to implement a frequency program for its customers in the U.S. The company's objective was to reward customers who purchased a minimum of 7 gallons of gas of any grade gasoline or diesel fuel for every purchase. When a customer accumulated 10 purchases, that customer received $2 off his or her next purchase of gasoline or diesel fuel. When a customer accumulated 20 purchases, the customer received $5 off his or her next purchase of gasoline or diesel fuel.

Company Overview

A petroleum company identified a need for the development of a strategic direction for customer loyalty. Currently, the company has a frequent fueller program in place, whereby customers receive a punch card. The program targets customers who purchase premium gasoline, whereas the frequent program is for users of regular gasoline.

The present frequent fueller program has the following features:

- The frequent fueller program has been in place for approximately 2.5 years, at an estimated cost of $4 million annually, of which $600,000 is estimated fraud expense.

- Customers currently receive $2 off gasoline or merchandise ($4 for premium) after receiving 10 punches; $5 to $10 for 20 punches. Convenience store purchases are not rewarded.

- Currently, the company redeems 100,000 cards per month at an average of $500,000 monthly. This information applies to company-owned locations. Approximately 500 branded distributors are participating in the program but are not reporting results.

- It is projected that 10 percent, or approximately $50,000 monthly, of redemption is fraudulent.

- Previously, the program was discontinued in one market and sales dropped markedly.

- The company is interested in installing an electronic tracking system to build a customer database and reduce fraud.

The petroleum company was unsure of whether to base the program on a smart card or magnetic stripe card and requested an analysis and comparison of both technologies. Figure 2-8 describes the analysis of the problems, goals, and cost analysis and proposed solutions and smart card operational flow.

**PROBLEMS, GOALS, SOLUTION, AND ANALYSIS
OF A PETROLEUM COMPANY**

Smart Card Reward Program

PROBLEM: Current frequent fueller program is not structured effectively.

A. It excludes anyone that purchases less than ten gallons, on average.

B. Convenience store purchases are also excluded from the frequency program.

C. The current system is visit-based, and therefore does not create an incentive to spend more dollars each visit.

D. The focus of the program is on increasing purchases of a low-margin product (gas) rather than high-margin products (convenience store items).

GOALS: Implement a frequency program that will:

A. Increase sales of highest-margin items (convenience store products).

B. Increase gasoline sales.

C. Make a loss leader (gas) profitable.

Figure 2-8. Smart card reward program.

D. Reward customers for overall dollars spent, not visits, to add incentives to incremental purchases.

E. Encourage customers for purchasing higher margin items (convenience store purchases) by rewarding them with lower margin ones (gas).

F. Identify gasoline versus c-store customers, and motivate the gas customers to become convenience store customers as well.

G. Eliminate fraud.

H. Increase overall customer loyalty for gasoline *and* convenience store purchases.

SOLUTION: Implement an *electronic frequency program* that will:

A. Track dollars spent rather than just visits.

B. Reward customers on total dollars spent so that they have an incentive to spend each incremental dollar.

C. Drive gas customers into c-store through targeted instant POS couponing in order to increase c-store sales and overall profit margins.

D. Increasing the number of average customer gas purchases (loyalty) from four per month to five per month will make gas a profit center rather than a loss leader.

E. Incentivise customers for purchasing higher margin items (c-store purchases) by rewarding them with lower margin ones (gas).

F. Sweeten the incentive to customers by offering catalog items in lieu of gas awards.

G. Increase profitability of program through fraud reduction.

COST ANALYSIS:

Assumptions: 900,00 cardholders

$0.14 profit margin per gallon

Avg. purchase = 10 gallons

Cost of hardware and cards: $600,000 (1st year)

$69,000 (2nd year)

Fraud savings: $600,000 (every year)

Variable costs: Transaction fees: $0.0188/trans.

Phone charges: $0.17/min.

(Each call lasts one min.)

Reward structure remains unchanged.

Figure 2-8. (continued)

Analysis: *Incremental Revenue*

Increase average visits per customer from four per month to five per month (does not assume any increases in c-store purchases).

= 900,000 incremental transaction/mo.

900,000 trans. x 10 gallons = 9,000,000 incremental gallons

9,000,000 gal. x $0.14 profit/gal=$1,260,000 profit/mo.

$1,260,000 profit/mo x 12 mo=$15,120,000 gross profit/yr

Incremental Costs

Transaction Fees:	900,000 trans x $0.0188/trans = $16,920/mo x 12 mo = $203,040
Phone Charges:	1 call per night x $0.17/call X 1,030 stores x 365 days/yr = $63,912
Total:	$266,952 incremental costs/yr

Total Incremental Net Profits = $14,745,048/yr

Figure 2-8. (continued)

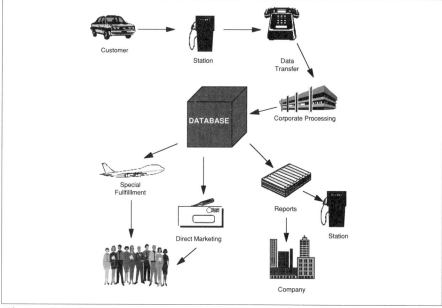

Figure 2-9. Smart card operational flow.

Smart Card System

A customer is issued a frequency smart card which can be used when buying gasoline. The customer's points are stored directly on the card. This smart card is always up-to-date and can be used at any location at any time with a current up-to-the-minute point total stored on the card.

Fraud Issues

- A smart card is tamper-proof and therefore cannot be duplicated.

- There is no lag time in redeeming awards because awards are a direct function of the customer's point total stored directly on the customer's card.

- There is no possibility of fraud with a smart card because a customer's entire point total is not resident in any terminal or hard drive but rather on the customer's card.

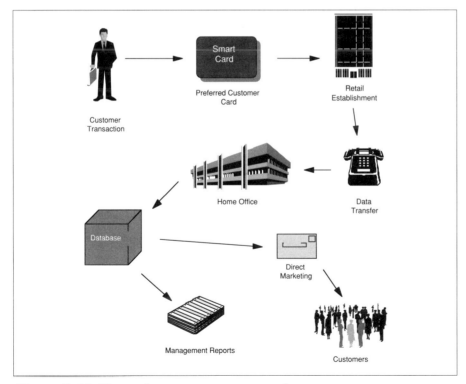

Figure 2-10. How a frequency program works.

Communication Issues

In a smart card system, transactional data is downloaded once a week from each POS terminal to a data center. This downloading merely backs up customers' point totals and is not critical in operating the frequency program because a customer's points are stored on the customer's card.

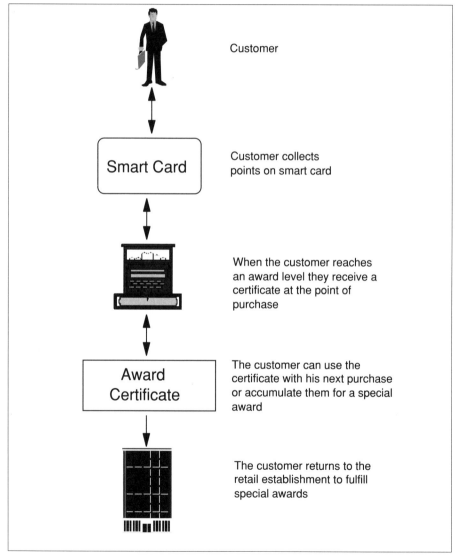

Figure 2-11. Fulfillment process.

Communication Charges

Communications charges (estimated): One call from each location once a week, 52 weeks a year.

How a frequency program works and how customers receive awards are shown in Figures 2-10 and 2-11.

On-line Mag Stripe System

A customer is issued a frequency mag stripe card which can be used when buying gasoline. The customer's point total is stored in a central database and can be accessed from any location through a phone call.

Fraud Issues

Like a smart card system, there is very limited possibility of fraud because a customer's points are resident on a central database and can be accessed only through a phone terminal at any location. Additionally, customers can use their card from any location, and like a smart card, they receive instantaneous awards

Communication Issues

In an on-line system phone charges are enormous because every time a customer comes into a location, a phone call must be made to the central database to access that customer's point total.

Communications Charges

One phone call for every transaction occurred.

Terminal Issue

Limited memory permits storage of 15,000 to 20,000 customers.

The solution and results for implementation are shown in Figure 2-12.

Objectives	Solutions	Results
Reduce cost of current Frequent Fueller program	• Install smart card system • Target program to most profitable customers • Drive purchase on high-margin products	• Definable method for ROI • Fraud control • Program decisions will be based on measurable objectives • Upselling opportunities
Make the program more enticing to independent retailers.	• Smart card driven program • Build database	• Fraud Reduction • Targeted marketing approach
Increase the value of the program for customers.	• Include C-store purchases in earnings • Segment payouts • Include partnership awards	• Increased earning potential • More valuable awards • Perceived value of smart card
Increase purchase of premium gas.	Segment payouts: • Unleaded 1% • Mid-grade 2% • Premium 3% • C-store 5%	• Reinforces consumers switching to premium gas
Reduce fraud.	• Install electronic tracking system • Train employees	• Fraud will be minimal and traceable

Figure 2-12. Objectives, solutions, and results.

Off-line Mag Stripe System

A customer is issued a frequency mag stripe card which can be used when buying gasoline. Customer point totals are stored at every location either on the POS or on a standalone terminal. Every night each location downloads its daily transactional data to a central data center. The following evening after consolidation of the data at the data center, updated information is then uploaded to all participating locations. This system has a 24-hour time lag in updating all locations with each customer's point totals.

For example, if a customer uses his card in station A and then goes to station B on the same day, the first purchase will not be reflected on that family's point total in the second location—or, for that matter, any other location—until the next day when all locations are updated with the new information.

Fraud Issues

If a customer has reached an award plateau, that customer could hypothetically redeem an award at every single location because the system has a 24-hour delay. Because a customer's point totals are not resident in either a central database or on the customer's card, this fraud issue arises.

By requiring customers to redeem points only at a single store (home store)—meaning a customer's point totals are resident at only one location—this fraud issue can be avoided. This obviously limits the ability of customers to redeem points at any location. A customer who makes a non-home store purchase would have to wait the obligatory 24 hours until the non-home store location downloaded to the data center and then updated at the customer's home store the next day.

Terminal Issue

The database must be very large.

Communications Issues

Every night each location downloads its daily transactional data to a central data center. The following evening after consolidation of the data at the data center, updated information is then uploaded to all participating locations.

Communications Charges

Over all 1000 locations dial in once a day, 365 days a year, resulting in high phone charges.

END NOTES

1. *Chip Cards—The Competitive Edge.* Feb., 1995. MasterCard International background document (internal), pp. 1–5.

2. "A La Carte' Menu in French School." June, 1995. *Smart Card News.* p. 111.

3. Fung, Noel. May, 1995. "Schlumberger Teams Up with Chinese Project." *Smart Card Bulletin.* p. 1.

4. "Spain Gearing UP EBT Social Security Project." May 10, 1995. *EFT Report.*

5. "AMICA Loyalty Card in Italy." May, 1995. *Smart Card News.*

6. Aranda, Antonio. June, 1995. "The RATP Ticketing Project: A High Tech Electronic PUrse Solution for Public Transport in Paris." *World Card Technology.* pp. 6–10.

7. "Have Card, Can Fly Delta Shuttle." May, 1995. *Smart Card News.* p. 87.

8. "Stored Value Application." March, 1995. MasterCard International. p. 1.

9. Giakoumis, Alex. 1995 Interview. "Smart Card Opportunities."

10. Keenen, William. June, 1995. US WEST Interview for Smart Card Opportunities.

11. Falk, David. July, 1995. "Using Smart Cards for Loyalty Programs."

12. Pulver, Gerald. July 1995 Interview. "Coin Laundry Equipment Using Smart Cards."

13. Weekes, Michael. June, 1995. "Getting Clients Involved in Smart Cards."

3

Card Technology Choices

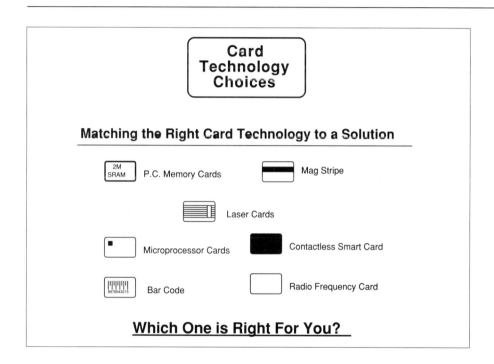

Technology used to have a 10-year life cycle. But the mean life span for much current technology is now about 24 months, and then you have almost a whole new technology base to deal with and apply.

—Stanley Harrison, CEO, BDM Inc.

INTRODUCTION

Almost everyone has a magnetic stripe card and understands its use. However, today's card technology will progress from a simple bar coded, single-purpose card to the multifunctional, large-storage smart card with the magnetic stripe card somewhere in the middle of a card spectrum. The purpose of this chapter is to explain card technology and possible applications in simple terms so that you can determine which card meets the needs of your market. Cards may combine multiple technologies. This will be prevalent as smart cards and mag stripe cards are combined on one card for a transition card while card terminals are upgraded worldwide to handle both card technologies.

When looking at the various implementations of card systems, we can see that the magnetic-stripe technology and memory cards using integrated logic are the two technologies on the market today that create big volumes. Until now and for most applications, these technologies were sufficient to fulfill the requirements stated.

Today, however, one can see that:

- There is an increasing amount of fraud with the existing technologies.

- There is a demand for multi-application functionality in the card, in order for the issuing company to be more cost-effective when issuing cards.

- Applications are appearing that require a high security structure in the card (data integrity, authentification, and so on).

- There is a demand for high-storage memory capacity.

- There is an increasing demand for interoperability between similar applications in different countries, and even between various applications. This demand is pushed by the standardization work being done by various groups.

When looking toward the future and taking into account the above-mentioned considerations, one cannot neglect the increasing need for a standardized card offering a maximum of security, and at the same time, the possibility to have several completely independent applications on the same card.[1]

TECHNOLOGY STANDARDS

No discussion on technology usage would be complete without the standards issue. Indeed, standardization has become a key issue in the development of information technology (IT) for the financial sector and telecommunications worldwide. It has become one of the crucial issues for the future of both the IT industry and of all the other sectors that now use IT. This includes the use of smart cards.[2]

Before we examine which technology is right for your company, let's understand some common industry characteristics to be aware of during the selection process.

COMMON INDUSTRY CHARACTERISTICS

Although industries vary in size and development, the smart card industry has certain characteristics that are common to industries that are emerging. The most important of these characteristics are discussed next.

Technological Uncertainty

There is usually a great deal of uncertainty about the technology of an emerging industry: What product configuration will ultimately prove to be the best? Which production technology will prove to be the most efficient? How difficult will it be to develop this technology? How difficult will it be to copy technological breakthroughs in the industry?

Strategic Uncertainty

Related to technological uncertainty is a wide variety of strategic approaches often tried by industry participants. Since no "right" strategy has been clearly identified, industry participants formulate different approaches as product positioning, advertising price and the like as well as different product configurations or production technologies.

First-Time Buyers

Buyers of an emerging industry's products or services are first-time buyers. The marketing task is thus one of substitution, or getting the buyer to make the initial purchase of the new product or service.

Short-Time Horizons

The pressure to develop customers or produce products to meet demand is so great in many emerging industries that bottlenecks and problems are dealt with expediently rather than on the basis of an analysis of future conditions. Short-run results are often given major attention, while long-run results are given too little consideration.

Barriers to Entry

In addition to the structural hurdles an emerging industry faces, there are also barriers to entry. These barriers may include proprietary technology (expensive to access), access to distribution channels (limited or closed to newcomers), access to raw materials and other input (e.g., skilled labor), cost disadvantage due to lack of experience (magnified by technological and competitive uncertainties), or risk (which raises the effective opportunity cost of capital).

Some of these barriers decline or disappear as the industry develops; however, it is still important for you to be aware of them.

HOW TO SELECT A TECHNOLOGY FOR YOUR APPLICATION

The following pages outline the important characteristics and applications for various card technologies. By reviewing these characteristics and advantages it should help you to determine which card technology is best suited to the solution you are seeking.

So, keep in mind the following seven guidelines to help you select the technology for the application.

1. What service are you trying to provide and in what market?

   - How much memory do you need to store data?
   - What type of security protection is necessary?
   - How much data is updated?
   - Do you need to maintain a centralized database, or must all the data fit on one card?

2. What are the environmental issues that might affect your choice?

3. What are the performance speeds, failure rates, and other factors relating to technology?

4. What is the area of interest? What best fits the market segmentation? For instance, is your potential customer a university looking for a campus card or a business examining a specific application?

5. How is price as a factor a component of the system? Who pays for the cards?

6. How committed is the corporation to the technology or product offering?

7. Does the industry have a standard for the card of your choice?

Bar-code card

Bar-code technology is visible throughout the retail arena. The series of dark parallel lines on almost all retail products represent a code that can be entered into a system either manually or automatically with a scanner or reader. This line-and-space identification system can be printed on almost any item using any computer or printing system. Bar-code systems allow low margin industries to control costs through careful inventory tracking.

Technology

- Simple technology since code is static and can be printed on any medium
- Bar-code is screened onto card
- Does not require standardized plastic
- Requires centralized database

Data Storage

- Limited capacity of 10–12 characters

Security

- No security built into card; anyone who has it can use it

Cost

- Inexpensive to produce—less than $0.10 per card

Card Reader

- Optical reader required, typically laser scanning
- Wide range of scanning technology is available to interact with large databases
- Standards are well established for reading the bar-code

Uses

- Identification (library, check cashing)
- Inventory and product tracking
- Supermarkets

Advantages

- Universally accepted in many locations
- Implemented on a worldwide basis

- Very cost-effective

- Easy to use

Radio Frequency Card

The radio frequency card is intended for single applications that require speed of transaction over all other considerations. It does not require contact points so the card does not have to come into direct physical contact with the reader. Remote readers are used on highway systems for toll collection. Data contained on the card can be similar to that of any of the other cards.

Technology

- Uses radio wire wraps within the card as well as microprocessors to handle transactions

- Contactless reading

- Not ISO standard; can be any size or shape

Memory

- Memory capacity can range from 0 to several hundred bits

Security

- No security built into card. Anyone who has it can use it or read it

Cost

- Wide range—$5–$15 per card

Card Reader (Transceiver)

- No on-board intelligence, intelligence must be in reader or host. No standards exist among manufacturers; each manufacturer governs its own card and reader

Uses

- Public transportation, toll roads

- Physical access

- Secure inventory (e.g., retail clothing)

Advantages

- Faster usage—no insert

- Rugged construction

Disadvantages

- Higher costs

- Closed systems

- More expensive system integration

- No security features

- Requires special devices

Magnetic Stripe Card

The ubiquitous magnetic stripe card may seem unsophisticated when compared to the seemingly brilliant smart card, but its simple, inexpensive technology and widespread use force anyone considering card use to review its capabilities. It can be used for many of the same applications as other cards, and even when considering its limitations, it may be the card of choice. When security or corruption of data due to magnetic fields or other forces becomes an issue, thoughts should turn to another card type.

Technology

- Most widely used card technology in the world today

- Cannot process data or compute but can activate a computer connection

- No onboard power or battery

- Intelligence resides outside the card

- Requires centralized database

Data Storage

- Limited to maximum of 75 characters

Security

- Unsecured; anyone can read and counterfeit stripe data
- Easily erased or corrupted

Cost

- Inexpensive—about $0.25–$0.50 per card

Card Reader

- Reading standards are well established, and many inexpensive readers in use are capable of reading this card with no modifications

Uses

- Bank numbers
- Serial numbers
- Secure door access
- Identification
- Credit/debit transactions

Advantages

- Accepted worldwide
- Implemented worldwide
- Cost-effective
- Easy to use

Memory Card

This card is a memory-only card and not considered a smart card. It is the least expensive form of storage using integrated circuit (chip) technology. Information stored is electrically erasable programmable non-volatile memory (EEPROM or non-erasable EPROM). This technology requires power to alter data within the card, but data is sustained when power is removed.

Technology

- No computational capability; intelligence resides outside the card in a reader or PC

- EEPROM capability allows data changes up to 10,000 times

- Same size as magnetic stripe card

- Requires physical connector to reader for communication

Memory

- Capacity ranges from 1024 bits to 65,536 bits

Security

- Unrestricted access, so there is no security in the card. Security can be in the PC or the reader

- If data can be read, it can be duplicated

Cost

- Medium price—$1–$3 per card, depending on memory size

Card Reader

- Available in many forms

- Throat for reading can be put in any intelligent device (e.g., telephone, computer, vending machine)

Uses

Use anywhere a portable data file is important:

- Telephone prepaid cards (the biggest use of card)

- Car warranty programs

- Supermarket programs

- Insurance

- Education (student records)

Advantages

- Stores value on the card
- Low cost (as an IC card)
- More memory than mag stripe
- Portable data file

Secure Serial Card

This card is similar to a memory card, except that it has a chip that contains a hardware-coded secure field which allows use of a password to control access. It fulfills the same functions, but is the card of choice when data integrity is a high priority.

Technology

- No computational capability; intelligence resides outside the card in a reader or PC
- EEPROM capability allows data changes up to 10,000 times
- Same size as magnetic stripe card
- Requires physical connector to reader for communication

Memory

- Memory capacity of 4096 bits

Security

- Controlled access through password

Cost

- Moderate cost ($2–$5)

Card Reader

- Available in many forms
- Throat for reading can be put in any intelligent device (e.g., telephone, computer, vending machine)

Uses

- Physical access

- Limited computer terminal or network access

- Financial (e.g., debit card)

Advantages

- Password-protected for access

- More memory than mag stripe

- Portable data file

- Read and write capabilities

Microprocessor Card Smart Card

Definition of a Smart Card

A *smart card* is defined as being an *intelligent device* containing a microprocessor that has both built-in processing power and three different kinds of memories (ROM, RAM, and EEPROM), and which is capable of being packaged in the card format defined by ISO.

Advanced microprocessor technology embedded within the smart card permits the storage of several thousand bits of data on this type of card. Reusable memory available through the chip allows data to be changed whenever necessary during the life of the card. Data in the card is retained when power is off or until it is overwritten. Data areas within the card can be programmed with different security access.

Technology

- Contains CPU, RAM, ROM, and EEPROM on the card

  - **CPU**—Central processing unit; computer serves as intelligent gateway from reader to memory.

  - **RAM**—Random-access memory. Becomes like a notepad during transactions and when making calculations. Is active only when power is being supplied from an external source. Contents disappear when card is removed from the terminal.

- **ROM**—Read-only memory. Memory that stays with the card; it is entered during manufacture of the chip and cannot be altered. It usually contains a specialized program (operating system) that controls the CPU.

- **EEPROM**—Electrical erasable program. Memory that can be electrically erased and rewritten up to 10,000 times allowing data changes over the life of the card.

- Interacts (send and receives data) with another processor (reader or host).

- Eight-bit microprocessor built into card.

Existing Smart Card Masks

A *mask* is defined as the software that is coded in the corresponding microprocessor's assembly language that is implemented into the ROM of the silicon chip at a very early stage of its manufacturing phase. The operating system, security algorithms, programs or subroutines needed for the EEPROM management, byte and block protocols, and so on, are usually coded and are masked in the ROM.

There does not presently exist any smart card on the market that is truly a standardized one, and which allows creation of applications into the EEPROM memory during the utilization phase of the card. The only standardized smart card at this time is the one that contains the GSM/SIMEG application. This card contains, however, only one standardized application which has to be written completely into the EEPROM memory during the personalization phase of the card. Afterwards, during the utilization phase of the card, it is impossible to create new applications.[3]

Memory

The memories used can be classified into two categories that correspond to whether or not they are capable of keeping the data after the power supply is cut off. If the memory keeps the data it is called *non-volatile* memory and if it does not keep the data is it called *volatile* memory.

In smart cards, the only volatile memory is the RAM, which is used exclusively for data manipulation and data transfer. It is considered as the working area. The non-volatile memories are the ROM, the EPROM, and/or the EEPROM.

The term "mask" also is often associated with the software development or code that is to be stored in the ROM of the card's microcomputer. Obviously, the term "mask" does not mean the same for chip and card manufacturers. Therefore, it has to be used with a lot of caution.

There are two families of CPU architecture that have been widely used in the smart-card applications. These are the ones that have been derived from the Intel 8051 and the ones that have been derived from the Motorola 6805 family. As of today, all microcontrollers used for smart cards have an eight-bit word.

In the programmable ROMs we can find the EPROMs and EEPROMs.

All EPROMs available today require an external power supply for programming. The first-developed CMOS EPROM processes require 20 to 24 volts where the latest ones have reduced it down to the region of 10 to 15 volts, depending upon the semiconductor manufacturer.

As significant current is required to program an EPROM cell, this limits the chip size due to power dissipation and, consequently, thermal effects. This high current requirement of EPROM memories makes them undesirable in the contactless card applications, where there is a restriction with respect to the power that can be transmitted to the device.

Another disadvantage of EPROM technologies is that its cells cannot be reprogrammed individually. To change the content of some memory cells, the entire memory has to be erased and this is only possible by exposing the device to ultraviolet light. In cards though, the special window opening for the penetration of the ultraviolet light is often omitted, hence the change of the EPROM content is impossible.

The EEPROM is a more recently developed technology that offers a certain number of advantages compared to EPROM. The biggest advantage is that *individual* bits theoretically can be written and erased an infinite number of times. In reality, most manufacturers today warranty a minimum of 10,000 read/write cycles.

Another advantage is that EEPROM needs only a single power supply for DC biasing and programming and it uses considerably less current. Hence it consumes less power.

Security

- Each application can be secured differently
- It is difficult if not impossible to emulate
- ID codes can be embedded in the card
- It is difficult to obtain data from the card or alter data contained on the card
- The card can store cumulative transaction records

Cost

- Medium price—$5–$10 per card.

Card Reader

- Uses same contact points as serial card. Can come in different forms, from simple communication to point-of-sale terminal (POST) which can be external to or embedded in the host.

Contactless Smart Card

The contactless smart card is a secure portable computer the size and thickness of a credit card. A reliable intelligent peripheral, it can communicate directly with a host system. It is the balance between the needs of a sophisticated system and the requirement for user convenience.

The contactless smart-card technology available today was developed by AT&T and is functioning reliably as a secure system peripheral.[4]

Rugged Construction

The smart card is physically designed for multiple applications with their long-life usage requirements. It has no metal contacts, assuring longer wear, and multi-layer construction makes it rugged. It can withstand ordinary credit card handling, as well as the heat and stress of ID laminating systems.

Simple, Secure Capacitive Data Transfer

The smart card uses simple, straightforward capacitive data-transfer techniques to achieve a high level of security. Limited components add reliability and reduce maintenance cost.

Efficient Inductive Power Transfer

The smart card is powered from the terminal to the card. Minimum power means small, portable readers and terminals.

Flexible Reader Interface

Small circuits for easy integration and no moving parts means longer life. Surface-read for hostile environments.

Multiple Applications

The powerful, feature-rich operating system provides a secure and efficient way to handle multiple applications.

EEPROM for Extended Life

3K- (24K bits) and 8K- (64K bits) versions are available

Systems Compatibility

Meets or exceeds ISO mag stripe, embossing, and smart card standards. It will coexist with contact readers and supports multiple communications protocols for added compatibility.

Laser Card

The laser card optical memory card is an updatable, credit-card size, plastic, multi-megabyte data-storage card for storing and carrying up to 2000 pages of information. It is based on optical recording technology—the process of writing and reading with light.[5]

The laser card contains a wide, reflective optical recording stripe encapsulated between transparent, protective layers. Information is stored digitally on the card in a binary code consisting of 1 or 0 bits that are represented by either the presence or absence of physical "spots" on the recording stripe. The spots are microscopic in size—as small as 2.25 microns. (The smallest-size spot that the human eye can see is about 20 microns.)

The card user inserts the laser card into an optical card reader/writer attached to a personal computer, where light from a tiny laser (about the size of a thumbtack) records the data by creating dark spots on the card's shiny surface. Using a keyboard or other means, the card user writes, reads, and deletes data as if the laser card were a floppy disk. Yet deleted data remains permanently stored on the card as an audit trail of all changes.

Although it is only the size of a consumer credit card, the laser card has a digital data-storage capacity of book-size proportions. The standard laser card has a total capacity of 4.1 megabytes with user data capacity of 2.86 megabytes. The 6.6-megabyte laser card has 4.2 megabytes of user data capacity. Thus, a single card holds thousands of text pages, hundreds of document images, or up to 80 medical images such as MRIs or CT scans.

This unique card also offers high security. The card has non-erasable and nonvolatile memory, it flexes easily, it is not affected by magnetic or electrostatic fields, and it can be manufactured to withstand temperatures of up to 212°F. The card has ample memory to store personal ID numbers (PINs), biographic data, a color photo, and biometrics such as signature, voice print, fingerprint, and hand template. This makes it possible to verify that the person using the card is the authorized cardholder. Also, data encryption and unique card/equipment interface codes can be used to protect the data from unauthorized access.

The laser card optical memory card can be used to store text, graphics, voice, pictures, software—virtually any form of information that can be digitized. The laser card system can be used with communication networks (on-line) or with standalone personal computers (off-line). The laser card is an ideal storage medium for health card systems, publishing, consumer transaction systems, document storage, ID card systems, bank debit cards, and many other business, consumer, and government applications.

Compatible with Other Technologies

High-density magnetic stripes, bar codes, machine-readable text, and even I.C. chips may be added to the optical card if desired for specific needs. This allows the optical card to function compatibly with already existing technologies, and to provide a future migration path to the optical card.

Additionally, since the card is the functional equivalent of several high-density floppy disks, the card is also compatible with conventional computer data-storage media, allowing a direct method to back up, copy, or add data to and from optical cards.

Laser Card Applications

There are a number of applications and market possibilities for the laser card optical memory card. For example, cards are currently being used in the following important application areas:

- Banking

  - Prepaid debit card (computerized consumer payment card)
  - Security access control (including armored cars, vaults)
  - VIP customer card (customer identification)

- Medical

  - Patient record card (medical records and insurance)
  - Prenatal care records, ultrasound recordings
  - Medical image card (MRI centers—MR & CT archiving)
  - Immunization history (childrens' immunization records)

- ■ Dental records (patient records and X-rays)

- Automotive/Transportation

  - ■ Auto distributors (warranty and maintenance records)
  - ■ Transportation (freight-container manifest documents)

- Education

  - ■ University student card (I/D and medical records)
  - ■ High school student card (performance and achievement)

- Government

  - ■ Special U.S. Government Department of Logistics Applications
  - ■ State welfare services (ID and service distribution)

PC Memory Cards

One of the most promising developments in the area of low-power storage devices is PC memory cards. PC memory cards are smaller, lighter, and more convenient than existing floppy and hard disk drives. They are also considerably faster. Data access from a PC memory card is hundreds of times faster than from a floppy or hard disk. PC memory cards are more reliable than other forms of data storage because they contain no moving parts or rotating media. They are virtually impervious to liquid spills, are inherently shockproof, and are not subject to bending like a floppy disk. Because of their size, one or more PC memory cards can be easily transported in a shirt pocket or a billfold. One of the most significant features of PC memory cards is the fact that they require very little power in comparison to a floppy or hard disk. This feature significantly extends a laptop computer's battery life.[7]

Standard Cards

Standard PC cards are blank cards that can be written to (programmed) multiple times and used as logical replacements for floppy diskettes and/or hard drives.

SRAM

SRAM (static random-access memory) cards contain the same type of high-speed memory used in a typical cache memory application. SRAM cards can be written to or read from at any time by the user. SRAM cards contain a replaceable battery which protects their contents when removed from the computer.

Flash EPROM

Flash EPROM cards can be written to over and over again, yet retain their data until erased. Flash EPROM cards do not lose their contents when removed from the computer. Flash EPROM cards require far less power than SRAM or EEPROM cards.

EEPROM

EEPROM cards can be written to, erased, and rewritten in place. EEP-ROM cards do not lose their content when removed from the computer. EEPROM cards are most often used in specialized applications requiring small amounts of storage.

Specialty Cards

Mask ROM

Mask ROM (read-only memory) cards are programmed one time, during the manufacturing process, using data and/or programs supplied by the customer. The contents of a Mask ROM card can never be erased.

OTPROM

OTPROM (one-time programmable read-only memory) cards can be written to only once, but read a number of times. An OTPROM card can be programmed in place on the user's computer. An OTPROM card does not lose its contents when removed from the computer.

Combo

Combo cards contain a combination of SRAM and OTPROM or Mask ROM. The contents of the Mask ROM portion of a combo card is programmed with user-supplied data at the factory. A combo card contains a replaceable battery, which protects the contents of the SRAM portion of the card when the card is removed from the computer.

CONSULTANT'S EVALUATION OF HOW TO CHOOSE A CARD TECHNOLOGY

A former consultant of smart card programs, Joseph Schuler of Stored Value Systems, a Division of National City Processing Co., evaluates smart card technology for companies. This is a brief example of how a consultant assists a company in determining the best technology to use.

In the past, the choice of card technologies was essentially limited to magnetic stripe and some elementary close proximity cards for opening doors. Today, several new sophisticated card technologies deserve serious consideration in the design of transaction processing systems. These include:

- Smart cards

- Wired-logic integrated circuit (IC) cards

- Memory-only IC cards

- High-coercivity magnetic cards

- Optical memory cards

So, which technology should you use? That depends on your application. There isn't any right or wrong card technology. There are just right and wrong *applications* of technology. The best technology to use is the one that most closely meets the requirements of your application. Your application should ultimately define the technology, not vice-versa.

The reason many organizations have developed smart card applications is because they require more capacity, more security and greater reliability than magnetic stripe cards are capable of delivering. Smart cards are ideally suited to applications where a small amount of secure, portable data is desirable, especially when data needs to be frequently updated at the point-of-service location.

Security

Smart cards are based on the most secure existing technology, the self-programming single-chip microprocessor. This type component is extremely difficult to defraud and the cost to defeat one component is very high with no guarantee of success. Smart cards are able to program their memory under their own control. They can, therefore, lock or otherwise restrict any of their functions when the established authentication procedures are not fulfilled. Some smart cards can even commit suicide when they come under security attack.

Smart cards have not yet been compromised. At least, there is no record of any successful reverse-engineering attack. That does not mean that they never will be compromised. But they do offer the greatest protection available today, as well as the flexibility to implement a variety of different sophisticated protection schemes over time. What's important to recognize is that smart card technology alone does not guarantee a secure system. It's part, albeit an important part, of an overall security scheme. The critical question concerning protection against fraud is a business one ... Does the cost problem justify the cost solution?

Updating

The content of smart cards can be quickly and easily updated using low voltage (5v), solid state card acceptor devices with no moving parts. This is a distinct advantage over magnetic cards which usually require a motorized device to move the card across a read/write head.

Reliability

Recent studies on the reliability of French bank cards shows that fewer than 1.5 percent of their smart cards fail because of "chip-related" problems while over 3.7 percent must be replaced due to magnetic stripe failures. The magnetic stripe failure rate is consistent with figures from Visa, MasterCard and Mag-Tek which shows between 3 to 4.5 percent of magnetic stripe cards fail worldwide.

Enabling Technology

From a marketing point of view, smart cards give companies new possibilities for unique product differentiation and a high-tech image. Smart cards are an enabling technology—one that allows new solutions that were not possible beforehand. They are being used in pay telephones to replace coins, in banking to replace "less-secure" magnetic stripe cards and to offer new services, in health care for emergency patient information and entitlement rights, for secure access control to buildings and computers, to scramble pay television signals, in mobile telephones, in lotteries, for electronic transfer of welfare benefits, in parking meters, vending machines, as city or town cards and as multiple application student identification cards on college campuses.

Smart cards provide the opportunity to rethink current transaction delivery systems. For example, processing every transaction on-line may not be necessary for most payment systems. This is because the card can maintain up-to-date information about its use which can help determine when an on-line session is necessary.

Smart Cards Are Not the Product

It's not unusual for an organization to get caught up in the fascination of smart card technology and momentarily forget what business they're in. This sometimes manifests itself in words such as, "Let me show you our plans for a smart card product." Very few organizations can legitimately lay claim to having a smart card product. Nearly all are card and terminal manufacturers or system integrators. Your organization may have Stored Value Card products, Frequent Shopper Card products, or Health Benefit Card products that are delivered using smart card technology but they are not smart card products. Remember what business you're in. Let your product define the choice of technology. Then, market your product benefits, not the promise of technology.[8]

END NOTES

1. Giakoumis, Alex and Jean Paul Schelkens. SOLAIC Group. 1992. "High Security Card." p.2.

2. Ibid, p. 3.

3. Ibid, p. 5.

4. "AT&T Contactless Smart Card." 1994. Description of Product. pp. 1–3.

5. Drexler Technology Company, Lasercard Systems, 1992-. DTC 029-2094.

6. Hondlob, Fred. 1994. "Advantages of Contactless Card." *Smart Card Technology Intensive.*" p. 37.

7. Panasonic. 1994. *Panasonic Memory Card Description*. pp. 1–3.

8. Schuler, Joe. 1995. "Selecting a Technology." Stored Value Systems, Division of National City Processing Co. pp. 1–3.

Part 2

Managing for Success

4

Successes and Failures in the Smart Card Industry

You may have to be obsessed with an idea or vision to turn it into a reality. Especially if you are establishing a new technology paradigm such as the smart card business. The vision is always parent to the reality.

—Arlen Richard Lessin

KEY FACTORS IN SMARTCARD INTERNATIONAL, INC.'S SUCCESSES, FAILURES AND FUTURE

Data and documentation provided by Arlen Richard Lessin
Chairman & CEO, SmartCard International, Inc.

Arlen Richard Lessin is the Distinguished Professor, Chair, and Founding Director of the Allan P. Kirby Center for Free Enterprise and Entrepreneurship at Wilkes University. He is concurrently Chairman/CEO of the Lessin Technology Group, Inc. (LTG), a NY-based consulting firm specializing in the facilitation of technology innovation, entrepreneurship, and the management of change and of SmartCard International, Inc., which consults and is developing, defining and designing smart card applications and solutions.

Mr. Lessin has advised or consulted in strategic marketing of various applied technologies, products and services, and in advanced telecommunications to the U.S., French, British, Austrian, Swedish, and Japanese governments, and to major commercial organizations internationally. He serves on various boards, lectures internationally and writes extensively, and is currently working on three books, *Exploring the Anatomy of Innovation—The Smart Card Story*; *Entrepreneurially Creating Entrepreneurs; and Everybody Hates Change*; *How To Make Them Love it*."

He is an alumnus (B.A.) of the University of California at Berkeley in Political Science, Economics and Business. He has pursued graduate studies at the University of California School of Law, the Aspen Institute, Columbia University, and a certificate management program at Harvard/MIT/TUFTS, among others.

Arlen R. Lessin: Smart Card Pioneer

Arlen R. Lessin discovered smart card technology in 1980 and had intense faith in its future. He was a pioneer in the industry, is currently regarded by many and has been publicly cited internationally as the father of smart card technology in the U.S. where he established a seminal company, SmartCard International, Inc. He was instrumental in its success, challenges, decline, and current rebirth.

The story actually began in the early 1970s when a young French computer enthusiast, Roland C. Moreno, became enthralled with the notion of putting a computer in a card. Mr. Moreno formed Societe International pour Innovatron. The *carte á memoíre* was first patented in France by Innovatron in the mid-1970s.

By 1980, the card was in the early prototype testing stages by several manufacturers in conjunction with the French government. *Carte á memoíre* was part of a larger program to combine videotext and an electronic telephone service into a national effort to bring computer and telecommunications technology to the home and office.

Intelmatique was an international organization chartered by the government of France in 1979 to promote and market carte a memoire memory cards and videotext technology. Roy D. Bright, an early developer of videotext, was its head. He coined a more descriptive, American-style name, "the smart card," and enlisted an American entrepreneur and information technology pioneer, Arlen R. Lessin, to introduce the technology to North America.

Mr. Lessin had himself discovered the smart card in 1980, tucked away at an exhibit at an international telecommunications conference. "I knew the moment I saw the card demonstrated that it would revolutionize the way we conduct both our business and personal lives," said Mr. Lessin in describing what was to become "a quest to bring *smart card* technology to the U.S."

But there were problems. The high price of the card and the need for special card readers mean a large investment for American financial institutions which were firmly entrenched in magnetic stripe systems. "The smart card had to be customized to the needs, applications, and culture of each country," Mr. Lessin said. "And, it needed to be self-contained with more memory."

With these objectives, Mr. Lessin persuaded Mr. Moreno to license the smart card patents to Mr. Lessin's new company, SmartCard International, Inc. (SCI). It became the first non-French company to receive the prestigious and necessary patents from Innovatron. The year was 1983. The next 10 years would be "dramatic and frustrating as we watched the company go both uphill and downhill," said Mr. Lessin.

Mr. Lessin struggled to raise capital to fund development in the U.S. He succeeded, first with a private placement of some $500,000 in early 1986 and on September 10, 1986, SmartCard International, Inc., became a public company. Its securities were traded the same day on NASDAQ. The company raised in excess of $5 million by going public and close to $7 million by 1987.

SmartCard International, Inc. (SCI)

SCI Focus

SCI was committed to the development of smart card technology, and offered smart card systems, hardware, and software.

SCI saw potentially rapid and material growth in an international market that would want smart card systems because they could provide workable answers and meet five basic criteria:

1. Applications that *satisfy needs*

2. Cards that *customers want* to use

3. Cards that are *flexible and secure* in operation and that require *minimal, if any, modifications* to in-place customer systems

4. *Self-powered cards* that are not dependent on new and expensive hardware infrastructures

5. *Cards that can work* at home, in the office, while traveling—anywhere

SCI Products

UltiCard. A complete series of the first interactive, self-powered, large memory, reprogrammable, display-readable smart cards. They are essentially self-contained systems.

MagnaCards. A complete family of the most advanced current generation smart cards with greater memory capacity than current cards of this type. Using more powerful chips, these cards have multipurpose operating systems, a better user interface, and a wider range of applications than other cards. They can be reprogrammed. SCI readers and writers provide for uploading and downloading data.

SCI Systems. Support systems of software, interfaces, and terminals.

SCI Five-Phase Approach Program. A sensible, cost-effective approach to the design and implementation of applications systems at the lowest possible cost, and with a minimum of financial exposure.

Systems Integration. Delivery of a total package or "turnkey" system to customers. Includes all required hardware and software.

SCI identified market segments that could benefit most from its knowledge and products. SCI identified 84 separate and distinct applications in these varied market segments. The most significant applications can be found in Table 4-1.

Table 4-1. Market Segments and Applications

Market Segment	Application
Universal cards	As in current card applications.
Retailing	*Charge accounts*, *customer profiling*, *direct store delivery*.
Health and Medicine	*Preventive medicine*: lipid control; weight control; hypertension; anti-smoking; stress control.
	Home health care and rehabilitation: Hospital administration: in-patients, out-patients, admission, checkout.
Health and Medicine	*Health insurance*: Insurance underwriting and actuarial data.
	Medical equipment/treatment support.
Banking and EFT	EFT POS, withdrawals, transfers, payments, remote interactive financial services.
State/Local Governments	*State residents' card systems.* *Social services and human resources departments*: Benefit transfer systems.
	Department of transportation: Public transportation, vehicle registration, drivers' licenses, dealer car tracking.
	Department of natural resources: Hunting, fishing, boating, recreation, and the like. Licenses and personal services.
	Department of voter registration: Registration, poll control .
	Department of vital statistics: Birth certificates, death certificates.
	Department of health: Medical records.
	Department of correction: Parole monitoring.

Short Form SCI Business Case: Overall Critical Issues, Decisions, Outcomes

A Chronological Capsule Case History

by Arlen Richard Lessin

The primary elements in the history of SCI's founding, rise, and subsequent decline and restructuring involved the following key factors and events:

SCI Successes

1980–1983

> Under the aegis of the French Government's new technology marketing arm, Intelmatique, the SCI founder's firm, Communications Consulting Corporation (CCC), is retained to pioneer the introduction to North America of the carte á memoíre. The new technology is soon to be renamed the smart card (credit-card-size computer). And it is claimed by its French innovators that it will be the world's most advanced version of personal, packaged microchip technology. The CCC premiering process creates a growing global recognition of the essential technical validity and future applications potential of a then only prototype state, transactional/information technology. Smart cards are at this point still at the beginning of a long journey, not untypical of the experience of many new technologies (including magnetic stripe cards, ATM's, fax machines, and even now-ubiquitous television).

1983

> SmartCard International, Inc. (SCI) is incorporated in New York City, under NY State law. SCI becomes the first wholly dedicated smart card company in the world.

1983

SCI successfully concludes complex negotiations for, and acquisition of, licensing for North America of the four (and later five) smart card technology controlling patents from the French originators, Roland Moreno and his company, Innovatron. Moreno joins the SCI Board of Advisors, along with other internationally prominent transaction, banking information, and security technology experts. This agreement constitutes the fourth Innovatron patent license awarded in the world and the first outside of France. (As of 1995, some 200 licenses are estimated to have been granted.)

1983–1986

SCI demonstrates the ability to build, enhance, and sustain public interest in smart card technology via consulting, conferences, seminars, speaking engagements, and media support. These activities take place during more than three years of self-funded operations and outside funding activities. These funding activities require aggressively prospecting for, identifying, pursuing, and educating potential financial sources. They include private investors, corporations with potential symbiotic interests, venture capitalists, newly emancipated telephone utilities, and French and Japanese companies involved in, or close to, the technology. Among them, various funding candidates are identified.

1985–1986

Recognizing the potential marketing/funding opportunity via bank card issuers, SCI negotiates a seminal contract with Visa to develop the prototype of a super-smart, standalone (terminal-independent and active) type of smart card (ULTRACARD/ULTRASMARTCARD). It is probable that the Visa decision is intended, in part, to supersede and divert attention from a MasterCard announcement of its own scheduled field testing of a conventional (terminal-dependent and passive) type of French smart card—set to take place in two U.S. retailing malls.

1986

Both a private placement funding and a subsequent public offering (IPO/NASDAQ) are completed. They total some $7 million (and include attached exercisable warrants, potentially providing $14 million in additional SCI funding in the 1987–1989 time frame.)

1986–1987

SCI develops a proprietary design, single microprocessor chip, and operating system. Shortly thereafter, the company produces the first U.S. commercial, conventional, reprogrammable (16KB EEPROM) smart card. It is named MagnaCards™.

1986–1987

SCI develops a proprietary microprocessor chip circuit board, and operating system. It then produces the first U.S. commercial prototype versions of the reprogrammable, super-smart type of card (64 KB EEPROM Supercard) for Visa and others. SCI's version is named ULTICARD.

1986–1989

SCI establishes a European market development office in London and liaison offices in Paris and Tokyo.

1983–1989

Briefing, consulting and development contracts are signed by SCI, including a major project with AT&T. In it, SCI contributes smart card and videotext (interactive video terminal) data and analysis to AT&T for its 10-year Strategic Business Plan for Public Communications. Among other contracts are those with Texas Instruments, Visa, the U.S. National Security Administration (NSA), Baylor University College of Medicine and Houston Medical Center (via a U.S. Small Business Innovation Research Grant [SBIR] from the National Institutes of Health and the Department of Health and Human Services), Thomas Cook Travel/Midland Bank (U.K.), Kodak (France), Avis (U.K.), Infomed, Connecticut Mutual Insurance, Robert Morris College, Security Pacific Bank, State of Hawaii Department of Human Services (pilot applications to include food stamps, Aid to Dependent Children [ADC] and health care).

1983–1989

SCI's multifaceted ability to interest and excite the media and the public regarding the technology is pursued and successfully demonstrated. The result: over 1500 smart card and SCI-focused stories in newspapers, magazines, radio and TV in the U.S. and globally in 1989. SCI is publicly recognized as probably the highest profile smart card company in the world.

1986–1989

SCI lobbies extensively and successfully to encourage vocal U.S. government and state legislative support from many sources. Among positive actions, Senator Robert S. Dole (R, KS) and Senator Daniel Patrick Moynihan (D, NY) jointly introduce a non-partisan U.S. Sense of the Senate Resolution, directing the U.S. Department of Agriculture (DOA) to implement actively smart card technology applications in food stamp and related trials. The Senate passes the resolution unanimously. Some

DOA pursuant action is taken, (but much is still pending, or in process, as of l995).

1989

SCI is awarded a U.S. patent for the UlTICARD/ULTRASMARTCARD.

SCI Failures

1983–1986

SCI marketing activities are negatively impacted by the underlying difficulty of attempting to make incursions in the market of the previously long delayed, and just implemented, magnetic stripe card technology (adopted by Visa, MasterCard, AMEX, Diner's, and others). As a corollary result, the company finds funding to be a difficult and extended process. Funding candidates are resistant to investing in a technology still unproven in the U.S. and as yet unendorsed by what are considered its foremost potential issuers.

1984

Progress towards business strategy funding needs is severely damaged by the U.S. Justice department's refusal to allow one of the newly divested Baby Bells and Southwestern Bell, both to invest $1 million in SCI and to act as a diversified SCI pilot field-testing participant. This denial is attributable to the Department of Justice's (DOJ's) interpretation of the AT&T Divestiture Decree of 1983, banning involvements in "Information Services."

1985

The achievement of funding goals is impeded further by already delineated factors and, again, by the U.S. Justice department's refusal to allow Southwestern Bell to loan

SCI, as opposed to invest, $3 million–$5 million. This action is once more allegedly based on the previous DOJ rationale. Essentially, the decision is rendered (as stated by DOJ staff) because the DOJ wants to keep it completely dedicated to their telephone businesses and out of other, even if peripherally related, potential information technology businesses which could become engaged in manufacturing.

1986–1989

SCI marketing activities are substantially and negatively affected by the refusal, probably politically based, of French smart card companies to allow SCI to act as the primary agent for any one of them in the U.S. This forces the company into very expensive, originally unintended product development and manufacturing activities of its own. It is a critical and substantive diversion from the company's founding premise of acting: (1) as a smart card technology marketing, applications, and system solutions company; and (2) as a smart card value-added reseller (SCVAR) of a matrix of various international smart card products (hardware, firmware, and software).

1987

The stock-market crash of October, 1987, essentially eliminates the value of SCI stock warrants by radically reducing SCI's common stock price to an unredeemable price level. In this regard, the attached stock warrants (which holders might have exercised for as little as 20 percent of SCI's earlier common stock share's peak value) could have brought in as much as $14 million in additional cost-free funding for SCI in the 1987–1989 exercise period. (SCI has a projected minimal capital requirement of $10–$15, to carry out its marketing strategy. Its needs therefore are unmet and its strategy is stymied.)

1988–1989

> The 1987 stock market debacle, deeply depressing the value and marketability of nearly all new technology stocks, further prevents SCI from pursuing its planned market development program—based on investing in selected, qualified, high-profile market potential applications in vertical market sectors. Very critically, it also substantially diverts the company management's energies into fund raising and capital-intensive "crash level" product development, rather than into market development. The company's treasury is being substantially depleted, while viable investment opportunities prove to be very limited; and SCI revenues are well below its operational overhead.

1989

> Compelled to reduce its overhead, SCI reluctantly closes its key European office in the U.K. This jeopardizes implementation of U.K. and French pilot contracts.

1989

> Choosing to preserve SCI's assets and future growth potentials, its founder dilutes and sells much of his personally held controlling stock assets to acquiring interests and resigns his company management offices. He remains on SCI's board, later resigning from it to avoid any conflict of interests arising from his new venture activities.

1989–1991

> Following the departure of the founder, the company's new controlling interests and management radically change SCI's business course and concentrate nearly entirely on developing smart card terminals, essentially abandoning both cards and SCI's current customer base.

The targeted emphasis becomes health care applications, which have yet to surface in the U.S. SCI revenues continue to decline. The company changes its name to IX Systems.

1994

The company exhausts its funding and suspends its operations. IX Systems remains passively in business, discussing mergers, assets disposition, and so on.

1995

At this writing, despite clear signs of significant growth in the U.S. smart card industry, IX Systems' future is cloudy and unresolved. SCI's founder takes an initiative, based on a realistic U.S. smart card marketplace in formation. A number of major U.S. and international players are beginning to commit to smart card implementations. SmartCard International is re-formed as a smart card applications and software solutions firm with Arlen R. Lessin as Chairman and CEO.

The original venture was a substantial though carefully planned and calculated gamble on the part of SmartCard International (SCI). Its plan was to introduce a product in the United States that was the result of new and unique French-flavored technology. The product—smart cards—cannot be distributed directly to its end users—the public—without substantial endorsement, support, and financial commitment of middlemen—government, banks, large corporations, credit card companies, etc.

In addition to these built-in hurdles, the SCI project also violated the general marketing principle which discourages the making of a market, as opposed to meeting one. It is virtually impossible to create a market without sufficient amounts of money and luck. At critical junctures, SCI had insufficient amounts of either.

SCI's aggressive strategic business and marketing plans had been carefully designed to overcome these hurdles and establish the SCI marketplace. We defined SCI markets and pursued selected seed funding in them. Investment funds, however, proved to be unavailable for SCI to achieve our objectives. An alternative funding plan was formulated so that potential smart card issuers could take substantive, committed positions in programs involving financing, marketing, and implementation.

Smart card technology received positive media exposure and initial public indications of support. Compared to magnetic stripe cards, smart cards had substantially greater memory, intelligence, and applications flexibility. One billion smart cards have been issued in Europe in the 10-year period beginning in 1985, and millions more in Asia, Australia, and Africa. But the American smart card was saddled with drawbacks: relatively new (and untried in the U.S.) technology, and the high cost of smart cards and terminals that, because of low volume, made them too expensive to compete in the marketplace with magnetic stripe cards.

SCI did not solicit monetary investments from selected high-profile customers. The growth plan was mapped to avoid the pitfalls that had befallen the first French manufacturers (and later players such as Toshiba, IBM, and AT&T). But from 1983 to 1994, no major U.S. issuing entity was willing to take a significant position with smart card technology that would have involved a minimum purchase of 500,000 to one million cards, plus associated peripheral equipment.

What was going wrong? SCI's managers were not novice entrepreneurs. They were well aware how reluctant hard-headed organizations can be when it comes to investing in still-unproven technology with unplotted cost-effectiveness. To circumvent this mind-set, SCI intended to create its marketplace by investing its own money and seeding its own selected market sectors. SCI would research and then choose designated pilot customers; then together, they would target viable pilot applications that carried high probabilities for success. Based on the success of the test-market application, the customers would then order product (known as the "Integrated System Solutions") in quantity from SCI.

A major breakthrough was imminent for SCI in 1984 when Southwestern Bell Corporation (SBC) agreed to invest $10 million in the company. A controlling equity holding was not requested by SBC at that time. But the flow of this capital to SCI was impeded by the U.S. Department of Justice's position regarding SBC investments.

At about this same time, SCI was disappointed by French smart card manufacturers who had an apparent change of mind or strategy regarding product commitments to this small U.S. company still navigating a foothold in a difficult market environment. Then, the 1987 financial crash prevented shareholders from exercising their warrants and the resulting capital infusion into SCI of approximately $14 million. SCI had budgeted these monies to fund its critical development program.

The ripple effect of these setbacks was felt in SCI's ability to support its expansion plans. Some contracts were negotiated, but the potential for the company's growth was shaken.

Finally, the abandonment in late 1989 by SCI's newly installed controlling interests of the SCI strategic business plan, customer base, and essentially smart cards themselves, made the enterprise unable to build on the substantive understructure laid by the company since its founding. This outcome occurred despite the infusion of millions of dollars in additional funding from 1989 to 1994. The total investment in SCI is estimated at about $11 million to $12 million since its inception. Capital infusion was irregular after 1986.

Lessons Learned From the Failure of SCI

1. Too early in a reluctant "prove it to me U.S. marketplace"

   Although research studies by such organizations as Arthur D. Little and MasterCard International indicated that smart card technology made economic sense at mass levels, its broad acceptance has been long in coming to the U.S. For SCI, delays during its first critical three and one-half years (1983–1986) in growth and development were based on an unconvinced, wait-and-see investment community and a technology looking for a solution.

2. Lack of sufficient capital to overcome this recognized obstacle

   SCI had to prove the technical and financial viability of specific smart card customer applications in order for SCI products to attain critical mass, cost effectiveness, and profitability levels. Had adequate funds been available to fund its initial business strategy, SCI would have had an excellent chance at making smart card utilization happen commercially.

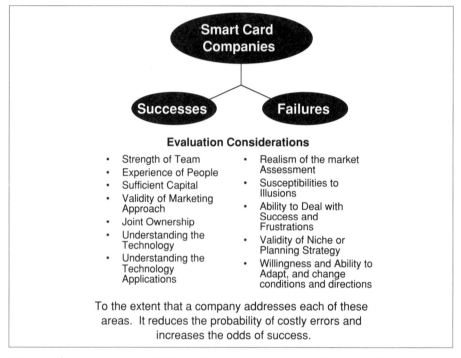

Figure 4-1. Success and failure factors for smart card companies.

Future of Smart Cards

Although its applications have been primarily single functions (telephone, toll, ID cards, etc.), I believe today, as in 1980, that the ultimate success of smart card technology will be substantially based upon its multi-functional capabilities. Its key technological assets are:

- Using the technology as with multi-functional flexibility and functions possible within one card. This long-term position has been vindicated by the formal visions of both Visa and MasterCard to pursue their strategy.

- Potentially unlimited reprogramability and updatability.

- Developing the programs to be used in marketing solutions like combining several cards into one card case.

These built-in capabilities will take smart cards out of competition with other card technologies and give them a recognized, powerful edge for applications and cost-effectiveness.

THE FUTURE OF THE NEW SMARTCARD INTERNATIONAL, INC. (SCI)

The 1995 re-forming of SmartCard International, Inc. (SCI), which I originally initiated in 1983, will hopefully prove to be of significant value to the U.S. and international smart card applications marketplace. SCI is being structured essentially as an applications definition, design and turnkey solutions implementation company. We will write customized software for clients and obtain hardware from appropriate suppliers, of which there are now many around the world. Applications activities will be enhanced be utilizing personnel with 10 or more years of hands-on smart card experience, and capitalizing on the benefits of having learned through both successes and failures.

Smart cards have come a long long way since 1980 when I first saw prototype cards as a potentially very significant technology—even though manufactured smart cards did not then exist.

Perhaps this chapter and, in particular, this segment about the new SmartCard International, as deja vú all over again, can most appropriately be capsulized with words relevant to SCI's original founding years. The "Introduction to the SCI Marketing Plan" as completed in August, 1984, (two years before SCI became a public company) included the following statement of SCI purpose:

> "It is evident from years of hands-on research that the smart card will happen with or without SCI. Of course there will be competition. However, no other company in the world today is totally dedicated to which SCI plans

to actively position itself in the marketplace, we fully expect to exert a dominant position in the future multi-billion dollar smart card system industry.

It should be further stated that it is SCI's clear intent to be flexible in its approach in the marketplace. We will pursue all logical avenues in product packaging, distribution, and development. In the beginning, we plan to operate as a smart card systems integrator, obtaining products from French and other sources. As soon as possible, we will have proprietary products of our own.

SCI will utilize a strategical and tactical marketing mix. It will range from providing consultative service to full turnkey system. We will strive to meet the market requirements in keeping with our profit and growth goals.

This then was part of SCI's 1984 statement of purpose, which funding problems prevented from coming to fruition in its first life. Much of it is still applicable to the new SmartCard International and its future. Since this statement, of course, in the intervening years, some one billion chip cards of all kinds have been produced in the world. Still, in my professional analysis today, this number represents just the tip of the smart card proliferation iceberg. To use an analogy to a U.S. presidential campaign slogan of the 1930s, promising "A chicken in every pot." A likely development in the twenty-first century may well, if belatedly, prove to be "a smart card in every pocket."

HEALTH INFORMATION TECHNOLOGY

Smart Care Health Service Case Study

There are several common reasons for failures of smart card companies, like limited capital or poor management, but these are too general and require a much more detailed explanation.

Most smart card business fail during the first three years of operation, a third as early as the end of the first year, due to a small, limited market. As we observed from previous chapters, the market in the U.S. is just beginning, and a company needs sufficient resources to become a player in this marketplace.

Small Limited Market

A good example is Mark Landis who formed Health Information Technologies in 1987 to offer card services in the health care marketplace.[1]

Mark Landis, a successful entrepreneur who graduated from Cornell University and went on to earn a J.D. from the University of Pennsylvania, had a vision for a smart card health service. His previous experience was well suited to kickoff a new smart card company. He had been chairman and CEO of Computer Application Systems, Inc., (CASI) a computer security firm that developed electronic systems for physical security using magnetic stripe cards. CASI systems were marketed to commercial clients on a nationwide basis.

Mr. Landis' personal skills included negotiating initial acquisition of an 80 percent interest in an existing start-up company; guiding the company through significant growth from losses to profitability; and negotiating the sale of the company in 1987 at a return on investment to investors of 500 percent. He was an excellent candidate to launch a smart card business and build a company with a strong position in this marketplace.

Mr. Landis planned to offer a medical emergency database service using a smart card to identify a patient's medical history at hospitals participating in the service. Patients would pay $25 for the service, fill out a medical questionnaire and have the medical and insurance data entered into a Smart Card and backed up in a central database. Additionally, Mr. Landis envisioned the card to be used in displaying insurance information such as policy number, expiration date, and types of insurance plan offered. The justification for the service was simple—help hospitals and physicians to get paid sooner, and provide a faster method to identify a patient's medical history. Other benefits for both patient and hospital were:

- Eliminate duplicate or unnecessary tests

- Reduce insurance carrier administrative costs

- Most important, save lives

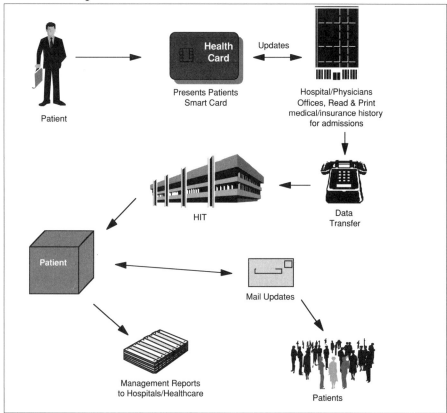

Figure 4-2. How a health smart card frequency program works.

Pioneering a New Service

As Mr. Landis soon discovered, the medical profession and insurance companies had other ideas. They viewed the service as a big investment in the cost of smart cards because they felt that patients would not pay for the service, but would expect the card free of charge. Liability of accurate data began to emerge as a key item, and the fact that new smart card readers were necessary at all locations to read and write to a smart card.

Mr. Landis did succeed in signing up local hospitals and began offering the smart card health service to insurance firms and credit card companies that would offer the service as an additional benefit to their members. Visa International showed interest and talks were underway to launch a test program within a defined region. "I was on my way," said Mr. Landis. "I was moving forward to launch a big campaign and to build up the smart card business. I invested heavily in the business and sold shares in the company to offer this program throughout the U.S. market."

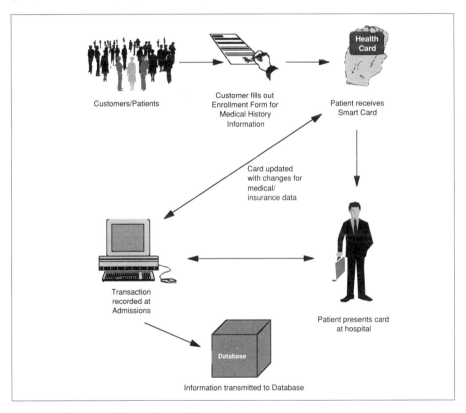

Figure 4-3. Health card enrollment.

Decline of Service

Mr. Landis quickly found out that smart card was a "technology looking for a solution." After several months of negotiations, Visa International backed out of the program. Furthermore, insurance companies were not willing to pay for the cost of smart cards and readers at hospital locations. "The infrastructure was too big of a nut to crack," said Mr. Landis. "No large company was willing to step up to the plate and support the system. Maybe when the cost of the cards comes down, there might be a market for us to explore."

As costs rose and expenses increased, Mr. Landis changed the direction of the company by substituting magnetic stripe cards for smart cards and focusing more on a physician insurance service. The company, after two years of effort, began to offer an electronic data interchange service to permit doctors and other providers of health care services to communicate with insurers that operated managed care plans.

Providers can verify eligibility, inquire about plan rules, file claims, make referrals, and produce a variety of management reports. Smart cards were offered as an option as a platform to gather data, making the service more feasible and cost-effective.

Managing Flexibility and Growth

It is most important that smart card companies remain flexible and know how to deal with growth. Most smart card businesses have to recognize the industry changes to stay competitive in the volatile marketplace.

Take as an example, a smart card manufacturer who begins production using a chip capacity of 8K byte for its initial business. Frequently the dominating force in the business is the technologist who wants to bring the product sold and into use. In this case, a smart card with 8K bytes of memory is expensive—$5 to $10 per card—and has to be integrated into the marketing and sales processes.

When crucial decisions have to be made, share the responsibility with a second group to gauge the marketability of the product. Determine what you collectively think will sell, based on price and demand.

Operationally, the product should perform flawlessly, and all the bugs will have been worked out of the service. It will be expensive to produce a different chip for the card, so evaluate the potential for further refinement. Keep in mind that a feasibility analysis may be needed to find ways to make the business more adept at coping with change and growth.

This is a good example of becoming infatuated with a service without really understanding whether or not there is a market.

END NOTES

1. Landis, Mark. Feb., 1995. "Health Information Technology. Interview on Smart Card Users."

5

The SWOT Analysis—Develop the Strategy for Managing a Smart Card Business

How to use SWOT to analyze your internal and external business environment.

Do it now, before you plan to utilize smart card technology.

PREPARING THE SWOT ANALYSIS

Whether you are in the banking, health care, telecommunications, or any other field, smart card technology can increase the value of your company's products and services. Once you have come up with a promising smart card opportunity, what next?

Before committing the company to prepare a business operation plan, you must do a SWOT analysis. SWOT stands for:

- Strengths
- Weaknesses
- Opportunities
- Threats

The SWOT analysis looks at the internal and external environments that face you and your group. Externally, what is the structure of the industry? Who are your competitors? Will you be the first to launch a new technology? Is governmental regulation an issue? In the case of smart cards, could your idea be perceived to invade an individual's privacy?

Internally, how consistent is your product? What new products are in the pipeline? What kind of sales force will you use? What are your start-up financial requirements?

This analysis is sometimes called a marketing analysis or feasibility study. No matter what name you use, you assess where you are both internally and in the outside world. This process will help you develop a strategy that leverages your strengths and accounts for your weaknesses.

For instance, the SWOT analysis may reveal that your product is superior but your industry contacts are weak. Considering this reality, you had better plan to market your product through a direct sales force rather than through an alliance with a major company.

In this chapter, we will present the SWOT analysis model, and then apply the model to a case in the financial services industry. Most existing smart card applications to date are telephone cards and communications, financial, followed by health, retail, education, security, government. For our purposes here, the SWOT analysis has a financial application. The framework is general enough, however, to be used for any industry analysis.

We will first examine the external environment. The external environment must be taken as a given; it includes factors such as existing players and government regulation, over which we have little control.

External Environment—Threats and Opportunities

In what kind of environment is your firm functioning? By assessing the outside conditions, you can tailor your firm's behavior to best leverage the current situation. In developing your smart card idea, first you need to ask, "How will industry standards affect my product?" or "Will competitors soon make my technology obsolete?" "How healthy is my industry at this time? Does it have the resources to make new investments in smart card technology?" Several factors make up the dynamics of an industry: competition, technology, economic conditions, and political and social factors.

Competition

First, you should identify your competitors. What other companies are out there doing something similar to what you want to do? Finding out who they are and what they've been doing can: (1) help you avoid mistakes they have made and (2) design your product to a niche theirs does not cover. As Casey Stengel once said, describing the key to his fantastic batting average, "I hit 'em where they ain't." You can learn about potential competitors by doing database searches, calling and requesting press kits, conducting informational interviews, and networking at trade shows.

Once you know who your competitors are, you can begin to analyze the competitive environment. In *Competitive Strategy* (Free Press, 1980), Michael Porter speaks of the "Five Forces" that make up the competitive environment: Barriers to Entry, Degree of Rivalry, Bargaining Power of Suppliers, Bargaining Power of Customers, and Substitutes.[1]

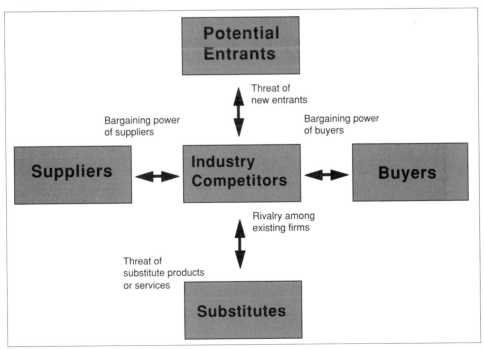

Figure 5-1. Evaluating the competition.

Forces and Barriers to Entry

Certain industries might be less desirable to enter based on industry structure. Factors that make low or high barriers to entry are the following:[1]

1. **Economies of scale**—Unit costs decline as volume increases. Are competitors already doing a smart card product? Do they already have a high volume? Can they sell it for less than you can produce it?

2. **Product differentiation**—This refers to brand identification and customer loyalties from past advertising or customer service. How different are the other products in the industry? Smart cards give issuers new opportunities for product differentiation and expansion.

3. **Capital requirements**—This includes up-front costs from product development and advertising as well as facilities, inventories, customer credit, and start-up losses. How well-capitalized are your competitors?

4. **Switching costs**—These are one-time costs the buyer faces when switching from one supplier to another. Must buyers obtain a new bank account or credit card to use your product?

5. **Access to distribution channels**—Do competitors have favorable ties, based on long-range or exclusive relationships or high-quality service, that will affect your distribution plans? Is there one premier distributor you must have, or several potential distributors of similar size and reach?

6. **Cost disadvantages independent of scale**—Disadvantages could be such aspects as proprietary technology, favorable access to raw materials and location, government subsides, and learning and experience. Where does your firm stand in this process?

7. **Government policy**—This is government regulation you must consider, including licensing, limiting access to raw materials, and standards for product testing and pollution control. In the past, in

order to maintain public trust and economic stability, the government has closely monitored banks for adequate cash supply in proportion to deposits, etc. Because of the security risks in electronic commerce (in 1993, $600 million was lost in electronic transactions to fraud, as we will discuss later), it is likely that the government will carefully monitor smart card commerce.

8. **Industry standards**—For open system applications (applications with a general-use rather than a proprietary-use card), no standards and specifications exist that would allow all smart cards—regardless of their branding—to be accepted in a single POS device. You need to get involved in the development of these guidelines, or forever accept standards tailored to someone else's advantage.

9. **Protection through patent or lead time advantage**—If you are marketing based on innovation, how will you defend against copycats? Will you have the next generation of products ready for introduction as the competition is bringing out its first?

Rivalry

If you decide to enter an industry despite barriers to entry, how will your competitors react? Will they ignore you and continue to pursue their own strategies, or will they react swiftly to drive you out of the business before you can gain a toehold? The intensity of rivalry is based on the following factors:[2]

1. **Numerous or equally balanced competitors**—Several banks, including Chemical Bank and Citibank, have invested considerable money in becoming the smart card leaders. How will you catch up to their lead?

2. **Slow industry growth**—Banks grow slowly, often by stealing market share from competitors. Thus, rivalry is cutthroat. To make matters worse, many non-traditional players such as General Motors (GM Card) and insurance companies are innovating in the financial services industry with varying degrees of success. Can you steal sufficient market share from other players?

3. **High fixed or storage costs**—Financial services firms have confronted deep downsizings to reduce fixed back-office costs. They are more cost-effective than ever before. Are you?

4. **Lack of differentiation or switching costs**—Are customers indifferent when choosing between the competitors' products and yours?

5. **Capacity augmented in large increments**—How much unused capacity will your competitors have if they allow you to succeed?

6. **High strategic stakes**—How important are smart cards to your rival's strategy?

7. **High exit barriers**—The stability of financial services firms is so important to the national economy that the government will intervene to keep them afloat. This special position serves as a powerful deterrent to exit.[3] A summary of rivalry factors in evaluating the competition is shown in Figure 5-2.

Evaluating the Competition

FACTOR	ATTRACTIVENESS	
	HIGH	LOW
Rivalry among existing firms	Imperfect competition or emerging industry	Few players; mature or declining industry
Bargaining power of buyers	Individual buyer volume low	Product undifferentiated; buyer faces few switching costs
Bargaining power of suppliers	Many substitute sources	Limited supply; products differentiated
Threat of substitutes	Few, different alternatives	Many perfect substitutes
Threat of new entrants	Complex barriers to entry	Few simple entry barriers

Figure 5-2. Evaluating the competition.

Technology: First Mover or Second Mover?

In this section we will concentrate on the role of technology in new applications. Smart card technology has existed since the 1970s, yet its use has not become widespread.

Two contrasting strategies can be employed by different companies regarding technology—being a leader or being a follower. Either works for individual firms, based on a firm's internal strengths and weaknesses (the SW of our SWOT analysis). Being there first can give a firm a lead on competition that is difficult for others to overtake. AT&T has not yet made money from smart cards, but it will be way ahead when other firms enter the market. AT&T's strategy involves a continuing commitment of considerable time and money with the always-present risk of failure to produce a product that will create a viable profitable basin. Firms considering smart card applications must either fund their own research or have a source from whom they can buy or license it.

The second technological strategy of being a follower can work because you can learn from the leader's mistakes, and then position yourself so you're not in direct competition with the leader. In financial services smart cards, AT&T and Chemical Bank are in a position to be leaders. In November, 1993, they announced an alliance to introduce smart card banking applications into the New York City market. In their first trial, a number of Chemical Bank employees were issued smart debit cards to be used for purchases in the company cafeteria. The employees were able to transfer cash value to the cards from their bank accounts at select Chemical ATMs, which were equipped to read smart cards. Other major leaders are MasterCard and Visa, who have both announced financial stored value programs in a pilot environment.

On the other hand, companies who wait to see how these trials turn out will learn from their mistakes.

Economic Conditions

Economic conditions both in the U.S. and internationally are an important external environmental factor. While a smart card firm might perceive itself to be helpless regarding the economy due to its small size, it is important to consider this area. Economic growth information by location and by industry can help you choose your industry and location. Interest rates also affect your attempt to secure funds for your firm, as well as consumption. For instance, when interest rates are high and housing starts are down, one does not launch a home security smart card application. Unemployment affects you in terms of the availability and salary requirements of the types of workers you need.

Finally, demographics affect the market. The "graying of America" offers great opportunities financial or health applications for seniors. Remember that analyzing these trends in foreign countries gives you the opportunity to export.

Political and Social Factors

Smart card applications have touched on highly regulated industries such as health care and telecommunications. The effect of the government's intervention in your business, therefore, should be taken into account. Deregulation has opened up the banking industry to new players, which have turned the competitive structure of the industry on its head.

Several groups are lobbying for measures that make it a crime to access a person's smart card records without proper approval or purpose. Privacy must be maintained, although people differ on what constitutes privacy. The smart card must be launched carefully for end-users to understand the safeguards for their privacy.

Privacy: An Explosive Issue

The issue of privacy and smart cards, especially for financial and health applications, is potentially explosive. As long as smart cards are less than 100 percent secure, sensitive financial or health information could be plundered by cyberpirates. Furthermore, a smart card holder may lose control over the information even when the card is willingly released. For instance, a woman admitted to a Catholic hospital may prefer not to tell the doctor she had an abortion, but may have no choice if the information is on her smart card health history. Or, if an individual's financial history is centralized on a smart card, the information could conceivably get back to an ex-spouse, the IRS, the college financial aid office, or other ruinous destinations.

Privacy advocates will vigilantly protect individuals' rights against businesses harvesting credit histories or market database information for profit. Their methods range from letter-writing campaigns to offending companies, threatened boycotts, and lobbying for protective legislation. (For further information, see the "Privacy" section in appendix D.)

Security

The growth of television home shopping and PC-based information services, illustrates consumers' increasing comfort with self-service and automated access devices. The point of service is moving to where the customer is, increasing the reliance on the card as the only link between the customer and the service provider.

Today, there is inadequate security to protect payment information for transactions originating at these remote points of service. Information is passed through telephone lines, cable, or satellite. Hackers can listen, steal, then fraudulently use financial data.

The migration in the use of credit and debit cards to remote mediums (as compared to face-to-face transactions) requires that a secure access device be provided that can guarantee to the issuer the authenticity of the card and the cardholder, as well as protect the integrity and privacy of the transaction. Security will certainly become a go/no go assumption for your venture.

Internal Environment—Strengths and Weaknesses

In developing a smart card application, the internal environment includes the individuals involved and the resources they can muster to support the project. This depends on their support within the company, the company's strength in the various functional areas (marketing, manufacturing, service, etc.) and the importance of the project to the company's overall strategy. Often technology firms are characterized as being market-driven or product driven. Apple Computer Co., under Steve Jobs, was considered product-driven. It released the products it wanted to release, believing that a market would follow. By contrast, Apple under John Sculley was market-oriented. John Sculley, who came from Cocoa-Cola, believed in tailoring products to suit perceived customer needs. He increased the number of new models released in order to catch all market segments. However, the strategy failed because the consumer realized that the new models were window dressing, not significant technological advances.

Throughout the rest of this section, "product" refers to both smart card products, services and/or applications.

Marketing: The Four Ps

We will use the classic "Four Ps" (product, place, promotion, and price) to evaluate a firm's marketing.[4] The firm's products should be compared to products offered by competitors in terms of quality and features. Unique attributes that are important to customers should be identified and highlighted. The products should be considered from the physical standpoint, for size and appearance can be important attributes. On the other hand, the service element of smart card applications is as important as the product itself. A smart card, at a minimum, needs a read/write machine to be of any use, and in banking applications, for example, smart cards require a back-office network service as well. Without this infrastructure, the card is useless.

Important marketing characteristics for your smart card idea will be introduced here, and discussed in more detail in the case analysis.

- **User-friendliness**—Will non-computer-literate people feel comfortable using your smart card product?

- **Reliability**—Will the card work? Will the user feel 100 percent confident that the card works? What backup system is in place in case the card does not work?

- **Versatility**—Can the customer use your card for services involving a different vendor? In the customer's eyes, how useful is your card?

- **Cost-effectiveness**—How does delivery cost compare to the customer's perceived value of the service?

- **Compelling use**—The initial smart card application must be universal and valuable, to compel a critical mass of people to accept it.

Smart Card Marketing—The Four P's

- **Product**
  - Compelling use: application must attract critical mass of users
  - Versatility: does the product have multiple uses?
  - Cost-effectiveness: is service's perceived value worth the delivery cost?
- **Price**
  - Start up: new high-tech products command price premium
  - Transition to maturity: price to cover costs; eliminate unprofitable lines
  - Maturity: Competitive price cutting begins
- **Place**
  - Direct sales force vs. distributors: smart card sale complex; direct reps give you better service and control
- **Promotion**
  - Smart card's promotional issues: a. industry must create a need for new technology (remember VCR's?) b. installed base of magnetic stripe cards

---

Figure 5-3. Smart card marketing.

Pricing: Influenced by Cost and Competition

Firms can price products according to their costs, or they can price them by the market. Ultimately, competition exerts a strong influence on pricing. Product differentiation can moderate or minimize the influence of competition, but it can never completely insulate the company. Even if one financial smart card product monopolized the market, substitute products such as cash would compete. Pricing takes into consideration features offered compared to competitive products and the value perceived by the customer. In general, customers seem to be willing to pay more for perceived superior quality.

Place: Technical Products Require Direct Sales Force

Smart cards cannot be distributed through retailers. Nor could distributors effect the complementary network of smart card-compatible ATMs and other read/write devices. The complexity of the product and necessary accessories requires a well-trained, technical sales force.

Selling carried out by an internal sales force, rather than using agents or brokers, is important for a small firm if it is financially strong and can handle the administration of a sales force, if its products are similar and use the same marketing channel, if sales territories are concentrated, and if it wants to retain primary control of distribution. Other issues to be considered are the use of specialists versus generalists as salespersons and the assignment of territories which may be exclusive, overlapping, or unassigned. The number of accounts to be assigned to an individual salesperson must be determined, as well as the use of house accounts. In turn, compensation could include a salary, a commission, or some combination of the two. Incentives are important with an increased emphasis on individual achievement.

Promotion: Educate Public before Selling to Them

Promotion is often identified with advertising. Advertising can inform customers and induce them to buy the product being advertised. However, with a complex product such as smart cards, you need a more sophisticated promotion approach. Visa and MasterCard have started the education process to promote the use of smart cards through trade shows, press junkets, demonstrations, and other promotions.

It took 10 years for VCRs to achieve mass penetration in the U.S. It may take smart cards longer to penetrate, considering the established base of magnetic stripe cards. Market research is particularly important for a new product like smart cards to determine what people want or will be willing to try.

Product Development: One-Hit Wonders Need Not Apply

One-product companies are unlikely to survive. Any product has a limited life, although some products have longer "legs" than others. Product developers must be able to establish and extend a line of products.

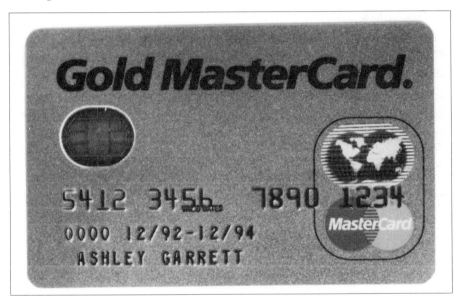

Figure 5-4. MasterCard smart card.

MASTERCARD'S NEW SMART CARD—A CASE STUDY

MasterCard International, a global payments franchise company with offices in 20 countries and headquarters in Westchester NY, comprises more than 22,000 member financial institutions worldwide. Through its family of brands, MasterCard, Maestro, and Cirrus, MasterCard offers a full range of credit and debit products and services supported by a global transaction processing network. MasterCard has nearly 290 million credit and debit cards issued and its cards are accepted at nearly 13 million locations worldwide.

The Role of MasterCard

In 1994, the MasterCard International board of directors unanimously approved a plan to build a foundation for the acceptance of microchip cards ("smart cards") anywhere the MasterCard brand is accepted.

Member banks (a member is the bank issuing the MC or Visa-branded cards) wanted MasterCard to take a leadership role in chip technology offers many benefits to the banks including improved fraud control, authorization flexibility and value added services.

The smart card's increased storage capacity enables members to tailor products and services to a single cardholder to strengthen and expand the customer relationship. Provided the capacity is sufficient, all these products and services can be maintained on one card, increasing the cardholder's utility. New opportunities for smart cards are shown in Figure 5-5.

Card Feature	Product Opportunity	Profitability Impact
Card authentication and cardholder verification	• Enhance security of existing products	• Expand into new geographic markets • Expand into new retailer environments (e.g., unattended terminals)
Intelligent microprocessing power	• Cardholder-specific, issuer-controlled authorization parameters	• Lower fraud losses • Reduce authorization cost • Extend credit to higher-risk customers
Increased storage capacity	• Support multiple applications on one card	• Enable members to tailor products/services to a single cardholder
Upgradable	• New security measures • Support new complex, memory-intensive products	• Maintain control over risk • Maintain/expand customer base

Figure 5-5. New opportunities with smart cards.

Adapting to a Changing Industry

Over the last ten years the plastic payments industry has changed dramatically and chip technology is clearly necessary to help members combat new fraud problems, reduce costs, and support new products and enhanced services.

As more cards are used at unattended terminals and other remote points of sale the potential for fraud impacts cardholders and issuers. The fraud issue and criminal use of technology dictates that a long-term solution needs to be chip-based for optimal card security.

Competition Heating Up

In the meantime, thanks to deregulation, competition has intensified among the major card providers and new players may enter the businesses, cable companies, and other pre-paid service providers.

Also, technology is changing the delivery of payment products and services. The proliferation of ATMs, unattended POS terminals, and global networks has allowed consumers to tap financial services and information anywhere in the world. Furthermore, technological advances are providing new payment product opportunities for retail customers that involve new, more sophisticated card products. The result is that plastic card volume and usage has climbed. MasterCard sales volume alone totaled $389.9 billion in 1994.

As more consumers use cards at self-service machines or to make remote payments, they are selecting service providers whose plastic payments products offer optimum access, utility, convenience, and financial control. In light of this trend, "chip technology is the best long-term product delivery solution and one that will help MasterCard and members maintain a competitive edge."[5]

THE BENEFITS OF CHIP TECHNOLOGY

The microchip in cards is similar to those in computers and other electronic products. One advantage of the chip is that it can be embedded into a plastic card without affecting its thickness or other dimensions. It is also more upgradable than the magnetic stripe. The more memory a chip has, the more (and increasingly complex) functions it can support.

Because the plastic payments business demands a high level of security and flexibility, a microprocessor chip (as opposed to lower-capability memory-only chips or chips having memory with hardwired logic) is the most appropriate to support MasterCard applications. Microprocessor chips can "think" using information provided during any transaction, which explains the origin of the name "smart card."

These chips, like small computers, are extremely difficult to compromise. In fact, many manufacturers have a built-in "self destruct" mechanism that activates in the event of tampering.

As a risk-control tool, the microprocessor chip can support a card authentication method (CAM) that is secure and operates off-line and on-line. Also, it employs a card-holder verification method (CVM) that encodes a cardholder identifier (e.g., a PIN or biometric, such as a fingerprint) in a secret area of the chip. This means the CVM can be verified off-line as well, which offers a distinct security advantage.

Credit and Debit Applications

New products, such as stored value cards, can be introduced safely without requiring an on-line transaction. Because a chip can store transaction information and send data in batches to a terminal or through the network, a card can be given a pre-determined value and used in low-ticket purchases.

Other products or services can be programmed onto the card. Smart cards also offer the ability to add value to existing credit and debit cards. For example, loyalty programs, electronic couponing, financial/information data and transportation are among the types of applications the industry is considering. This can be done on a debit or a credit product, which makes a card that more valuable and useful to a cardholder than ever before.

Moreover, the chip allows issuers (banks that issue payment cards) to securely and cost-effectively introduce products into new geographic markets. And because the chip is so secure, it is ideal as an access device for remote electronic services such as home banking and cellular telephones.

Risk Control Tool

As a risk control tool, the MC smart card combats counterfeiting by authenticating the card securely—off-line as well as on-line. It can verify the cardholder's identity off-line as well, using a PIN typed in by the cardholder at the merchant's register. The ability to remain off-line securely reduces transaction costs and allows MC to expand into new geographic markets that may have unreliable telephone infrastructures such as Eastern Europe, and new retailer markets such as home banking, cellular telephony, and unattended terminals.

From the issuer's point of view ("issuer" refers to member banks), the more services the card offers, the more market share and customer information the issuer gains. All card issuers strive, and usually fail, to approximate share-of-wallet. Share-of-wallet is the proportion of transactions the customer puts on this particular card versus other cards, checks, or cash. The approximation difficulty arises because issuers have no way of knowing a customer's payment card ownership or total spending. If an issuer can approximate share-of-wallet, it can target their efforts to lure a larger percentage of transactions to the issuer's card. In an iterative manner, increased payment options on one card further increases an issuer's share-of-wallet, which provides more transaction information to allow microtargeting, etc.

Since the card is upgradable, issuers can add memory (and services) in the future to existing cards. Since its introduction as a 1K version (1000 characters, compared to a magnetic stripe card's 140-character capacity), it is now available with up to 8K of memory. AT&T recently announced a 100K chip for 1997. MC managers believe that increasing the size of the card's memory will provide additional functionality.

Authorization Flexibility

MC's smart card has an advantage in authorization as well as security. Issuer-defined authorization parameters can be programmed to the card based on the risk characteristics of the cardholder. The parameters determine whether on-line authorization is required, based on information such as transaction value, the number of transactions which have already occurred off-line, etc. This capability affords the bank the opportunity to extend credit to higher-risk customers. The issuer can reset or modify these parameters whenever a transaction is on-line in order to adjust for a cardholder's spending and payment patterns.

Credit /Debit Cards versus Stored Value Cards

MC's payment products have traditionally consisted of credit and debit cards. Now it intends to launch a new type of application, a stored value service linked to an existing credit or debit card. Because the MC smart card can store transaction information and transmit data in batch form to a terminal or through the network, the card can be loaded with value and used to replace cash in small value transactions such as buying a newspaper or a soft drink.

Participant	Advantage	Description
Cardholder	Convenience	• No need for correct change • Safer than carrying cash
Merchant	Reduced Cost	• Reduced cash handling • Reduced vandalism/theft
Issuer	Additional Revenue	• Float/Interest • Unused balances • Additional fee income • Expanded cardholder base
Acquirer	Additional Revenue	• Additional merchant service charges • Expanded merchant base

Figure 5-6. Advantages of stored value cards.

Stored Value Card Benefits

All participants benefit from the stored value product: for cardholders, there will be no need for correct change. It is safer than carrying cash. They may choose to pay for some transactions with the stored value feature to reduce the size of the end-of-the-month credit card bill or to make quick convenient payments previously paid for with cash.

For the issuer, additional revenue grows from the interest on the unused balance, additional fee income, and an expanded cardholder base. The capture of a large chunk of transactions previously conducted with cash increases the issuer's information about the cardholder's spending behavior and the efficacy of its marketing efforts. For merchants, human error and theft associated with cash handling will decrease.

MASTERCARD'S IMPLEMENTATION STRATEGY

Implementation Assumptions

The smart card product line implementation makes the following assumptions:

Card—The smart card would contain a microprocessor chip in addition to the magnetic stripe, understanding that these technologies would coexist for the foreseeable future.

Terminals—Both POS (point-of-sale) and ATM (automated teller machine) terminals would be replaced or upgraded to support PIN and read both magnetic stripe cards as well as smart cards.

Risk control—The smart card chip would authenticate cards to control counterfeit, verify card users to prevent fraud, and authorize transactions according to issuer-set parameters to control credit risk. These tasks could be performed on- or off-line, depending on conditions of the given transaction.

Cardholder and retailer education costs—These costs are primarily related to the use of PIN at the point of sale.

Terminal acquirer/retailer infrastructure costs—Costs for terminals, systems enhancements, and retailer education to be divided between issuers and terminal acquirers/retailers in a manner to be negotiated. The issuer portion will be split 50/50 between MC and Visa, assuming that Visa members will receive similar benefits once smart card is implemented.

The conversion period: Phase-in is expected to take seven years, to approximate the average life of a post terminal.

Standards: MC and other stakeholders will develop standards and specifications for financial interchange transactions in open systems (where the service provider accepts cards from many card issuers).

Smart Card Implementation Strategy

MasterCard suggested the following implementation strategies:

For MasterCard:

- Commence building the infrastructure to support the orderly migration to the smart card platform.

- By early 1996, write standards, modify rules and procedures, and provide enhanced systems specifications.

- Seek cooperation with Visa and other card associations to support implementation of smart card and PIN at the point of sale.

- Promote the use of smart cards, PIN at the point of sale, and issuer-controlled authorizations to terminal acquirers/retailers as a means to reduce transaction costs and control risk.

- Develop new, smart-card-based products.

- Implement incentives to motivate terminal acquirer and merchant participation.

- Provide the flexibility for upward migration to more advanced smart card technologies as the need arises (e.g., biometric user verification, expanded memory, cryptography).

For Public:

- It is envisioned that by 1996, terminals that accept both magnetic strip with PIN and chip cards that conform to MC's rules will be available to merchants.

- It is envisioned that by 1996, terminal acquirers/merchants will be incentivised to upgrade to the newly available POS devices.

- By 2000, virtually all of MC's branded payment products and acceptance locations will include smart card technology in some form.

Manufacturer Requirements

Manufacturers require clear specifications in order to produce equipment, develop software, and design microprocessor chips for smart card implementation. MC, Visa, and Europay are drafting specifications intended to provide manufacturers with enough to develop competitive solutions for this need.

ATM/POS Terminal Manufacturers

MC is calling for terminal conversion to smart cards over a four-year period. One of the largest smart card terminal producers (40 percent market share) estimates that it would require six months to ramp up production levels equivalent to 600,000 smart-card-capable terminals. Given this estimate, it is likely that the industry could ramp up to 1 million terminals produced within 1 year.

SWOT Analysis—External

The smart card also helps MC expand its product line to include stored value service and other payment products, open new markets, offer services competitive with other providers, and offer cost-effective and secure product delivery.

In embracing smart cards, MC has made a number of implicit assumptions. These assumptions deal with product, cost, time, cooperation, and security/privacy.

External Factors—Measuring Your Industry's Opportunities and Threats

FACTOR	ATTRACTIVE	
	HIGH	LOW
Technology	One technology; it will not soon become obsolete nor do customers believe that it will	Several technologies; lack of standardization impedes customer adoption
Economic Conditions	Expanding industry	Declining or cyclical ind.
Social Factors	Uncontroversial product	Media has sparked debate
Government Regulation	Little	Much

Figure 5-7. External factors.

Product

First, we will examine what qualities users seek in a smart card. Then we will look at MasterCard's proposed product and measure it against our criteria.

User-Friendliness

Everyone, not just computer nerds, must feel comfortable using smart cards. The interface characteristics are currently unknown, but in adopting a seven-year phase-in, MC seems to account for the slow user acceptance curve.

Reliability

The cards contain an individual's financial information. Chips are more complex than magnetic stripes, and thus more vulnerable to breakdown. Already, chip manufacturers have had to prevent chip malfunctions due to users folding the cards in their wallets.

The industry will face important issues under two kinds of chip malfunctions: (1) the chip loses transaction information not backed up online; and (2) hackers break in and decode the information on the cards. Thus, the project will not tolerate even a minute rate of chip failure. To date, the technology has not undergone a large-scale reliability test.

Versatility

Cards have proliferated in today's marketplace. By the end of 1993, over 60 percent of the population in the U.S. possessed an average of 9.2 plastic cards in their wallets, one-third of which were bank cards. As cards increasingly become the means of accessing self-service copiers or making remote payments, consumers will seek out those service providers who can offer the greatest utility and convenience with a piece of plastic. By including high memory and upgradability, the smart card will be able to offer more services and compete for space in a customer's wallet.

Cost-Effectiveness

Stored value smart cards, will replace low-value, cash-based transactions, and are gaining momentum in closed out environments. Several prepaid smart card pilot programs, known as electronic purses (see chapter 6), are also being conducted in open environments (where there are multiple service providers). However, for credit and debit cards, delivery costs must be examined closely when determining the feasibility of an application. Historically, the delivery costs, including authorizations, clearing, and statement production, are too high to make entry into the smart card market profitable.

Compelling Use

The initial smart card application must convert a critical mass of users. For example, France's Minitel system was successfully launched as France's only national telephone directory. In this compelling use, the smart card is used to access data and identify the user.

Timing Risk

The technology for smart cards and terminals has existed since the 1970s. However, the specifications for the international financial smart card envisioned by the industry will provide interoperability, the same as the magnetic stripe that is enjoyed by technology today. Then other companies must agree to accept these specifications.

As with any innovation, be it ATM cards, the fax, the CD player, or the VCR, this diffusion process will take years. Even seven years sounds like an optimistic estimate. The complexity of the tasks and number of people involved could stretch out the transition to ten years. This situation would falter the dynamics. For example, the 18-month delay in opening the much-touted Eurotunnel cost its owners millions. MC must continue to analyze its expertise and continue to create a competitive advantage.

Savings Estimates: A Mirage?

MC's smart card plans to overcome the constraints of high delivery costs because it can cost-effectively control risk, does not require 100 percent on-line authorization, can be reloaded with additional value or units as required, and can accumulate transactions for efficient statement production.

MC has not disclosed how much it will save through reduced fraud. In 1993, risk costs were beginning to decrease due to risk-prevention methods other than smart cards, so MC's fraud savings calculation should be re-evaluated against declining fraud levels.

Similarly, MC savings due to reduced transaction costs are being reviewed. It is likely that actual card and terminal costs will exceed estimated costs. It is possible that the criteria for off-line credit authorization will be too lax, and credit losses will ensue. Or the criteria will be too stringent, most authorizations will continue to be performed on-line, and cost reductions will be less than hoped for. Finally, it is likely that the cost of upgrading cards and terminals be passed onto the user through higher card fees or interest rates. This rate hike may adversely affect card enrollment.

Security and Privacy

Smart cards in the financial services area generate serious privacy issues. Privacy watchdogs attempt to block any innovation that allows outsiders to watch one's personal business in the perceived manner of George Orwell's Big Brother. In their eyes, the imprint of one's credit information on a smart card unfurls a red flag. In order to appease them, the privacy issue must be addressed clearly *before* the product is introduced. The smart card developer must put the right spin on its product introduction. Even wildly untrue rumors regarding product privacy could sway market perception and sink the product.

Aside from the marketing spin, card programmers must create sophisticated encoding methods to protect the information on the cards if they are to satisfy privacy advocates.

SWOT Analysis—Internal

Cooperation: MC Wields Clout

MC's plan calls for cooperation from card issuers, transaction service providers, and merchants. Each party has different priorities. The same members who conceptually support the upgrade to smart card technology will be given incentives to help pay for the new terminals.

On the other hand, MC is one of the only players that could coordinate the many stakeholders. MC is involving members from the start in creating its smart card plan. This process will introduce members to the new technology as well as build support for the final plan. MC will ultimately benefit if it takes time to listen rather than force on the members a plan to pay for new terminals.

Those Who Create the Standards Make the Rules

In current smart card use, many closed systems exist in which the service provider is the card issuer. Examples include university cafeteria, telephone, and subway cards. MC is participating in a joint effort with Europay and Visa to develop specifications for IC Cards and Terminals. Furthermore, to the delight of European financial service providers, smart cards permit stored value in multiple currencies. The worldwide specification leadership allows EMV (Europay, MasterCard Visa) to limit competitors using non-competitive system specifications.

Internal Factors—Measuring Your Firm's Strengths and Weaknesses

FACTOR	ATTRACTIVENESS	
	HIGH	LOW
Management team	Proven	People with right skills not available
Financing	You have comfortable cushion or can raise capital if needed	You have a narrow time horizon to make money
Product development	Complete product line	One product of limited life
Sales force	Strong contacts; specialist skills	Limited contacts; generalist skills
Marketing	Deep and tightly-focused	Untargeted
Operations	Strategic alliances help improve execution	Learning in a vacuum

Figure 5-8. Internal factors.

MC's Stored Value Product: Does It Add Value?

Though the unique MC stored value application sounds compelling, flaws exist in the plan that could prove fatal. In the credit card business, banks make their revenue on cardholders' large unpaid balances. The fees on a stored value card are yet to be determined, but the issue of float has to be addressed by comparison, as will profits.

For both debit and stored value transactions, banks may charge a transaction cost. However, compared with credit card transactions, the average size of stored value transactions will be smaller, and the number of stored value transactions will be higher, since people make more small purchases than large ones. So the profit potential for stored value cards is realize through fees, but additional securities such as company loyalty and information-based securities can mean a revenue stream.

How much will people pay for a stored value card? A charge of $5.00 for every $100.00 put on a stored value card may sound reasonable, but will people pay an additional fee? People may balk at a fee. And unless the stored value card were accepted *everywhere*, one would still need to carry cash, so how convenient would the stored value card be? MC is currently examining pricing and acceptance issues.

CONCLUSION

There is no doubt that the introduction of smart cards will mean that the longevity of card products and supplier roles in the industry will change. The card industry is at the point of reinventing and even redefining the types of products it develops and distributes.

As a technology enabler, smart cards will not become the one new product that stimulates new growth in the financial card industry. Instead, the introduction of smart cards will force change in the nature of competition in the card industry as a whole. These changes will in turn force banks and others to identify the next trend for the card industry. In the new environment, successful card issuers and other players will foster a simplified user interface and offer "multi-branding" products where the cardholder selects the brands. Simply, the cardholder will be addressed as an individual and not as a credit risk.

MasterCard is leading this migration to smart card technology that will enable consumers to be targeted as individuals and therefore strengthen the relationship between banks and their customers.

END NOTES

1. Porter, Michael. *Competitive Strategy*. Free Press 1980. p. 20.

2. Ibid. p. 35.

3. Ibid. p. 50.

4. Ibid. p. 7.

5. Chipcards, the Competitive Edge, MasterCard International Document.

6. Ibid.

6

World Tour of Smart Card Applications

by Robin C. Townend—MasterCard International

PROFILE

Robin C. Townend in 1994 joined MasterCard as senior vice president of chip technology from a career at Barclay's Bank, U.K., where his responsibilities involved retail banking, specializing in the automation of plastic cards. While at Barclay's Mr. Townend held various managerial positions within the plastic cards division, including internal audit, debt recovery, and fraud prevention, culminating in the overall responsibility for research and development, with a focus on the business application of emerging card-related technologies. He has been instrumental in the implementation of various card programs, including Dallington Country Club's multi-functional smart card, the Barclay's/Mercury one-2-one mobile telephony alliance, as well as pioneering Barclay's work on biometric identification.

Mr. Townend is the former chairman of the APACS IC Card Working Group in the U.K. and was both the U.K.'s representative on the European Committee for Banking Standards and the International Organization for Standardization. Previous appointments include the chairmanship of International Association for Microcircuits Cards (INTAMIC) Working Group, formulating standards and application guidelines for smart cards within the banking sector.

Mr. Townend has presented papers at all the major smart card and card technology conferences and events in Africa, Asia, Europe, and the United States on the subjects of worldwide prepayment cards, smart card developments and applications, standards, and different card technologies.

PREDICTING THE WORLD MARKET

The widespread use of smart card applications is now running at an all-time high. Throughout the world, announcements of new applications are becoming more frequent as the real potential of the solutions they provide is being recognized. Europe is continuing to play the largest role in sustaining the industry's growth, followed by the Pacific Rim as the region with the second highest number of smart card applications. Latin America and the Middle East/Africa will follow, with Canada and the U.S. to be the last to convert to using smart card technology. But in the U.S., speeding up the development of smart card systems, especially for banking services, could help head off future competition from firms who offer consumer services like banking from the home or office. Bank card customers who use personal computers, interactive television, and smart phones for home banking could also be potential customers of such companies as Microsoft, Apple, GE, AT&T, regional telephone carriers, cable television operators, etc. These companies could preempt the retail banking relationships that already exist between Visa and MasterCard members and their customers by creating proprietary smart card-based remote banking systems of their own.

The assumptions that follow predict a total worldwide installed base over 3.0 billion cards in 1999. It is interesting to note that Europe will have only 30 percent more cards than the rest of the world.[1]

Table 6-1. World Smart Card Market

World Smart Card Market (Estimated in 1999 By Units) (RoW = Rest of World)					
Applications	Europe	Pacific Rim	North America	RoW	Total
Financial	415m	15m	77m	440m	1,037m
Identification Cards	110m	160m	80m	30m	380m
Telephone	250m	205m	—	165m	620m
Customer loyalty	165m	85m	18m	80m	348m
Health record cards	130m	43m	32m	1.5m	206.5m
Pay TV	63m	62m	10m	35m	170m
Student record cards	38m	26m	2.5m	1.5m	68m
Transport ticketing	16m	17m	18m	—	51m
Employee cards	16m	16m	11m	5m	48m
Government benefits*	10m	—	10m	4m	24m
GSM	11m	10m	3m	8m	32m
Health insurance	8m	4m	4m	—	16m
Car parking	—	2.4m	2.4m	1.2m	6m
Road pricing	2m	6m	1m	1m	10m
Sports/leisure center	2m	4m	3m	2m	11m
Town cards	2m	—	—	—	2m
Utilities	4m	—	—	3m	7m
Total	1242m	745.4m	271.9m	777.2m	3036.5m

* EBT Social Security Food Stamps, etc.

A new research report, The Smart Card, written by Ronald Brown of Post-News in the U.K., bases its five-year market forecast on continued growth for an adoption of a national electronic purse system. Smart card applications today are split into three sectors; financial transaction applications, personal ID applications, and portable file applications. *The Smart Card* concludes that there will actually be far fewer cards in circulation than many people have anticipated. Once the electronic purse concept is developed in a country, then the need for individual companies to issue their own prepayment cards diminishes strongly. Looking five years ahead, it is clear that most European countries and many in the Pacific Rim area, as well as elsewhere, will have nationwide electronic purse systems.

In five years time, all countries using separate cards for telephone cards, cash cards, and prepaid cards will begin to consolidate all of these cards into one system. This will be called an electronic purse system. In countries where no national electronic purse program has been established, issuers of smart cards in these application areas will still be required to provide their own cards. Given this plan, countries with a national electronic purse system are likely to see fewer cards in circulation than countries which are less developed with regards to the smart card.

Highlighted below is a description of the opportunities and concept of an electronic purse.

ELECTRONIC PURSE: A WORLDWIDE OVERVIEW

History of Money

Today we all take for granted the use of bank notes, coins, checks and a whole array of plastic card products as a means of everyday monetary exchange. But these payment instruments have evolved from the early forms of barter, exchange, and truck. We can trace the evolution as follows:

- Records in Iraq made some 5000 years ago reveal the first references to *units of exchange*.

- *Coins* first appeared in Libya some 2700 years ago.

- *Paper notes* were first introduced in Sichuan Province, southwestern China some 800 years ago.

- *Invisible money* came about when England and Holland first floated a joint stock company some 300 years ago.

- *Prepaid tickets* can be traced back to 1891 with the Bayern Telephon-Billets in Germany—the concept is just as it is today.

The customer simply paid funds in advance of using the service, with different denominations according to the duration of the telephone call. This *ticket* was thick paper and remained in service for many years until the German Public Payphone network was developed based on coin-operated pay phones. As with most prepaid systems, the ticket offered the operator the benefit of float and the security benefits of reduced cash handling as well as providing the user with a more convenient method of payment. It was not until 1983, nearly 100 years later that the Deutsche Bundespost began trials with plastic cards and *the rest*, as they say, *is history!*

It is estimated that between 2 percent and 5 percent of GDP in many economies is absorbed by the movement of cash. So, the search for a more efficient, cost-effective way of handling cash is on. However we look at this problem, one cannot help reflect on the fact that cash, as we know it today, is a very useful payment instrument—any cash substitute would not only have to have the same (or improved) security features and properties but also its universal appeal.

What Is an Electronic Purse?

"Electronic purse: An application for effecting prepaid card transactions, intended for small amounts." this definition is taken from the ISO 9992 series of standards—"Financial Transaction Cards—Messages between the Integrated Circuit Card and the Card Accepting Device." On its own this definition perhaps does not go far enough, as there are numerous terms that have been used to describe prepayment instruments:

- Change cards

- Cash cards (also referred to as "petty cash cards")

- Electronic purse (also referred to as EP)

- Electronic wallet

- Prepaid or prepayment cards (also referred to as PPCs)

- Stored value cards

Basically, *units of value* are stored on the card, either tokens or the electronic equivalent of cash. In the cases of change cards, cash cards, stored value cards, and prepaid cards (which are different names for broadly the same product) these tend to have the following characteristics:

- Be of fixed denomination or value

- Are not personalized to the user

- Fully transferable

- *Throwaway* when fully decremented

- Usually non-refundable

Mostly, these cards are used in single service/single service provider environments. However, schemes like the Danmønt system in Denmark have multiple issuers and multiple service providers, but as they all participate in the same common scheme to the same common standard, cards issued by one player can be used in applications managed by other service providers. Nonetheless they still conform to the characteristics above. Prepaid card systems have existed for a number of years and have been implemented all over the world in various applications right across industry. There are no standards for prepaid cards, so many different card technologies are used—magnetic, optical and electronic.

Why service providers should wish to upgrade their public service systems is best illustrated by the telecommunications operators, and I will use them to illustrate the commercial drive for prepaid card services. With over 170 PTTs around the world, the telecommunications pay phone operators are already the largest issuers of prepaid cards. This market will continue to grow with a trend towards the use of wired logic and in intelligent memory smart cards as the delivery mechanism. Enhancements to the pay phone will also occur over the next five years, and we will begin to see public videophones, smart phones, and videotext services in on-street pay phones.

Cards are being preferred to coins by pay phone operators because they offer a number of benefits:

- The network operators no longer need to send two staff people (dual control) to collect the coinage from the pay phones.

- Transactions do not need authorization, unlike credit and debit cards.

- There is less vandalism and theft because there is no money in the pay phones.

- With pre-payment the operators receive their funds in advance of the service and benefit from the management of "float."

- The operators receive third-party income from advertising carried on the cards.

- Many cards are never redeemed because they are lost or stolen or held by collectors, where the value of a collectible card can vary depending on whether or not the card has been used. Unused cards tend to be rarer and trade at a premium on the collector's market.

- The operators have the ability to do remote servicing and diagnostics of equipment.

For the user, prepaid phonecards offer:

- The convenience of not having to carry large quantities of coins.

- The precise cost of the call.

- More service availability as fewer phones are vandalized.

Most but not all prepaid card applications have the value stored at card level, however, a significant number of prepaid cards store the value centrally on account and use the card as an access device to that account. This concept is growing in popularity among the U.S. telecomm operators. Such cards are collectively known as "remote stored value cards."

The ISO definition described the electronic purse as relating to small amount payments. This 9992 Standard goes on to describe the wallet as, "An application for effecting prepaid card transactions, intended for large amounts." Either way these concepts tend to have different characteristics from prepaid cards:

- They are issued empty of value—the user decides how much, or little value is loaded onto the card.

- They are rechargable.

- They are usually personalized to the user.

- They are usually linked to a bank account.

- Transactions are usually tracked within the system.

- They are usually managed on *hybrid* cards (smart and striped—the integrated circuit to manage the EP and the magnetic stripe to make it compatible with current banking systems and to enable the gate on ATMs to open for EP reloading).

Interestingly, we can use Danmønt as an illustrative example of the EP—they are currently rolling out rechargeable cards. So the Danmønt EP implementation will allow prepaid cards to co-exist within the same system as its EP rechargeable version. In fact, Danmønt plans to extend this concept even further by incorporating the EP integrated circuit into current bank card products. This is consistent with the vision of a number of EP systems designers around the world. The big question regards the economics—is there a business case to support this approach? See Danmønt application for more details in this chapter.

The Mondex Global Electronic Cash scheme, currently being trailed in Swindon, U.K., takes the EP concept to its ultimate conclusion by designing a new global payment scheme entirely based on smart card technology. Supporting the Mondex card are an array of technology devices which make up the system. One of these devices is the electronic wallet; in this context the term is used to describe a hardware device. This wallet functions as a personal communicator to provide cardholders with the ability to examine the card's contents, interact with other services on the card, and perform *person-to-person* (purse-to-purse) payments. So this approach is a long way from the single service/single service provider systems relating to prepaid cards, in which value is controlled within the system by the same party, and each transaction is traceable. With Mondex this does not happen. Transactions are not cleared by the system. This clearly places a heavy dependence upon the scheme's security. Another feature of the Mondex card is that it can simultaneously hold up to five different currency purses—a multiple EP card! See Mondex application for more details in this chapter.

Electronic Purse Terminology

Like any new concept or technology the EP has its own jargon. While many definitions exist for these terms, some are described here:

Closed Prepaid System

A prepaid card system that includes any of the following scenarios:

- Single issuer/single service provider (which can be either one entity or different entities.)

- Multiple issuer/single service provider.

- Single issuer/multiple service provider.

Open Prepaid System

A prepaid card system that has a common set of operating rules which permits the scheme to support a multiple issuer/multiple service provider environment.

System Operator

The prepaid card or EP scheme authority who defines the scheme's operating rules and conditions and also has responsibility for the clearing and settlement of transactions (if applicable).

Truncated Transactions

There are three options in terms of transaction-processing and interchange for EP systems:

- **Truncation to the Issuer**—this follows the traditional approach of most card payment schemes in which transactions are treated individually and data is routed from the point-of-sale terminal via the acquirer to the issuer.

- **Truncation by the Acquirer**—also referred to as *aggregated truncation*, the service provider passes the transactions to the acquirer who totals the value for each issuer prior to settlement.

- **Terminal Truncation**—the terminal accumulates the EP transactions and passes on to the acquirer a single total for reimbursement. In this scenario the transactions are anonymous.

Anonymity and Privacy

The whole question of anonymity and privacy in EP systems is an issue of major concern. Identification of the user tagged by the auditable transaction may be acceptable with credit, debit, and check-based payment instruments, but it arouses emotions when related to EP transactions.

Some proposals for free flow (no barriers) road pricing schemes, where users pay for the use of the roads or motorways, are finding this topic to be a constraint. Users and consumer associations do not like the idea that an individual can be tracked in real time while driving about his or her business.

So authentication of the purse (usually carried on a smart card), verification of the user, and validation of the value in an anonymous manner are issues that have taxed the EP system designers. To achieve this and deliver a system in a cost-effective way has been the Holy Grail.

Who's Doing What?

It has already become a difficult task to document all EP systems as there are too many of them, so those featured here relate to the national electronic purse schemes and other major operations of significance.

Table 6-2 shows the *who's who* and current position regarding implementations of National EP systems. Other countries known to be considering EP implementations include: Brazil, Korea, Poland, Lebanon, Canada, Indonesia, and Thailand.

Table 6-2. Who's Who Regarding National EP Systems

Country	Scheme Operator	Sector	Status
Denmark	Danmønt	Inter-sector	Roll-out
Finland	Avant	Central Bank	Roll-out
Switzerland	Swiss PTT	PTT	Planning roll-out
France	La Poste	PTT	Planning trial
Germany	ZKA	Banking	Planning trial
Bulgaria	BalkanCard	Banking	Trials
Holland	Chip Knip	Banking	Trials
Spain	SEMP	Banking	Trials
Portugal	SIBS	Banking	Roll-out
Belgium	Banksys–Proton	Banking	Trials
UK	Mondex UK	Banking	Trials
Latvia	Union Baltic Bank	Banking	Trials
South Africa	Inter-bank SCC	Banking	Trials concluded
Taiwan	FISC	Government	Roll-out
Singapore	NETS	Banking	Trials
Australia	Various Banking	Transit/Campus	Trials
MasterCard	Project Canberra	Banking	Trials
Visa	Regions	Banking	Planning trials
USA	EPS (Smart Cash)	Banking	Planning trial

Summary

Senior Retail Banking Executives now understand the concept and their questions are more searching. E-money has arrived and with it the rules of engagement and players have changed. It is clear that the we need secure on-line money to service the customer of the future. Electronic commerce has arrived and with it related concerns of security and privacy. The winners will balance these issues and ultimately the consumers will dictate the pace—very much as they have always done.

A conclusion from this review of EP systems and E-money is that there is no standard approach and therefore no unique blueprint for either the business case or the implementation. Issues will vary from one approach to another, even within the same country, as issuers all start from a different perspective.

We will clearly need some standardization and rationalization. This issue is well recognized by the payment associations, and MasterCard along with Europay and Visa plan to develop specifications for stored value cards. All three associations recognize the importance of this work and see this as a major deliverable for the future.

Although the commercial banks appear to have grasped the initiative, other industry sectors see opportunities too. This may cause pre-emptive responses from the central banks to regulate operators, thereby ensuring tighter control through licensing and closer monitoring of the impact of EPs on the money supply. Such action should also ensure proper consumer protection.

The choice of technology is no longer which card technology but *"which chip"* and *"whose e-money will I put on my EP card?"* Both the market and the consumer demand is there for a low-value coin replacement. We have seen magnetic stripe debit and credit cards become established replacements for bank notes. Are we are now witnessing the smart card as the replacement for coins? Can we now herald the *changeless* society?[2]

DANMØNT-DENMARK: PREPAID CARD SYSTEM

Danmønt A/S was established June 18, 1991, by KTAS (Copenhagen Telephone Company), on behalf of all Danish telephone companies, and PBS (Danish Payment Systems A/S), on behalf of all Danish banks and savings banks, with share capital of DKK 80 million.[3]

Danmønt A/S will play an important role as system operator. The purpose of Danmønt A/S is to develop and introduce a general purpose prepaid card based upon IC (Integrated Circuit) technology, which in a secure and economical way can be used as means of payment of small amounts in vending machines and other sorts of self-service automates.

The conceptual idea behind the system—to introduce an IC card, which can be used as payment of small amounts in, for example, vending machines, telephones, trains, buses, stamp issuing machines, POS terminals and parking meters—is easy to explain and already accepted by a large part of the population.

In the initial phase, the Danmønt A/S system uses non-rechargeable cards. At a future stage, the system will use multifunction cards.

The role of Danmønt A/S is to:

- Be the system operator.

- Design the concept.

- Make specifications, and keep the clearing system under surveillance.

- Make specifications, and keep the security system under surveillance.

- Make specifications for cards and terminal equipment.

- Market the concept.

The purpose of the system operator is to take care of the implementation of the concept. Danmønt A/S has developed specifications for the IC cards and the terminals and will perform tests and authorization of the equipment, as well as perform the financial transaction clearing.

Consequently, it is possible to be a service provider without also being a card issuer. This enables small merchants to get access to the system, even though they do not have the necessary size to be an independent card issuer.

Security Issues

In connection with prepaid cards, security is an issue about which everybody is concerned. Danmønt has combined the knowledge from the debit and credit card environment with the latest IC card technology to ensure a very secure clearing and settlement system. This gives the system operator total control over the entire system at a low cost level, and it gives the authorities the necessary data for their audits.

Unlike many other prepaid card systems, Danmønt is clearing the transactions on an individual as well as on an aggregated level. This is very important in large and/or open systems, where public authority wants to be able to supervise the system.

Furthermore, a clearing of the individual transactions makes it possible for the system operator to:

- Determine the redemption value on the individual cards in circulation.

- Detect possible double transactions, which can occur either as errors in the card accepting device or as fraud.

- Detect if fraud occurs with the cards.

To clear the individual attractions implies added cost in operation of the clearing system, but Danmønt has developed methods to allow the system operator to clear transactions on an aggregated level if appropriate.

The requirements from the consumer have been thoroughly investigated through consumer research both prior to and after the field trial in Naestved.

The trial has also given solutions to many problematic technical issues which occurred during the pre-launch period, as none of the equipment and software to open a prepaid card system existed before. It was concluded that the market and technical issues had been solved, and that a national implementation could proceed as stated in the original plans for Danmønt.

EUROPEAN UNION-MONDEX: GLOBAL ELECTRONIC CASH

The National Westminster Bank has developed a new electronic payment service called Mondex, which became operational in July, 1995, that uses smart cards as an alternative to cash. Innovative features of the system enable customers to use the value on their cards for making payments by telephone, as well as to store up to five different currencies on a card. The new service is a joint venture with Midland Bank in conjunction with British Telecommunications company (BT). Mondex will use the bank's 11 million customers to initiate the project. The intention is to invite other financial institutions to join the program under the name of Mondex International.[4]

While there are many smart card electronic purse systems beginning throughout the world, the Mondex concept is an open payment system, like using real cash. When a customer pays with a Mondex card, the money is paid instantly to the retailer or service provider and the transaction does not go through a clearing system as in other electronic purse applications. The banks have no records of the transactions and know only the amount issued, in the same way as banks issue cash.

Mondex appears to be the first system in the world to offer very special services like:

- Twenty-four hour banking and access to electronic money by telephone, either public telephones or a home smart card phone.

- A multi-currency card capable of holding up to five different currencies separately.

- A personal secret code number to lock the card, preventing value in the card from being used without re-keying the code.

- An electronic wallet to which value from the card can be transferred for safer keeping at home, and to enable payments to be made from one card to another.

- A personal key-ring card reader to check the balance on the card at any time.

Customers can also use the card to make payments over the telephone in the same way as they would pay at a point-of-sale terminal, except in this case the transfer is the telephone line.

The Mondex project is probably the most technically advanced project of its kind anywhere in the world and will offer unique services for customers and service providers.

Mondex is a unique new payment scheme for consumers, merchants, and banks. The heart of the payment scheme is the "electronic purse," in which monetary value is stored. The electronic purses are typically held on a standard-sized plastic card, so the card will look much like any other payment card.

Loading and reloading value onto the card is easy. The cardholders are able to transfer monetary value directly from their bank accounts to the card at cash machines, bank counters, and public telephones displaying the Mondex sign.

Payment Methods

Cardholders are able to make payments wherever a sign for Mondex is displayed. All payments are simple transfers of value, just like paying with ordinary cash—quick, certain, and with no need for paperwork, authorization, or signatures. To pay, the card is inserted into a point-of-sale terminal and value is immediately transferred from the card to an electronic purse inside the terminal.

Unlike other card-payment products, the system also enables person-to-person payment. Using a special wallet, two cardholders can transfer cash between their cards. With a special telephone, person-to-person payments can be made across the world.

Mondex Benefits for Consumers

Consumer benefits include 24-hour electronic cash via special Mondex phones which may be available at home or at work and is a convenient alternative to cash and safer to carry.

Retailers and other cash-handling businesses will benefit from an efficient, faster, and more secure way of handling money that is economical to operate.

The Mondex system was developed, tested, and validated through an extensive market research program in France, Germany, Japan, the U.K. and the U.S. The research highlighted the following consumer benefits:

Convenience

- Payments are quick and easy.
- No authorization or signatures are required.

Figure 6-1. Modex Benefits for Consumers.

- Cards can be reloaded from ATMs or by telephone, either at a pay phone or from the comfort of home.

Flexibility

- Like cash, the system is suitable for both large and small purchases.
- The Mondex Wallet allows consumers to make person-to-person payments.
- Instant electronic payments can be made remotely by telephone.

Control

- Mondex allows exact payments for any purchase amount.
- Expenditure is limited to the balance held on a card, viewed with a simple balance reader.
- Unlike cash, a Mondex card keeps a record of transactions as they are made.

Safety

- The Lock function keeps money secure and transactions private.
- A consumer can choose and change the lock code.

Figure 6-1. (continued)

Mondex Benefits for Merchants

Mondex benefits for merchants have been tested in a major research study involving 35 leading U.S. retail and public service corporations and 16 smaller single or multi-unit retailers. The following benefits were identified:

Greater Efficiency at the Point-of-Sale

- Customer identification, signature, or PIN entry is not required
- Payment authorization is not necessary
- Payments are exact so there is no need to give change

Flexibility for All

- Because payments are fast and cheap, they are suitable for all types of merchant and size of payment.
- The pocket-sized Wallet can be an inexpensive and compact point-of-sale terminal suitable in environments where a Retailer Terminal is not appropriate, market stalls and taxis, for example.

Figure 6-2. Mondex benefits for merchants.

Marketing Opportunity

- The system will allow merchants to capitalize on the opportunity offered by smart cards to run customer loyalty schemes. If customers choose to join a loyalty scheme, a merchant can automatically record each use of the cards. With such detailed information, merchants can offer sophisticated discounts and special offers to reward their loyal customers.

Extra Security, Lower Costs

- Value held in merchant terminals can be electronically locked reducing both the cost and security risks associated with storing, counting, and transporting physical currency.

Figure 6-2. (continued)

Mondex Functions

Balance Know-How

Consumers want to know how much cash they are holding. All cardholders will be able to use a key-ring-size balance reader to check the values in their cards at any time. Cardholders will also be able to check their balance at telephones, ATMs, and in the wallet.

Statements Prepared

An electronic purse maintains a record of a cardholder's last 10 transactions. A statement inquiry will show the cardholder the nature of the transfer (a payment or a credit), the currency and amount of the transfer, when it took place, and the identity of the other party involved.

Lock Code Functions

An electronic purse contains a four-digit "lock code." By pressing the lock key on devices such as a wallet or telephone, the cardholder's money is kept secure and the transactions private. In lock mode, transfers out of the card are barred and statement entries cannot be displayed. To unlock the cards, the cardholder simply enters his or her four-digit lock code. The choice of lock code is up to the cardholders and it may be changed whenever the cardholder wishes.

Currency Flexibility

In the future, Mondex will facilitate payments in most major currencies. A Mondex electronic purse can, at any one time, hold up to five different currencies in separate "pockets" inside the purse. When the value of any one of these five currencies is reduced to zero, a new currency may be held in that pocket. A currency inquiry will display the balances of all the currencies held on a Mondex card and identify each currency both by means of its local currency designator (e.g., FF, $) and its unique ISO currency code, standard throughout the world.

Special Devices

All devices work together with the card to deliver the vast potential of the Mondex Payment System. They include four key components: the balance reader, a special telephone, the wallet device, and retailer terminals.

Balance Reader

The balance reader is a key-ring-sized device containing a card reader and small screen. When a card is inserted into the reader, the balance is displayed on the screen.

Special Telephone

A special Mondex telephone operates just like a normal phone, but includes a card reader and screen to enable functionality. The telephone, whether public, home, or office, becomes a 24-hour cash dispenser—cardholders can transfer money to or from their bank accounts at any time. Cardholders will also be able to order and make immediate payment for goods and services and transfer money to friends, family, and business associates across the world.

Wallet Device

The wallet is a pocket-sized device that contains its own internal electronic purse along with a card reader, keyboard, and screen. Wallet holders can transfer money from their cards and store it in the electronic purse inside their wallet. By transferring money from the wallet to another individual's card, person-to-person payments are simple.

The wallet can be used as a secure bank of value, so that some consumers need only carry enough money for a day's purchases at any one time. Like a telephone, the wallet provides balance, statement, and currency-inquiry functions, as well as the lock facility. These functions can be used in conjunction with either the wallet's own internal electronic purse or any card inserted into the wallet's card reader.

Retailer Terminal

Retailer terminals will range from small, low-cost, portable units to integrated systems for larger retail chains. The basic component of the retailer terminal is a card reader, into which a customer's card is inserted, and an internal electronic purse, to which the amount payable is transferred.

The Mondex cashless electronic purse is probably the most advanced system today and will offer a unique service for all customers and service providers.

GERMANY—NATIONAL HEALTH CARE CARD

In 1988, the German government mandated the introduction of the smart card for citizens collecting public insurance benefits. That year, Germany's AOK social insurance fund launched a pilot project in Wiesbaden. In the course of the project some 160,000 insurance holders received for use with all the health care providers in the district, a "health card" embossed with identification data.

The health care provider could print all the insured people's information on required administrative forms by swiping the health card through a traditional credit card receipting machine. After two years, the experiment had achieved significant results: its acceptance was total, and the savings on management costs exceeded 35 percent.

German Health Care System

Germany practices a version of socialized medicine. All physicians belong to provincial *Kassenartzliche Vereinigung* (KV) that negotiates with provincial committees of sickness funds (public insurers) for a lump sum, and then pays all claims. Physicians do not bill patients directly. Provincial KVs have developed significant organizations to negotiate with funds; track members' utilization; and process and pay claims. A national association of KVs negotiates with national associations of sickness funds over reimbursable procedures, fee schedules, and approximate payment levels.

Sickness funds (public insurers) enroll members, calculate and collect premiums and social security pension contributions, communicate with and pay provincial association of KVs and hospitals, and cooperate with national and provincial audits.

National associations of sickness funds shoulder a large administrative burden: strategic planning, lobbying for reforms, negotiating at the national level, organization of health insurance in former East Germany, preparing reports, and publishing journals for members and the public. Private health insurance provides primary coverage for only 10 percent of the population.

The government mandated smart health cards in order to assuage the administrative burden of the medical provider and insurer organizations, cut management costs, and improve the services provided to insured people.

National Healthcard Roll-out

After the successful test in Wiesbaden, the national roll-out of smart health cards proceeded. One cannot overstate the magnitude of the project. The medical provider and insurance associations worked together to design standards for the health card, mandating the type of smart card technology, memory size, security, and acceptable failure rate. Next, the associations sought card-reader and smart card manufacturers up to the task of providing card readers for Germany's 200,000 doctors and dentists and cards for its 78 million population. The associations faced quite a quality-control challenge in the quest to make sure cards from 20 different manufacturers and readers from 5 different manufacturers operated identically. Finally, by June 1995, 78 million Germans were issued a health card.

Smart Card Advantages

Smart Card Advantages to Patients

- Smart cards replace bulky personal health record *passbooks*.

- Patients can obtain authorization for services from a sickness fund *in doctors' offices*.

- Patients can access preventive medical analysis.

Smart Card Advantages to Public and Private Insurers

- Smart cards supplant all use of paper forms for communication between insurers and medical providers.

- Management reduces administration costs significantly.

- Insurers can offer individualized and highly effective service to their insurance holders.

Smart Card Advantages to Healthcare Providers

- Office administrators enjoy a simplified sickness insurance form.

- Doctors enjoy more time to deal with patients themselves due to the reduction in the complexity of administrative tasks.

- Doctors feel a new motivation within their profession to make effective use of computerized systems.

Privacy Risks

The shift from paper to computerized record-keeping in Germany promises not only greater efficiency and cost savings, but increased concerns about the threat to patient privacy.

The creation of a national health card drastically increases the number of individuals with access to private medical information. This information can influence decisions about an individual's access to credit, admission to educational institutions, and his or her ability to secure employment and obtain insurance. It is not an exaggeration to say that inaccuracies in the information, or its improper disclosure, can threaten an individual's personal and financial well-being.

The German medical establishment has taken strict measures in its choice of technology and personnel procedures to protect the privacy of computerized medical information and the security of patients' records. Concerns about safeguarding patient privacy can only grow as medical advances bring with them new ethical challenges, such as those that concern genetic information collected from patients and their families.

GLOBAL SYSTEM MOBILE COMMUNICATIONS (GSM)

The new Global System for Mobile Communications (GSM) radio-telephone system started operation in 1992 and will cover all major European towns and motorways within the next five years. GSM will allow European travelers to keep in touch, because any GSM phone can be used anywhere in the served areas. (GSM is now being offered in the United States.) The GSM project is technically possible because of advanced radio and networking techniques, but is only feasible because logistics and security are managed by smart cards.

GSM Architecture

The standard sets, for the most part, the formation of the network, the functions that are to be performed by each element, the information that is to be passed between the elements over "interfaces," and the circumstances under which information is to be exchanged.

In some cases the manner of information exchange (the protocol) and the exact process to which the information is subjected is also defined; in some cases it is left up to the individual manufacturer. Thus some of the details are public and other details are proprietary. This compromise permits the manufacturers to exercise individual ingenuity to gain a competitive advantage, while protecting the subscriber and the service provider from incompatibility problems.

The primary parts of the architecture are the phone itself and a Subscriber Identity Module (SIM).

The phone consists of two parts; an electronics package that performs the communications functions. The SIM is a removable device in smart-card-like format that contains information on the subscriber's phone number, services subscribed to, and billing and security information. The SIM must be inserted into the phone in order to make the phone work (exception: emergency calls).

GSM SIM Card

The SIM card is a GSM-specific card carrying a microchip and contact connections. Originally designed to be the exact dimensions of a credit card, it now comes in two sizes; credit card and mini-SIM. The latter became necessary when, unexpectedly to the GSM founders, portable telephones became too small to accept a credit-card-sized device!

SIM cards contain non-volatile information embedded by the manufacturer related to security and identity, and a programmable memory (electrically erasable) to provide for optional and dynamically changeable information. The memory is partitioned by function, and a directory is provided.

SIM cards are not required to be removable, but at present most are. It is possible for mobile units to accept additional IC cards, for example to enable car-rental companies to rent phones and execute real-time billing; in this case the inserted IC card contains much the same information and overrides the SIM card until it is removed.

A GSM subscriber will be issued a smart card, which will be his or her key to the whole system. When the card is inserted into any GSM telephone, that telephone becomes the subscriber's own personal line. Calls to the number will reach that individual, and bills will be sent to the home or office account. If one has a list of abbreviated numbers for regular contacts, you will be able to use it with a car phone, the phone in the taxi coming from the airport, or the phone borrowed from the Italian office or rented for the day in London. The important information about the GSM subscription is held in the smart card, not the telephone.

This makes the logistics of the GSM project possible. Radio telephone operators can sell subscriptions to people in the form of a smart card and its PIN. GSM telephones can be bought or rented anywhere, so telephone operations do not have to be involved in the manufacture of telephones. To operate a GSM phone, the cardholder inserts the card, types in the PIN and the phone is ready to use.

Once the PIN has been correctly entered the GSM phone can hook itself into the GSM network so that calls can be made and received by the cardholder.

The GSM standard is now being adopted in Australia, New Zealand, Arab Emirates, Singapore, South Africa, the United States, and many Eastern European countries. Many other countries are expected to follow, and the GSM is becoming a world standard.

Will GSM Permeate the Americas?

The introduction of GSM equipment into the U.S. will likely break a logjam and herald more widespread use of the standard throughout the Americas.

But will this mean the use of a single phone, anywhere one goes? Unfortunately not. The phone purchased in the U.S. may operate in some other countries in the Americas (notably Canada, for example) but cannot be taken to Europe or Asia because the two "flavors" of GSM used there, though functionally identical, operate on two sets of frequencies different than those authorized in the U.S. And the volume of transoceanic GSM "roamers" is unlikely to reach sufficient proportions to justify the creation of a multiband handset.

Paradoxically, the problem will be worse for GSM subscribers within the U.S. than worldwide. While over a hundred nations have GSM internationally, its use within the U.S. and the Americas will continue to be spotty. Whole cities, states, and countries will not have GSM and may never have it.

SCOTLAND—THE SHELL OIL LOYALTY PROGRAM

Shell Oil in the U.K. has launched a customer loyalty program in Scotland using smart card technology to provide electronic points as a replacement for paper gasoline vouchers and stamps. Motorists will benefit from the new fuel promotion program, called Shell Smart. The program will give the smart card industry in the U.K. a major boost and provide the opportunity for many people to use the technology for the first time.[5]

In the Shell Smart fuel promotion, customers will use a smart card to collect "electronic points" for their purchases at Shell service stations. Customers can then exchange their points for free cinema tickets, air miles, tapes, CDs, or other gifts, or donate the points to charity.

The electronic points are stored in the smart card's memory and deducted when redeemed for gifts or given to charity. Shell Smart cards cannot be used to pay for fuel or other goods or services, but this may be part of future plans.

Points Support Charities—Shell Matches Donations

One Smart Point is given with every £6 (U.S. $9) spent on any grade of New Improved Shell Advanced Petrol, Shell Advanced Diesel, Shell Helix Motor Oils, or Aqua Valet car washes. Points collected at Shell service stations can be exchanged for a range of gifts (delivered via mail order) or British Airways flights, or can be donated to one of two British charities: The British Heart Foundation or The Save the Children Fund.

Shell will double the first 333,000 points donated by its customers to The British Heart Foundation, and the first 500,000 points donated to The Save the Children Fund, to celebrate the fund's 75th birthday. Shell's charitable donation is worth more than £600,000.

Open-Ended Run

Ian Sutcliffe, Forecourt Marketing Manager at Shell U.K. said: "Shell has opted for smart technology rather than traditional magnetic stripe technology still used by most credit card companies and banks because it offers scope to add extra offers in the future without having to change customers' cards. The promotion is designed to appeal to both high- and low-mileage drivers and will run indefinitely."

Initially, customers will be able to redeem their points for donations to The British Heart Foundation or The Save the Children Fund. As examples, Shell says 87 points pays for enough grain to feed a family of eight for a month in West Sudan, and 134 points hires a minibus for children from a family center in Britain to enjoy a day out.

Technology

The Shell Smart cards are personalized for each customer and carry the cardholder's name. If the card is lost, Shell can issue a new one with the same number of points. The old card will be electronically canceled.

SINGAPORE—CASHCARD: THE SINGAPORE NATIONWIDE ELECTRONIC PURSE

The CashCard system in Singapore is a government-initiated project implemented by the seven shareholder banks of Network Electronic Transfers (S) Pte Ltd (NETS). It is an electronic purse concept for a "cashless" society. The purpose of this project is to provide a convenient way to pay for small expenses. CashCard is also positioned to complement electronic-fund-transfer point-of-sale (EFTPOS) as an alternative method of payment.[6]

CashCard is an *all-purpose muli-service provider card* which is targeted to reach a wide spectrum of services.

More than 270 outlets were involved in the trial at a town called Ang Mo Ko, the financial district, and National University of Singapore. The CashCard payment was introduced in retail shops, pharmacies, bookstores, various vending machines, public telephones, and photocopy machines. Singaporeans were able to experience cashless purchasing in places like supermarkets, cafeterias, and hawker centers of factories. Current participants includes schools, universities, factories, and banks.

NETS plans to introduce the CashCard nationwide by 1996 and targets one million CashCard holders within the first year. As part of the program, the NETS shareholder banks are expected to introduce new bank cards that will combine CashCard functions with existing ATM/EFTPOS functions, credit-card functions, and even new value-added services. The system supports loyalty programs, bonus points, and lucky draw promotions. These features help promote the CashCard system at the merchants' level. Many other affiliated cards combining CashCard functions with different service operators are expected to follow, bringing the concept of a multi-service, all-purpose card to reality. Such operators include the National University of Singapore with the student/staff identity card and the Ministry of Defense with the military service identification card.

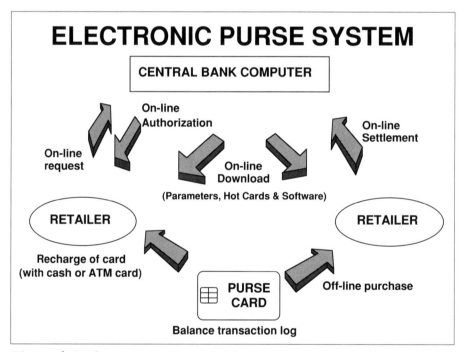

Figure 6-3. Electronic purse system.

Electronic Purse Features

CashCard is used mainly for two types of transactions: debit (purchase transaction, statement printing) and credit (rechard of cards, refund transaction). Debit transactions are performed off-line and credit transactions are performed on-line.

- CashCard is an electronic purse which can be used in a wide range of outlets such as retailers, payphones, self-service terminals, vending machines (drink and cards), multi-media service machines (public utilities, cinema ticketing, postal products), automated machines (tolls, public transport, car-park), photocopy machines, and games and arcade machines.

- Each CashCard has a unique card number and comes with an initial value of S$10 for students and S$20 for other members of the public. There is a S$2 deposit value. The template design is the same for all the standard cards.

- No PIN code is required. This means that payment by CashCard is faster than cash. A transaction log of the last 10 transactions is available on the card for statement printing.

- CashCard can be topped up, or recharged, to a maximum value of S$200. The maximum value is controlled by the bank during a credit transaction using an ATM/EFTPOS card.

- CashCards are unpersonalized and anonymous. No data about the card holder is stored. If lost, it is just like a bank note that anyone can use.

- All transactions are captured at the host where a central card balance is maintained. Settlement of all transactions can be performed on-line with the host, or off-line by downloading the transactions into a merchant card.

The CashCard project is another contribution to the IT 2000 plan which brings Singapore a step nearer toward fulfilling its vision of becoming an "Intelligent Island."

> **Note:** Ingenico has been involved in CashCard since the beginning of the project and is the "payment module" supplier and terminal supplier for this nationwide pro-

ject. Ingenico is a leading company supplying credit card and debit card terminals with a development and marketing program oriented exclusively toward electronic funds transfer systems. The parent company of the group, Ingenico S.A., is based in Paris.

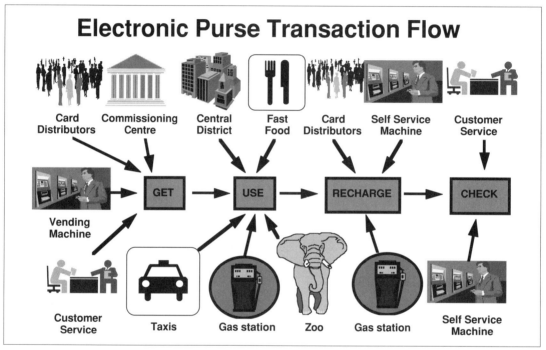

Figure 6-4. Electronic purse transaction flow.

MASTERCARD'S STORED VALUE SMART CARD PROJECT

MasterCard International is taking a giant step by reducing the need for consumers to carry cash by launching a stored value pilot in Sydney, Australia, for MasterCard-branded smart cards with five of the world's largest banks.[7]

Unlike other stored value cards under development, which are disposable or throw-away cards, MasterCard's stored value feature will be linked to existing credit and debit card accounts, thus enhancing the value of the cards that consumers already carry. This move will demonstrate a commitment by helping its member financial institutions use payment cards as a relationship-building tool to enhance cardholder loyalty. A stored value feature lets a cardholder load value that is equivalent to cash onto a card, and use the card for small-ticket purchases—those generally made with small bills or coins. A microchip embedded in the card calculates each transaction, thus making the card "smart."

"Changes in technology are giving consumers more choices for accessing and managing their money," said H. Eugene Lockhart, MasterCard president and CEO.[8] "Our objective is to stay ahead of that change by delivering a broader array of payment options and value-added services to consumers whenever and wherever they want them."

The capital city, Canberra, has been selected for MasterCard's pilot in Australia, which is scheduled for the fourth quarter of 1995, and will run for nine months. Australia New Zealand Bank (ANZ), Commonwealth Bank of Australia, National Australia Bank (NAB), and Westpac Banking Corporation, which together represent more than 70 percent of the Australian credit and debit market, will issue the smart cards, which can be credit cards, debit cards, or combination credit/debit cards, which are common in Australia. Credit cards issued will bear the MasterCard logo, while debit cards issued will carry Maestro, the company's on-line point-of-sale debit brand. Merchants accepting the cards during the test period will include gasoline stations, convenience stores, and specialty retailers.

"The markets of Asia/Pacific are aggressively pursuing new developments in the payment services," said James A. Cassin, president of MasterCard's Asia/Pacific region. "Our Australian members also provide an excellent combination of market scale and technical experience for this pilot. At the same time, the results of this effort will be valuable to all MasterCard members around the world."[9]

How the Program Works

A participating bank will issue to the cardholder a MasterCard credit card and/or a Maestro point-of-sale debit card with the stored value feature. The credit or debit function will be used as it is today. To initiate the stored value feature, the cardholder will go to a select merchant location or ATM later in the pilot, enter his or her PIN, and load value onto the card. Each time the feature is used, the amount of the purchase will be deducted from the card. Additional value can be loaded onto the card at the ATM, or even during a transaction at select point-of-sale locations. Each load transaction will be detailed on the cardholder's regular monthly statement.

As the program gains additional insight into consumer needs, more options will be added to the stored value feature. Cardholders will be able to:

- Load value onto the card from public telephones or their homes.

- Store up to 10 foreign currencies on the card at one time.

- Convert previously loaded value from one currency to another.

- Use the card at a wider range of locations that traditionally do not accept cards for payment.

The Australian members recommended Canberra to conduct a market pilot because it presents a high concentration of consumers who are early adopters of new products and a density of consumers and merchants.

SOUTH AFRICAN ELECTRONIC PURSE APPLICATION

Understanding the Environment for the Project

The total population of South Africa at the end of 1992 was approximately 40 million people—of whom 30 million are black, 5 million white, and 4 million colored and Asian.

During the 45 years of apartheid, the educational policies of the government contributed largely to the situation in which the education of black people lagged behind, resulting in limited work opportunities. As a result the average income of black people in South Africa is exceedingly low.[10]

- 60 percent of the urban population earns less than R2000 ($600) per month; 90 percent of these are black.

- 40 percent earn more than R2000 ($600); only 15 percent of these are black.

The future of the country is dependent on changing these statistics, on providing new generations of South Africans with education, housing, access to jobs, and light by which to study.

This is the environment in which the banks are trying to market their products.

The four major banks in South Africa have designed and developed an electronic purse application which provides the core of a multi-purpose banking card. The application and acceptability of the smart card will be tested in a pilot project. However, to best determine the results and outcomes of the project, we should first understand the South African environment for such a project.

Traditionally banks in South Africa have catered mainly to the needs of white customers, with first-world products such as check accounts and credit cards. Black people were seldom considered for these products and were offered savings accounts as a matter of course. Branches too were placed so as to serve the first-world customers. The deterioration of services and political instability in black townships discouraged bank management from investing further.

Research has shown that one of the aspirations high on the priority list customers is the ability to make purchases using a card. Very few black people presently qualify for a credit card because of low income. Therefore, other card mechanisms are needed to meet their needs. If the right products can be found maybe, black people can be directly converted from cash to cards without going through the check stage.

One of the major problems faced in offering card payment facilities was the instability of the communications infrastructure in South Africa.

Although it is relatively good in metropolitan areas, it is almost nonexistent in some townships.

Most electronic purse applications being implemented around the world concentrate on the lowest-value payments, i.e., transport, telephone, newspapers, vending machines, etc. South Africa's needs are greater than that. The black customers presently make the majority of their payments by cash, whether they be for clothing, groceries, household goods, or rent. Muggings on trains, in townships, and even at ATM's are commonplace. A means to replace all cash transactions is needed.

Smart Card Pilot

The pilot will take place in one shopping complex in Alberton, a town close to Johannesburg. All the participating banks will issue a minimum number of cards to customers of their local branches and upgrade existing POS equipment to accept the cards. Each bank will have to run its own tests internally before starting. The purpose of the pilot is both to test the acceptability of the application to customers and to ensure that technically the application is complete.

The pilot will run for approximately six months. Then, the products will be rolled out to the rest of the country, and POS terminals, ATMs and branch equipment will be upgraded. Ultimately, all ATM cards could be replaced by smart cards. Card numbers could therefore reach 15 million. The eventual number of POS terminals is approximately 100,000.

First Two Products

Two products will be launched during the pilot.

The first is an off-line debit card. The transactions on it will be processed against a check account. The card is used to:

- Allow off-line PIN verification

- To certify transactions

- To force an on-line authorization after a given number of transactions

There is no pin-protected balance on the card, however, it may be issued with an unprotected purse for low-value transactions.

As with credit cards, most terminals will have floor limits, transactions under the floor limit will take place off-line, and those over the floor limit will be authorized.

The product is aimed at present checking account customers, offering an alternative to credit cards and check payments. It will be issued at the bank branch manager's discretion.

The second product is an electronic purse. It will contain both PIN-protected and unprotected purses and is the product that the majority of the banks' customers will be offered. The cardholder will not be able to transact unless there is sufficient value on the card.

Cardholders will be able to load value to a card from any existing bank account through an ATM or self-service device, or with cash through a branch teller. All transactions at the POS will be off-line. Maximum purse and transaction values can be set by individual banks on both of the purses.

The cardholders will be able to use both the debit cards and the electronic purse products to draw cash at ATMs. The electronic purse card will offer a choice, cash can be drawn either from a linked account or from the card itself.

All PIN-protected transactions will be transmitted in batches through the present credit card system, to the card issuer. This will be done either through the current dial-up service or by transporting the batches on a card to a bank branch. The last 10 such transactions will be held on the card for cardholder reference. Each bank will keep a record of electronic purse transactions in order to reconcile the card balance when a card is lost or stolen.

Non-protected transactions are not passed individually to the issuer. The terminals will be programmed to accumulate all transactions for each bank and pass the total as a single transaction at the end of each day.

VISA SMART CARD STORED VALUE CARD PRODUCTS

Visa has introduced a new alternative to cash called stored value cards. The stored value card, which looks like a traditional bank card, contains a microprocessor that holds and processes money in the form of electronic data. As the card is used, the exact amount of money is deducted from the chip, and the terminal displays the amount of value remaining on the card.[11]

Figure 6-5. Visa stored value card.

Visa is implementing a variety of stored value card pilots in selected cities in five regions: Asia-Pacific, Canada, Europe/Middle East/Africa, Latin America, and the United States. For example, in Europe, where chip cards are already established, many banks offer stored value programs for domestic usage. Visa will provide these institutions with multi-currency capability so the cards can be used internationally.

In Australia, a national stored value program has been supported by major banks in that country.

In Latin America, Argentina and Columbia will issue combination cards, which feature stored value as an added function for debit cards. In Mexico, TELMEX has started negotiations to launch a co-branded card that will contain a stored value chip that can be used at TELMEX pay phones.

U.S. Program Launches

First Union Bank, NationsBank, and Wachovia Bank have individually agreed to participate in the Visa pilot for the 1996 Summer Olympics to be held in Atlanta. After the initial pilot is launched, Visa will expand the program to include additional banks that wish to participate.

Visa will showcase this innovative new payment method with the two million visitors expected to attend the Olympic games in Atlanta.

SVC Advantages

Many merchant locations (including automated vending machines, parking meters, pay telephones, buses, taxis, toll booths, video game machines, fast food restaurants, and school cafeterias) do not accept payment products such as credit cards, debit cards, or checks as payment today. Nevertheless, Visa research showed they would derive benefits such as immediate payment for goods, increased sales, time savings in handling, sorting, and replenishing coins, and reduced cashier handling errors and theft.

A major advantage of stored value cards over cash and coins will be the acceptance of the card at unattended locations where exact change is required. With stored value cards, consumers will always have exact change; and automated machine vendors will realize greater profits due to theft reduction and reduced maintenance costs.

Visa Stored Value System

To support program activity, Visa has developed a stored value payment system that is integrated with VisaNet, the core payment system.

"Visa is introducing a complete line of stored value products. We support both disposable and reloadable stored value cards, whether used as a single-purpose cash alternative or when used as a reloadable feature on an existing Visa or bank product," said Carl Pascarella, president and CEO of Visa USA. "The Visa system combines the need for a highly efficient processing with the requirement for providing substantial fraud-tracking and customer service support information."[12]

Visa is also supporting pilot activity to provide its members with practical market experience with stored value. The pilot banks have agreed to share lessons learned and help the general membership understand the business dynamics of building chip-based stored value card programs. After the initial pilots are operational, Visa will support broader pilots and roll-outs of both member-operated and Visa-operated versions of the system.

Creating a Global Infrastructure

Stored value products have existed in some form for many years. These products, typically issued by phone companies, mass transit authorities, some universities and selected governments, have a common shortcoming. They have limited, or "closed-loop," functionality because they are meant for a single transaction, like a transit pass, or they can be used only at locations within a set geographical boundary.

An open system architecture is a critical element that differentiates Visa's strategy. While many current stored value products adhere to the ISO 7816 standard, they lack the commonality of implementation specifications and guidelines that would allow them to be interoperable, thereby making them closed-loop systems.

Visa has been working with the world's major stored value system operators, as well as key banks and payment systems, to develop industry-wide specifications for the global operation of stored value cards and supporting equipment.[13]

MASTERCARD'S POSITION IN SMART CARDS

MasterCard is endorsing smart card technology as the future platform for the general-purpose card industry.

Mr. Lockhart has stated that smart card technology is one of the core strategies for staying ahead in a changing world—and a technology that will be central to MasterCard's strategy for improved delivery and relationship maintenance, and offering consumers added value.

Stored Value Consumer Research

Newly released MasterCard International research indicates that its global stored value application—called MasterCard cash—not only has great appeal among Americans and Australians, but that many consumers in these countries would be willing to switch financial institutions to take advantage of this innovative payment method.

In the United States, 60 percent of respondents said they would switch banks to obtain the stored value feature and 55 percent of Australians surveyed would be willing to do the same.

The quantitative consumer concept studies, recently conducted with almost 2000 people in the United States and Australia, revealed other significant trends as well. First, consumer interest in stored value is largely based on a consumer's lifestyle and does not vary significantly across different demographic groups. Second, consumers consider the stored value application most valuable as complementary to coins and cash, and not as a cash replacement. Finally, mass market outlets such as convenience stores and gasoline stations are establishments where stored value is likely to have the greatest impact.

Stored Value Pilot

One of the association's first steps towards this migration process is a multi-bank, multi-merchant and multi-vendor pilot. The pilot, beginning in Canberra, called MasterCard Cash—with a stored value application on a credit card, debit/ATM card, or combination credit/debit card. MasterCard Cash will have the ability for multi-currency loading and cross-border acceptance in select areas. Participating banks view the pilot as extremely vital to the process of enhancing customer relationships as the smart cards will be linked to existing credit or debit accounts—without that link it is virtually impossible to gauge how customer relationships can be really enhanced.

To initiate the stored-value feature, the cardholder will go to a select merchant location or ATM, enter his or her personal identification number (PIN), and load value onto the card, and the amount of value loaded will be detailed on the cardholder's regular monthly statement.

Industry Collaboration

One of the keys to successful implementation is working openly with different segments of the industry. Two such examples of MasterCard's leadership in this area include the creation of MasterCard Vendor Forum and Merchant Council on Smart Card Technology.

The Vendor Forum—made up of more than 100 smart card vendors from around the world—was created to provide an open dialog and exchange regarding the association's strategy for smart card development, implementation, and industry specifications.

The MasterCard Merchant Council on Smart Card Technology is the industry's first organized effort to bring together leading multinational merchants to discuss the technology development and deployment of smart cards and terminals. Several major companies from retail, airline, hotel, fast food, convenience store, and petroleum industries across five regions are participating in this unprecedented forum.

The objective of the MasterCard Merchant Council on Smart Card Technology is to provide leaders from the merchant community with current information and to solicit input on MasterCard's smart card technology developments, particularly specifications and deployment of terminals.

Building the Foundation

For the last 18 months, MasterCard has been working with Europay International and Visa International on the development of global specifications for the integration of micro-chip payment cards. In June of this year, the EMV (Europay, MasterCard, Visa) working group released the card and terminal specifications. These specifications represent a stable base upon which the financial service industry can begin to develop chip card applications that are capable of functioning across borders and systems. It is intended that these specifications will be updated and issued annually to allow enhancements that support the dynamic evolution of chip card implementations.

The effort is the result of the three organizations' decision in December, 1993, to form a working group to develop a common set of technical specifications for the integration of microprocessor chips in payment cards and their interaction with chip-card-reading terminals. Since then, the group has met on a regular basis, making steady progress in a cooperative effort.

Financial Services Industry Leaders to Form SmartCash

Leaders from the financial, smart card, and payments industries are planning to form SmartCash, a for-profit company that will develop, finance, implement, and manage the first nationwide stored value card business. Participation in SmartCash will be open to all U.S. financial institutions, networks and technology providers. It is presently envisioned that the founding owners of SmartCash will include major banks like: Banc One Corporation, Bank of America, Chemical Banking Corporation, Nations Bank, Core States Financial Corporation, and First Union Corporation, along with other companies like Verifone and Gemplus.

SmartCash will speed the implementation of smart card technology and the stored value application throughout the United States. The stored value application, one of the many applications that can reside on the embedded integrated circuit chip, enables value from the cardholders' deposit or credit account to be loaded onto the card from an ATM or smart card terminal. The card is then used in place of cash and coins for purchases targeted at the $20 and under range.

The initial roll-out of SmartCash's stored value card will occur in 1996 in multiple locations throughout the U.S.

THE ROLE OF EUROPAY

Europay was formed in 1992 by merging MasterCard's partner Eurocard, a T&E competitor of American Express and Diners Club, with Eurocheque, the ATM card and paper-based check-cashing system operating in Europe and North Africa. Europay members issue 35 million cards with Eurocard-MasterCard logos and 20 million cards with Cirrus logos. Nearly all are tied to deposit accounts, making them much less profitable than cards tied to lines of credit, which makes Europay members a lot more sensitive to losses from fraud and bad debt. It will take at least two years before chips will be used for fraud and risk management on cross-border Eurocard-MasterCard transactions. Microchips not only offer Europay a way of improving security, but also will help it build a technology platform from which to launch applications for consumer payment products such as the cross-border electronic purse systems springing up throughout Europe.

Soon after Europay was formed, management and the Board initiated a study into the business case for introducing chip technology. Priorities were established to include:

Fraud—the most significant problem is the incredible rise in counterfeit fraud over recent years, and the threat that fraud poses to bank profitability and payment system integrity. There is an absolute need for a method to authenticate a cardholder and be able to positively identify the cardholder. A Cardholder Verification Method using a PIN is already in use for all ATM transactions and will be the basis for further analysis.[14]

However, since Europay is proposing to employ chip technology across all products, we must accept that most credit cardholders do not use their PIN today. The opinion is that the PIN usage will be at the option of the issuer, on a card-by-card basis, though a PIN is preferred.

POS terminals worldwide should incorporate a common set of characteristics, including a keypad for PIN entry at all chip terminals, a display for prompting consumers through the transaction and the capability to support both off-line and on-line authorizations based on card issuer decisions. Using a verification method will significantly reduce fraud losses, and set a procedure in place.

Europay seems committed to developing the payment system of the future from its present model using magnetic stripe to a dynamic system, utilizing a chip for plastic payments cards, and by taking advantage of a global network of intelligent point-of-sale terminals.

The Board of Europay has stated that cost effectiveness is the key. Europay believes it must be the best international payment system, providing members with a full range of payment services along with those related value-added services that enhance the profitability of the underlying payment product.

Presently smart card applications already in the market are operating under their own proprietary infrastructures. If the major trade associations and vendors do not act now to build a global foundation for financial applications and selected companies could be precluded from accessing the new market opportunities already being pursued by others. The threat of not responding could lead to erosion of market share to competitors to enter the market who can better deliver products and services.

THE ROLE OF VISA

Visa, the world's largest consumer payment system, is playing a pivotal role in developing and implementing new technologies that benefit its members and their cardholders, business, government and the global economy. Headquartered in San Francisco, Visa and its 21,000 member financial institutions serve over 12 million merchants and 402 million cardholders worldwide. It also operates Visa/Plus, the largest global ATM network. In 1994, Visa consumer card transactions (credit and debit) totaled more than $630 billion worldwide.[15]

Visa believes that the chip card has the potential to dramatically change how the payments industry will do business worldwide. The chip opens the way to increased data capacity, greater security, and more powerful capabilities at the point of transaction.[16]

The Future of Electronic Banking

The chip is being developed for its member financial institutions, and Visa's job is to make the chip platform a profitable product for its members. The ubiquity and capability of the chip will grow as financial institutions use it as a means of reshaping relationships with their customers.

The chip will help to improve the relationship between a financial institution and its customer and will allow access to the management of individual customer data. In essence, it becomes the key to the customer's bank.

Consumers will be able to access their accounts and perform various banking functions—whenever, wherever, and however they choose. Over the last decade, we have seen significant use of automated teller machines (ATMs) and magnetic stripe reading point-of-sale terminals. In the next ten years, these devices will be complemented by millions of personal computers, personal data assistants, touch-tone phones, interactive-television, advanced pagers and a host of other devices that will be used for initiating financial transactions. Most will be capable of accepting chip cards and processing secure payment transactions.

Enabling Technologies for Secure Payments

Technological advances in telecommunications will influence the delivery of financial services. "Visanet, Visa's global payment network, Internet, CompuServe and other national and global information networks are all pieces of the information highway that will deliver these services." It is this information highway that will provide remote banking access. Transaction growth will be fostered as a result of significant advances in encryption technology that are occurring today and that which will enable financial transactions to be securely transported over public and private telecommunications networks.

A Decade of Groundwork

Visa's effort and commitment to develop the joint IC Card Specifications for Payment System is the result of its support for chip card technology over the past decade. In the early 1980s, Visa recognized that chip cards would play a significant role in future financial services. The technology was at a very early stage of development and a great deal of effort was required to ensure that bankcards with chips would be used globally. To ensure its member financial institutions needs were addressed, Visa decided in 1983 to aggressively participate in the development of chip card standards by the International Organization for Standardization. Visa participated in each of the ISO working groups developing chip card standards, hosted international meetings, and chaired industry activities.

To test the technology and to gain experience, Visa cards containing chips were issued in Blois, France in 1983. The knowledge gained from this test was used as a model for future French applications.

In October 1985, Visa conducted a joint study with Groupement Carte Bleue, Bank of America, and The Royal Bank of Canada and concluded that the technology was not mature enough to support worldwide deployment. Chip card costs were high and value-added services had to be identified to make the issuance of Visa chip cards an attractive proposition for member financial institutions and their customers.

Based on these conclusions, Visa made a strong commitment to continue development of international standards, undertake experiments to test the chip card technology and initiate research to identify value-added services that would enhance member institutions' use of the technology.

The next major milestone was in June 1988 when Visa tested the world's first multifunction chip card, called the SuperSmart card in Japan. Developed by Visa International and Toshiba Corporation, the card combined a microcomputer chip and a calculator-like keyboard and display. The experiment allowed Visa to test technical aspects of the technology and evaluate the acceptance of value-added services by consumers.

In July 1990, further research was undertaken on value-added services with the issuance of the Visa International worldwide study on prepaid cards. This study provided Visa with an early understanding of worldwide developments of prepaid card systems and provided a sound basis for its present development of stored value products for its members.

Following the 1985 study, Visa understood that the successful introduction of chip cards would only take place when conditions in the industry changed to favor the chip card technology. These changes included the maturing of chip card technology; lower unit costs; increased level of interest by member institutions.

Visa Urges Global Chip Card Usage

In September 1992, in keeping with its earlier commitment Visa International's Board of Directors endorsed chip cards as an international payment service option. Following this endorsement, Visa set a course for a rational, business- and market-driven global introduction of the technology by its member banks. Management immediately initiated the development of the Visa International Functional Specification for Chip Cards. Visa, working with representatives from member institutions with chip card experience and worldwide manufacturers, successfully completed the specification in November 1993.

Visa's management quickly recognized that member financial institutions wanted an industry-wide global specification rather than individual and probably incompatible efforts by each major payment system. As a result, Visa formed a working group with Europay and MasterCard in December 1993 to develop common specifications for payment systems worldwide.

Poised for Global Chip Development

In November 1994, Visa announced its Vendor Partnership Program with signed agreements from twenty of the world's leading technology suppliers to the payment industry for the development of prototype chip cards and terminals. The availability of prototype equipment based on the joint global chip cards specifications will accelerate the development and implementation of chip card technology.

Visa's Vendor Partnership Program will occur in two stages. The first stage involves alpha development with Gemplus, Schlumberger and Verifone. The second stage expands development to seventeen other selected vendor partners for beta testing of cards, terminals, automated teller machines and personalization devices. This approach enables Visa to work hand-in-hand with key vendors around the world, ensuring their active participation in the development of equipment critical to the global introduction of chip cards.

In addition to the development and testing of prototype equipment, Visa expects to complete the necessary chip processing modifications to its VisaNet systems by the fourth quarter of 1996. The association will then be in a position to support members' chip card implementations around the world.

Visa is confident that these activities will ensure worldwide compatibility of chip cards. Visa's systems will be ready to fully support its members as they deploy chip cards to facilitate their successful entry into the next generation of financial services.

END NOTES

1. Brown, Ronald. Dec., 1994. "World Market." *The Smart Card Post News.* pp. *1–5.*

2. *Chip Card—The Competitive Edge.* MasterCard International. p. 9.

3. *Danmønt Marketing Description of Services.* Nov., 1994. Danmønt internal document. pp. 1–3.

4. Dec., 1993. "Mondex Release on Global Electronic Cash." European Union, *Smart Card News.* pp. 230–232.

5. "Shell Card Goes Nationwide." Nov., 1994. *Smart Card Monthly.* p. 4.

6. Chabanel, Jean Paul. October, 1995. INGENICO Singapore Cash Card Presentation Interview and Materials.

7. "MasterCard to Offer Its First Smart Cards." March, 1995. MasterCard International. pp. 1–3.

8. "MasterCard Questions & Answers for Canberra Smartcard Pilot." March 30, 1995. MasterCard International. pp. 4–5.

9. Ibid. p. 5.

10. Ras, John. 1994. *The South African Position on Smart Cards.* First National Bank of South Africa, pp. 1–7.

11. *Stored Value Cards.* 1995. Visa International. p. 6.

12. Ibid. p. 7.

13. Ibid. p. 8.

14. McKenna, Jean. May, 1995. "Building a Highway to the Future." Visa International. pp. 5–6. World Card Technology. Feb. 1995.

15. Ibid. p. 7.

16. Ibid. p. 56.

7

Preparing a Winning Business Plan

INTRODUCTION

When a CEO-founder of a computer software firm in Washington, D.C., recently visited his banker to request a $50,000 line of credit to enter into the smart card software world, he had his business plan tucked neatly at his side. When the president of a smart card manufacturer in France wanted to establish a set of five-year goals based on the company's current financial projections, he, too, had a business plan. And when the management team of a company on the east coast of Florida sought these outside investors to finance their expansion into a financial service for smart cards, they made sure that their business plan was first rate. All executives recognize the value of the business plan for securing capital and for growth in their companies for a smart card business.

This chapter establishes the scope and value of a business plan. It provides a step-by-step procedure for preparing a plan and discusses why certain information is required, how it may be best presented, and why it is essential in launching a smart card business.

Most of us underestimate the importance of writing a plan and how it can help a business raise capital, plan for the future, and keep tabs on how it is currently progressing. In this chapter, we will not only stress the important aspects of a smart card plan but help you prepare a well-organized document that will serve as a guide to raise capital and financing.[1]

Launching a smart card operation is a serious undertaking. While statistics on the failure rate of smart card businesses vary, all suggest a high incident of failure, particularly in the first three years. Acquisitions of existing companies and expansions of present operations for smart card opportunities enjoy a significantly higher success rate, due to the lesser degree of uncertainty. However, even in these circumstances, issues are complex and stakes are high.

In light of this, a company must act in whatever manner will improve the odds. In most cases, this means the careful creation of the business plan.

WHY PREPARE A BUSINESS PLAN?

The business plan serves as a blueprint for building a company. It is a vehicle for describing the goals of the business, why the goals are economically and technologically feasible and how these goals can be reached over the coming years. Moreover, the business plan is a means to:

- Delineate individual responsibilities

- Project sales, expenses, and cash flows

- Explain to employees what is expected of them

- Improve company performance

- Assist managers in decision making

- Plan for a new product development

- Raise capital for a business

Thus the business plan is not merely a report that is prepared and then left on the shelf to collect dust; rather, it is a working document that business managers should use on a monthly—or even weekly—basis to ensure continuity of the business.

Despite the many reasons for preparing a plan is described above, the single most important reason for preparing such a plan for a vast majority of entrepreneurial companies is in securing capital.[2] Investors agree than an effectively prepared business plan is a requisite for obtaining funding for any business—whether it is a new business seeking startup capital or an existing business seeking financing for expansion, new business activities, or a turn-around situation.

WHAT IS A BUSINESS PLAN?

A business plan is a written document that details a proposed business opportunity. It must illustrate current status, expected needs, and projected results of the new business. Every aspect of the venture needs to be described: the project, marketing, research and development, manufacturing, management, critical risks, financing, and milestones with a timetable. A description of all of these facets of the proposed business is necessary to give a clear picture of what the opportunity is, where it is projected to go, and how you plan to get there. In other words, the business plan is your road map for a successful enterprise.

The business plan is also referred to as a marketing plan or an investment prospectus. Whatever its name, a business plan is the document that is initially required by any financial source, and one that allows you entrance into the investment-seeking process. Although it may be utilized as a working document once the company is established, the major purpose of the business plan is to encapsulate strategic developments of the project in a comprehensive document for outside investors or senior management teams to scrutinize.

The business plan describes to senior management if you are expanding operations for smart card opportunities or to potential investors and financial sources all of the events that may affect the business being proposed. It is vital that the assumptions upon which the plan is being based are explicitly stated. For example, increases or decreases in the marketplace or upswings or downswings in the economy during the start-up period should be stated.

The emphasis of the business plan should always be the final implementation of the venture. In other words, it is not just the writing of an effective plan that is important, but also the translation of the plan into a successful enterprise.

Thus, a business plan should:

- Describe every aspect of a particular business

- Include a marketing plan

- Clarify and outline financial needs

- Identify potential obstacles and alternative solutions

- Serve as a communication tool for all financial and professional sources[3]

The business plan is the major tool used to guide managers in the formation of the business, as well as the primary document needed to manage it. But it is also more than a written document; it is a process that begins when gathering information and continues as projections are made, implemented, measured, and updated; that is, it is an ongoing process.

PREPARING A WINNING BUSINESS PLAN

Most managers can prepare an *average* plan without too much trouble. That would be fine if investors would fund *average* plans. Investors, however, fund only *A+ or the best* plans. In essence, an average business plan is no better than an ordinary plan because neither is likely to get funded. Thus the real skill is to turn a business plan into one that warrants an A+.

A first-rate business plan might only be a 10 to 20 percent improvement over an average plan in the eyes of the professional manager; it might also take 80 percent more effort to gain a 20 percent improvement. Yet that 20 percent improvement will seem like a 100 percent improvement in the eyes of the person that matters the most (i.e., the investor) and will therefore increase the likelihood of getting funded by close to 100 percent.

What separates an average plan from an A+ or first-rate plan? The key difference is the perspective of the investor! The A+ plan gets the investor to believe in your product or service, your target market, and your management team while it addresses the problems or the key concerns of the business. In addition, the A+ plan demonstrates that something is unique about this deal—something that distinguishes this investment opportunity from the scores of others that may be brought before a particular investor every week.

The simple rules that follow are designed to enable you to develop an A+ plan. You will know you have written an A+ plan when you have to turn away money.

THREE FUNCTIONS OF A BUSINESS PLAN

First, and foremost, it is a plan which can be used to develop ideas about how the business should be conducted. It is a chance to refine strategies and "make mistakes on paper" rather than in the real world, by examining the company from all perspectives, such as marketing, finance, and operations.

Second, the plan is a tool, against which you can assess a company's actual performance over time. For example, the financial part of a plan can be used as the basis for an operating budget, and can be monitored carefully to see how closely the business is sticking to that budget. In this regard, the plan can and should be used as the basis for a new plan. After some time has elapsed, the business plan should be examined to see where the company has strayed, whether that straying is helpful or harmful, and how the business should operate in the future.

The **third** reason for writing a business plan is the one most people think of first, that is, to raise money. Most lenders or investors will not put money into a business without seeing a business plan. There are stories of wild-eyed entrepreneurs and venture capitalists with pens at the ready who meet, scribble some projections on a wet cocktail napkin, shake hands, and become "partners" in this hot smart card technology business, but those are myths.[4]

HOW TO TURN INVESTORS ON

There are several specific guidelines to guidelines to follow when developing a convincing business plan for investors—one that will warrant an A+ rating in their minds. These guidelines will not only help you in the preparation of your plan, but will serve as valuable advice to you in operating your business and in planning for long-term growth.

For a plan to receive a favorable review by an investor, it must demonstrate the following four features:[5]

- A clear definition of the business

- Evidence of marketing capabilities

- Evidence of management capabilities

- An attractive financial arrangement

Let's examine each of these.

Definition of the Business

There are three basic questions regarding the business that, when answered, provide a working understanding of the "definition of the business"—also known as the "mission" or scope of operations of the business (i.e., what business are you in?):

1. What is the product or service?

2. What is the industry?

3. What is the target market?

These three questions underlie the basic strategy (or direction) of the firm.

No smart card business can be all things to all people. In the earliest stages of a business it is critical that the company develop a logical, somewhat stable business definition or strategy and avoid any dramatic changes to it. Any alteration of one or more of these features—the product or service, the industry, or the target market—results in a new, riskier, strategy for the firm. Of course, as the business expands, the only way to accomplish significant growth will be to alter its current business definition, whether by expanding the product line, entering a new industry, or seeking a new market for a given product or service. Investors, however, will want to see some initial stability in the company's strategy or business definition.

USE AS PLANNING DOCUMENT

Many people who think "business plans" think start-up company. Yet this is not necessarily accurate. Ongoing companies or companies that are considering expanding into the smart card arena should and often do create business plans.

AT&T Smart Card Company, one of the largest ventures, still prepares an annual business plan.

For an ongoing business, the business plan serves a number of functions. "It is a way of getting consensus and consistency throughout the company," says William Elliot, general partner at ATT Ventures. "While business plans are often written by one or two people, in an ongoing company—especially one that is larger—a number of people have a hand in writing our business plan. By the time a business plan has run through a number of revisions and is produced in final form, nearly everyone involved will be committed to the plan's vision for the company."[6]

A frequent complaint among smaller companies is that, because of the day-to-day management pressure, there is little time for planning. That is, of course, unfortunate, since a continuing effort at business planning is probably more important to the survival of a smart card business.

The business plan is, in many ways, a company's first crack at strategic planning. And, contrary to what many people think, strategic planning not only can be done in the context of a small company, but is as vital to a small company as to a large company.

The business plan is also an implementation tool. It can be used to test theories of how the company should be run and to calculate possible outcomes. Then the plan can be checked as those ideas are implemented to see if the projections were accurate. This step provides an early-warning system and allows for prompt action to correct problems.

An ongoing company has an advantage over a new venture when developing a business plan. The numbers it uses to make projections will have some basis in fact and in past experience. And the strategies outlined for the business's future will also be rooted in its past strategies, incorporating what the company gained from its successes and learned from its mistakes.

USE TO MEASURE PERFORMANCE

The constant updating of the business plan helps the plan fulfill its second major purpose that of being a yardstick against which to measure the company's actual performance.[7]

Last year's business plan can tell a company's performance and strategy and what implementation was effective or ineffective.

Simplicity is a virtue to the extent that it eases implementation. Often, however, what looked simple on paper when the previous business plan was being prepared became complex in implementation. Examining the business's actual performance against the business plan can identify the strengths and weaknesses in the organization—sometimes relating to the people—that separate strategy from effective implementation.

The financial section of the business plan can be used in an objective, concrete way to monitor the performance of the business. The financial projections made when the plan was drawn up became the basis for the budget under which the company tried to operate. Deviations from that budget point out areas where either necessary resources were misjudged or possibly controls were lax during the period the business plan encompassed.

Others besides management will use the business plan as a monitoring tool. Financial sources, both lenders and investors, will note deviations between the plan and the company's actual performance; they will ask why those deviations occurred.

This is one of the arguments against overly hyping a business in a business plan. Professionals—consultants, accountants, and lawyers who work with you in writing business plans and securing financing—often counsel their clients to make realistic projections. Why should you risk not meeting projections, when a little more modesty will produce projections that can much more easily be attained, or even exceeded, thereby keeping lenders happy and still providing investors with a healthy rate of return.

FINANCIAL TOOL

This is the role of a business plan most people think of first. While we list this role last, it too is critical. After all, if a business can't raise cash, all else may be moot. Although raising cash is a critical hurdle, it is only the first of many.

Thinking that the primary role of a business plan is to be a sales tool to raise cash can produce problems. This emphasis can lead managers to write a hyped-up plan that will not provide the objectivity necessarily for the plan to fulfill its other two roles.[8]

Plan Outline

A table of contents should be completed for any business plan. It serves as a guide to show exactly where each section begins and directs the user to capitalize on the issues and recommendations.

Eight important elements in the plan are shown in Figure 7-1.

Section	*Table of Contents*	Is the plan approximately 20–30 pages with minimal redundancy?
I	Executive Summary	Clear, exciting, and effective as a stand-alone overview of the plan
II	Company Overview	Business purpose, history, genesis of concept, current status, overall strategy, and objectives

Figure 7-1. Key ingredients of a business plan.

III	Products or Services	Description, features and benefits, pricing, current stage of development, proprietary position
IV	Market and Marketing Strategy	Description of market, competitive analysis, needs identification, market acceptance, unique capabilities, sales/promotion
V	Operations/Research	Plan for production/delivery of product of services, product cost, margins, operating complexity, resources required
VI	Management	Background of key individuals, ability to execute strategy, personnel needs, organizational structure, role of any non-student executive, which students will execute plan
VII	Financial Section	Presented in summary form. Consistent with plan and effective in capturing financial performance; monthly for first year (quarterly for years 2–3; annually for years 4–5 optional)
VIII	Offering (if appropriate) or Milestone Schedule	Proposal/terms to investors: indicate how much wanted, the ROI, the structure of the deal; possible exit strategies

Figure 7-1. (continued)

WRITING THE BUSINESS PLAN

The business plan could take more than 200 hours to prepare, depending on your experience and knowledge of the company. It should be comprehensive enough to give any potential investor a complete picture and understanding of the business. It will also help you and your team clarify the thinking about the business.

Most incorrectly estimate the length of time that an effective plan will take to prepare. Once the process has begun, however, you will realize that it is invaluable in sorting out the business functions of your company.

Make the Plan Readable

A well-written plan may often be more than 40 pages long, but most plans for smart card businesses are usually about 20 pages. Potential investors and lenders receive many proposals, but usually they need no more than the executive summary. Michael Matthews, managing director of Westgate Capital, states: "I first read the executive summary and if I like it, the financial section is next. Only if the concept is intriguing will I spend more time. I receive about a hundred proposals a week and it is quite difficult to read all of them thoroughly. For those few plans that capture my attention, usually about five percent, there is a more detailed complete study."[9]

This clearly means that you must be very careful to capture the readers attention early, yet provide a thorough business case analysis that occurs later in the plan.

Winning Plan Outline

There are five critical rules to follow when writing your plan, shown in Figure 7-2.

---

1. Present quality management team
   - Show talented team
   - Show how to retain team

2. Stress competitive advantage
   - Demonstrate distinct competence
   - How substantial is your advantage?

3. Focus on market-driven opportunities
   - Demonstrate how product/service meets market need
   - Define niche
   - Don't underestimate competition

Figure 7-2. Critical rules to follow in writing plan.

4. Support projections for growth
   • Show how company will grow
   • Identify milestones
   • Validate results
   • Be confidant with numbers
   • Never minimize capital needs

5. Generate positive cash flow
   • Show how founders will be repaid
   • Look to future—going public or corporate acquisition

Figure 7-2. (continued)

COMPONENTS OF A BUSINESS PLAN

A brief description of the sections of a plan follows.

Executive Summary

This is the most important section because it has to convince the reader that the business will succeed. In no more than three pages you should summarize the highlights of the rest of the plan.

The executive summary must be able to stand on its own; it should not simply be an introduction to the rest of the business plan. Investors who review many business plans may read only the executive summary, so if it cannot gain the investor's confidence on its own, the plan will be rejected and will never be read in its entirety.

This section should discuss who will purchase the product or service, how much money is required for a start-up, and what the payback is expected to be. You should also explain why you are uniquely qualified and skilled to manage the business.

Because this section summarizes the plan, it is often best to write it last.

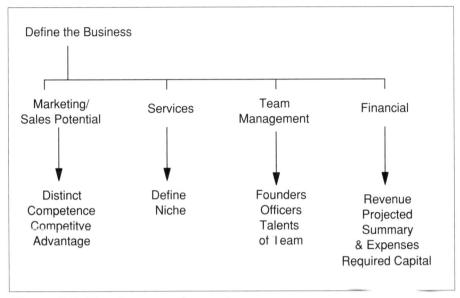

Figure 7-3. Key elements of executive summary.

Company Overview

This section should provide background information about your industry, a history of your company, and a general description of your new product or service. Your product or service should be described in terms of its unique qualities and value to consumers.

Specific *short-term* and *long-term objectives* must be defined. Clearly state what sales, market share, and profitability objectives you want your business to achieve.

Marketing Plan

Two major parts comprise the marketing section. The first is *products or services*. Here you should explain who will buy the product or service, or in other words, identify your target market. Measure your market size and trends and estimate the market share you expect to capture. Be sure to include support for your sales projections. For example, if your figures are based on published marketing research data, be sure to cite the source. Do your best to make realistic and credible projections. Describe your competition in considerable detail, identifying their strengths and weaknesses. Finally, explain how you will be better than your competitors.

The second part is your *marketing strategy*. This critical section should include your market strategy, sales and distribution plan, pricing, advertising, promotion, and public awareness. You should demonstrate also how your pricing strategy will result in a profit, identify your advertising plans, and include cost estimates to validate the proposed strategy.

Operations

Explain the process steps to be used to offer your product or service. A simple flow chart is often used to show how a product will be assembled. This section should also describe the advantages of your location in terms of zoning, tax laws, wage rates, labor availability, and proximity to suppliers and transportation systems. The requirements and costs of your production facilities and equipment should also be outlined in this section. (Be careful. Many people underestimate the importance of this part.)

Research, Design, and Development

This section includes *developmental research* leading to the design of the product. Industrial design is an art form that has successfully found its way into business, and it should not be neglected. Technical research results should be evaluated. Include the costs of research, testing and development. Explain carefully what has already been accomplished (e.g., prototype development, lab testing, early development). Finally, mention any research or technical assistance that has been provided for you.

I.   EXECUTIVE SUMMARY

Datamark Software Inc. ("Datamark" or the "Company") is an innovative customer marketing information company. Datamark utilizes smart card and magnetic stripe (interactive card) technology in conjunction with customized software to capture data for customer loyalty and marketing solutions.

Founded in 1992, Datamark pioneered the use of interactive card technology to develop marketing frequency programs for the restaurant and retail industries. Since this time, the Company has aggressively established itself as a leading provider of these programs to this market segment.

Datamark's programs operate similarly to the airlines' frequent flyer programs and are designed to increase a clients' profitability by building comprehensive customer databases and using the databases to generate highly targeted marketing campaigns.

Datamark differentiates itself in the marketplace by championing the use of smart cards in many of our systems. We believe that smart cards offer the most effective method for our clients to create added value for their customers and generate greater customer loyalty. Datamark's software products can be licensed as standalone products or used as the basic building blocks for our frequency products. Datamark's products can be integrated with most point-of-sale (POS) systems to develop comprehensive electronic marketing solutions.

To date, Datamark has successfully developed frequency pilots for several national restaurant chains and a regional sporting goods chain. A full scale roll-out anticipated for these three pilots is anticipated to include over 1,600 restaurants and retail stores by the end of 1995. Pilot programs have exhibited significant success for our clients, increasing both frequency of visits and average purchase amount by more than 20% (annualized) during the first year of implementation. Our successful entry into the restaurant market has provided Datamark with the opportunity to expand into other retail businesses. The Company is currently in the process of developing pilot programs for a company specializing in restaurants and a national hardware chain, which we plan to implement during early 1995. These programs have the potential to add over 5,000 stores to Datamark's customer base.

Datamark's long-term objective is to become a major provider of smart card marketing solutions to a broad market including the financial and health care industries. Datamark plans to specialize in multi-functional smart card applications, the use of a single smart card for multiple purposes, as we believe this represents the future of card technology. To help meet this

Figure 7-4. Executive summary example.

challenge, Datamark is aggressively pursuing copyright and patent protection for a multiple-application data card. Our patent, filed in December, 1993, is pending approval.

A key to Datamark's success lies in the strength of our strategic alliances and partnerships. Currently, the Company has formed partnerships with a direct marketing and promotional company, and a third-party database company. In addition, Datamark is negotiating an exclusive software licensing agreement with a software company to be the preferred smart card software vendor for its restaurant and retail businesses. These alliances further expand Datamark's sales and marketing opportunities and systems resources.

Market Potential

Smart card technology has been perfected abroad for over 10 years. Worldwide use of smart cards has more than doubled since 1992 to over 300 million cards and is projected to grow even more rapidly in the next few years. Management believes that smart card use is now ready to expand rapidly in the U.S. market.

Datamark's immediate opportunity lies in the growing demand for frequency programs and prepaid card programs in the retail market. Over the past two years, Datamark has experienced a tremendous increase in the number of inquiries from prospective customers and other companies interested in joining forces.

There are currently over 100,000 quick-service restaurants in the United States. Yet, only a handful of these restaurants offer any type of frequency programs or prepaid card programs. None, to the best of our knowledge, use smart card technology in conjunction with their programs.

In the market niche that Datamark is pursuing, smart card technology is the only interactive card technology available that can effectively combine a frequency program and a prepaid card program on a national basis. By combining these marketing programs, Datamark offers the restaurant and retail industries a very powerful solution to help generate customer loyalty and grow their businesses.

As a member of the Smart Card Forum, a multi-industry effort to accelerate the use of smart cards in North America, Datamark seeks to form strategic alliances and licensing agreements with other innovative companies to build for the future.

Figure 7-4. (continued)

Major Milestones

Datamark devoted Fiscal Year (FY) 1994 to software development. FY 1995 has been a year of Beta testing, product introduction and landing of several major accounts. In addition, Datamark has established strategic relationships to bolster the Company's systems integration capabilities and increase sales and marketing opportunities. We expect that FY 1996 will be our sales growth year.

Distinctive Competence

As a market pioneer, Datamark has gained expertise designing, developing, implementing, and operating successful electronic card programs for an impressive customer base. As a result, we offer one of the most advanced frequency card programs and have the opportunity to establish our product as the standard for the restaurant and retail industries.

In addition, Datamark's exclusive strategic alliances provide the Company access to a tremendous market potential and to resources that will allow it to be the number one provider of frequency programs for the restaurant and retail markets.

Financial Summary

Datamark derives its revenue through the licensing of our PC-based analysis software products, the development of customized frequency programs and card applications, and the processing of POS database information for clients on a per-use transaction basis.

The Company is projecting profitability in FY 1996 on a substantial increase in sales.

Datamark Software, Inc. demonstrated a strong financial condition as of the fiscal statement dated September 30, 1994. This assessment is supported by a favorable liquidity position and a favorable ratio of debt-to-equity relative to other companies in this line of business.

Figure 7-4. (continued)

The following is a four-year summary of the Company's financial projections:

Financial Projections (in '000s):

Fiscal Year (Feb)	FY 1994	FY 1995	FY 1996	FY 1997
Sales	$69.2	$158.0	$1,522.3	$5,925.7
Profit (Loss)	($125.5)	$201.0	$518.2	$2,012.1

Use of Funds

Datamark is seeking $1.5 million in investment capital over the next six months. These funds will be used to complete software development of the Customer Allegiance product, the smart card prepaid application, and transaction processing to offer a turnkey program to targeted restaurant and retail chains. In addition, Datamark will use these funds to expand its staff and Transaction Processing Center in order to meet its growth projections.

Figure 7-4. (continued)

Management and Organization

Start by describing the *management team*, the managers' unique qualifications, and how you will compensate them (including salaries, employment agreements, stock purchase plans, level of ownership, and other considerations). Discuss how your organization will be structured and consider including a diagram illustrating who will report to whom. Also, include a discussion of the potential contribution of the board of directors, advisors, and consultants. Finally, carefully describe the legal structure of your venture (i.e., sole proprietorship, partnership, or corporation).

Critical Risks

Discuss *potential risks* before investors point them out. Outside consultants can often help identify risks and recommend an alternative course of action. Here are some examples of potential risks: price-cutting by competitors, potentially unfavorable industry-wide trends, design or manufacturing costs that could exceed estimates, sales projections that are not achieved, production development schedules that are not met, difficulties or long lead times in procuring parts or raw materials, and greater-than-expected innovation and development costs needed to keep pace with new competition. The main objective of this section is to show that you can anticipate and control (to a reasonable degree) your risks.

Financial

This section of the business plan will be closely scrutinized by potential investors, so it is imperative that you give it the attention it deserves. Three key financial statements must be presented: a *balance sheet*, an *income statement*, and a *cash flow statement*. These statements typically cover a three-year period. Be sure you state all the assumptions you made when calculating the figures.

Determine the stages at which your business will require external financing and identify the expected financing sources (both debt and equity). Also, clearly show what return on investment these sources will achieve if they invest in your business. The final item to include is a break-even chart, which should show what level of sales will be required to cover all costs.

If the work is done well, the financial statements should represent the actual financial achievements expected from the business plan. They also provide a standard by which to measure the actual results of operating the enterprise and become a very valuable tool for managing an controlling the business in the first years.

WHY BUSINESS PLANS FAIL

Generally a poorly prepared business plan can be blamed on one or more of the following factors:

- Goals set are unreasonable.
- Goals are not measurable.

- The principal has not made a total commitment to the business.

- The principal has no experience in the planned business.

- No sense is given of potential threats or weaknesses to the business.

- No customer need was established for the proposed product or service.

Setting goals requires you to be well-informed about the type of business and the competitive environment. Goals should be specific and not so mundane as to lack any basis of control. For example, you may target a specific market share, units sold, or revenue. These goals are measurable and can be modified over time.

In addition, you should make a total commitment to the business. For example, it is difficult to operate a business on a part-time basis while still holding onto a full-time position. And it is also difficult to operate a business without an understanding from family members as to the time and resources that will be needed. Lenders and investors will not be favorably inclined toward a venture that does not have a full-time commitment. Moreover, lenders or investors will expect you to make significant financial commitment to the business even if it means a second mortgage or a depletion of savings.

Generally, a lack of experience will result in failure unless you can attain either the necessary knowledge or team up with someone who already has it.

END NOTES

1. Schilit, Keith. 1990. *Preparing A Business*. New York: Prentice Hall. pp. 3–11.

2. Crowner, Robert. 1991. *Developing A Strategic Business Plan*. Boston: Irwin. p. 3.

3. Kuratho, Donald. 1994. *Entrepreneurial Strategy*. New York: Dryden Press. pp. 53–58.

4. Timmons, Jeffrey. 1993. *New Venture Creation*. New York: Irwin. p. 220.

5. Hisrich, Robert. 1993. *Starting, Developing, and Managing A New Enterprise*. Boston: Irwin. p. 35.

6. Elliot, William. May 1995. *ATT Ventures*. Using Business Plans For Financing Interview.

7. Vesper, Karl. 1990. *New Venture Strategies*. New Jersey: Prentice Hall. p. 29.

8. Ernst and Young. 1995. *Business Plan Guide*. John Wiley & Sons, Inc. pp. 4–7.

9. Mathews, Michael. Sept. 15, 1995 (interview). Westgate Capital—Winning Business Plan.

8

Organizations Affecting Smart Card Standards and Understanding its Importance

"Without standards, nothing fits."

—Andrew W. Tarbox, Vice President
Chip Card Implementation, MasterCard

Standards for the smart card industry are generally not well understood or appreciated. This chapter is designed to identify the important aspects in standards development, indicate where the current gaps are, and what key organizations are affecting and establishing smart card standards to achieve global operability.

What is a Standard?

A standard is an agreement usually reached by a group of participants in creating a format and a set of protocols to communicate to smart card technology. The groups that usually participate in the creation of standards are manufacturers, industry associations, vendors and consultants.[1]

Why Standards are Important

From the outset, it was apparent that the industry needed to build a foundation and benchmarks for chip technology as well.

Today, it is assumed that magnetic stripe cards from many different payment systems can be accepted at the same terminal. But this capability did not happen by coincidence. It is the result of close cooperation among major providers that established global standards and specifications for magnetic stripe technology.

Perhaps the most important and recognized standards body is the International Organization of Standards commonly known as ISO. ISO is a worldwide federations of national standards bodies. All voting on standards is done by each country's standard body.

ISO standards cover a wide range of issues from things as diverse as quality control to electrical devices. Among the areas that ISO has developed standards for is smart cards.

Two major groups in ISO have developed standards that relate to smart cards. Joint Technical Committee 1—Standard Committee 17 is specific to smart cards. A related group is Technical Committee 68 which works on Financial Transaction Cards.

To fully appreciate, how ISO works, it is important that the reader understand the unique terminology used by ISO groups to refer to various working parties. The figure below show the abbreviations and their respective meaning.[2]

ISO Definiting

- IS—International Standard
- DIS—Draft International Standard
- CD—Committee Draft
- WD—Working Draft
- Work Item

Structure Terminology

- SC—Standard Committee
- TC—Technical Committee
- WG—Working Group
- TF—Task Force

Process Terminology[3]

Three major groups that are involved in standards development are ANSI, ISO and CEN. A brief definition of each is:

- ANSI—American National Standards Institute

  - X3—Information Processing Systems
  - X9—Security Standards for Financial Institutions
  - X12—Electronic Data Interchange

- ISO—International Standards Organization; *Geneva, Switzerland*

  - 70 Member Countries
  - No Ability to Enforce

- CEN—European Committee for Standardization; *Brussels, Belgium*

  - Liaison with ISO (no ISO voting rights)

Among the most commonly referenced ISO smart card standards is IS7816. 7816 is a part of Working Group 4 which is a part of SC17. IS 7816 is divided into several different parts as seen in Table 8-1. These various parts are in different stages of completion or revision at any point in time.

Table 8-1. ISO Contact Card Standards

NUMBER	TITLE
7816-1	Physical Characteristics
7816-2	Dimensions & Locations of Coupling Fields
7816-3	Electronic Signals & Transmission Protocols
7816-3/ AM1	Electronic Signals & Transmission Protocols: Block Transmission Protocols
7816-3/DAM2	Protocol Type Selection
7816-4	Inter-Industry Commands for Interchange
7816-5	Registration of Applications in IC Cards
7816-6	Inter-Industry Data Elements for Interchange

Another major group working on smart card within ISO is Working Group 7—IS10536. These standards relate to issues relevant to contactless chip cards. The major areas addressed by this standard can be seen in Table 8-2.

Table 8-2. ISO Contactless Card Standards

NUMBER	TITLE
10536-1	Physical Characteristics
10536-2	Dimensions & Locations of Coupling Fields
10536-3	Electronic Signals & Mode Switching
10536-4	Answer to Reset & Transmission Protocols

For readers in the United States who would like additional information on ISO standards you must contact ANSI (see Table 8-3) as they are the National body in the United States. For readers in other countries contact your appropriate agency.

Table 8-3. Other Useful Addresses

American Bankers Association (ASC X9 Secretariat)
1120 Connecticut Avenue, N.W.
Washington, D.C. 20036
U.S.A.   TEL: 202-663-5284   FAX: 202-828-4544

AFNOR Association Francaise de Normalisation
Tour Europe—Cedex 7
92049 Paris La Defense
France   TEL: [33] 1 4291 55 55 FAX: [33] 1 42 91 56 56

ANSI American National Standards Institute
11 West 42nd Street,
New York, NY 10036

APACS Association for Payment Clearing Services
Mercury House, Triton Court
14 Finsbury Square
London, EC2A 1BR
United Kingdom   TEL: [44] 1711 6200   FAX: [44] 1 256 5527

Table 8-3. (continued)

CEN European Committee for Standardization

Central Secretariat
Rue de Stassart, 36
B-1050 Brussels
Belgium

Europay International

Guido Heyns
Chausee de Tervuren 198A
B-1410 Waterloo
Belgium   TEL: [32] 2 352 59 34   FAX: [32] 2 352 58 39

ETSI European Telecommunication Standards Institute

Rue des Lucioles
06921 Sophia Antipolis Cedex
France   TEL: [33] 92 94 42 00   FAX: [33] 93 65 47 16

MasterCard International

Andrew W. Tarbox

Chip Card Technology

2000 Purchase Street

Purchase, NY 10577-2509

U.S.A.   TEL: 914-249-5360   FAX: 914-249-4308

Visa International

Jean McKenna

Technology Department

P.O. Box 8999

San Francisco, CA 94128-8999

U.S.A.   TEL: 415-432-3422   FAX: 415-432-3199

CPA Canadian Payments Association

50 O'Connor Street, Suite 1212

Ottawa, Ontario K10 6L2

Canada   TEL: 613-238-4173   FAX: 613-233-3385

Formation of EMV (Europay, MasterCard, Visa)

In late 1993, recognizing the importance of the chip technology to the future of the payments industry, MasterCard International, Europay International S.A., and Visa International Service Association joined forces to do this. The result is the Integrated Circuit Card Specifications for Payment Systems, commonly known as EMV Joint Specification.

Pooling Expertise for a Common Goal

Each of the payment associations brought considerable experience to the table. All had conducted pilot trials of chip cards and developed detailed specifications for chip cards independently. They realized that for chip cards to be universally accepted—for the good of card holders and the industry—it was essential that each organization share the specifications and agree on common specifications. The Organization for International Standards (ISO) was the frame of reference for the EMV Joint Specification, although its standards for chip cards was far broader because they were developed to support a wide spectrum of industries and interests.

The EMV team assembled and divided the specification into three parts. Part One deals with electrical and physical relationships between the chip card and the terminal. Part Two focuses an commands and data elements. Part Three addresses transaction flow and security. Before each part was released, experts reviewed what had to be done and give comments and recommendations.

With these specifications in place, the foundation has been established for the universal use of chip cards for financial transactions.

The Objectives: Global Acceptance

The goal was to create minimum requirements for chip cards and terminals that would assure global acceptance of transactions without creating a system that would be unrealistically expensive or cumbersome. The ultimate objective is that one terminal on a retailer's counter would accommodate all cards approved by the associations. All parties agreed to set aside the competitive differences between payment systems in order to find the best cost-effective technical solutions.

The EMV Joint Specification: Part One

Part One of the Specification addresses the following areas:

- Electromechanical interface

- Transaction session

- Physical transportation of characters

- Answer to reset

- Transmission protocols

Establishing specifications for the physical characteristics and protocols are essential before the terminal can be designed and manufactured. In the later sections, the group concentrated more on software-related functions since they are easier to change in terminals.

The specification for the Electromechanical Interface deals with numerous areas of an integrated circuit (IC) card's physical relationship with the terminal, including the card's strength and reliability under real life conditions, the location and function of the contacts, as well as electrical specifications.

The "Handshake." This area describes a critical stage of a Transaction Session, where the card and the terminal agree on the protocol for the conversation. The specification allows for either $T=0$ or $T=1$ protocol between card and terminal.. All terminals must support both techniques.

Byte or Block? Once a chip card is reset by a terminal, it answers with a string of data in bytes, known as the answer to reset. These bytes convey information to the terminal that defines certain operating characteristics of the chip card. The specification requires that both transmission protocols, the $T=0$ protocol, also known as the byte protocol; and the $T=1$ protocol, known as the block protocol, be understood by the terminal.

The byte protocol moves data byte by byte, while the block protocol allows data to move in blocks of up to 256 bytes. The card advises the terminal how it prefers to operate.

The Transaction Session specification is written to assure that no damage is done to the card as it proceeds through the various stages: insert card, reset card, execute transaction, deactivate card, and remove card.

Part Two: Data Elements and Commands

Part Two of the EMV Joint Specification defines data elements (information on a card such as a name and account number) and commands as they apply to the exchange of information between the IC card and a terminal. This includes:

Logically Structured Data describes how data is logically structured and coded so a terminal can read a card. Part Two of the specification can be thought of as a dictionary. It defines the data elements and commands but does not tell the reader how to use them, this will come later in Part Three. Information on a card is set up in a logical structure of files, records and data elements, almost like a file cabinet full of paper folders that contain documents, which, in turn, contain words. Files are units that have one or more records, while a data element is the smallest piece of information that can be identified by a name, a description and a format. The content of the files is very flexible. Most data elements defined by the joint specification are optional, allowing a great deal of flexibility.

The commands for the EMV Joint Specification are, for the most part, commands defined in ISO 7816.4—External Authenticate, Get Data, Read Record and Verify. The specification has elected optional ways of using these commands that may reduce chip costs. The specification also has created two new commands not defined by ISO—Generate Application Cryptogram and Manage Application.

Part Three: Transaction Flow

Part Three of the EMV Joint Specification covers the procedures that take place between a card and a terminal to execute payment. It provides an example of a transaction—and how to handle exceptions—to help a reader fully understand each step of the process.[4]

Standards for Identification Cards

Standards for identification cards usually are identified by the association and number which corresponds to the title defined. Examples are:

- ISO 7810—Physical Characteristics

- ISO 7811—Recording Techniques

- ISO 7812—Identification of Issuers

- ISO 7813—Financial Transaction Cards

- ISO 7816—Integrated Circuit(s) Cards with Contacts

- ISO 10536—Contactless Integrated Circuits Cards

- DIS 10373—Identification Cards—Test Methods

Profile of a Chip Card Transaction

Here is what takes place in a smart card transaction:

- When a chip card is inserted into a terminal, the two "handshake" or recognize each other and a dialog begins.

- The terminal selects and begins application, reads the cardholder data, and stores it in its memory.

- At this point, the terminal authenticates the card, verifies the cardholder, and stores the these results for subsequent action analysis.

- The terminal then records processing restrictions—as rules by the institutions that issue and process the card—in order to determine the compatibility between the card and terminal applications.

- The terminal risk management function is performed to protect the system from fraud. This includes data checking, floor limits and random selection or issuer host processing.

- The card and terminal analyze the action analysis function to process the issuer's card risk management specifications.

- After this analysis, the terminal decides whether the transaction should proceed on-line or off-line and issues a Generate Application Cryptogram command. A transaction certificate provides a digital signature proving that this transaction—and only this transaction—has been generated correctly.

- Should questions arise concerning the transactions validity or security, it may be sent on-line to the issuer for processing as well as authentication of both the chip card and issuer host terminal.

- If all analysis has determined that this transaction may be performed off-line, the transaction is completed by the terminal.

- The terminal, chip card, and issuer work together to determine if a transaction is approved or denied. The terminal requests from the card three types of cryptograms: Transaction Denied, Request to go On-Line or Transaction Approved.

- The last function performed by the terminal is the completion of the transaction, unless the transaction is terminated prematurely by error processing or exception handling. The card then verifies whether the transaction was completed off-line or on-line by generating a transaction certificate.[5]

DEVELOPING A STANDARD CHIP OPERATING SYSTEM

Inside each microprocessor smart card resides a small silicon chip. Inside the chip resides programmed logic called the Chip Operating System. Most smart card manufacturers and some system providers have designed one or more chip operating systems. Millions of smart cards have been issued worldwide, yet most of today's chip operating systems are considered proprietary products. None is compatible with another and there is no clear cut standard chip operating system in sight.

The situation in the smart card industry is best explained with an analogy. Imagine how chaotic the VCR industry would be if manufacturers had only gone so far as standardizing the physical dimension of tape cartridges, the position for a read head and some basic header information at the beginning of each tape. Suppose they had also maintained their proprietary tape recording schemes for the video image and sound tracks. All cartridges would look the same and fit nicely into any standard VCR. The read head would make contact with the tape as described in the standard and it would be possible to initiate some basic operations, such as rewinding the tape and reading the header information. However, viewing the tape would be impossible unless the electronics in the VCR were compatible with the recording scheme on the tape. Under this scenario, companies could manufacture standard VCR units and other companies could manufacture standard tape cartridges but there would be no guarantee that a given tape would work in a given VCR.

What's the Answer?

Today, several companies manufacture ISO standard smart cards and other companies manufacture standard read/write devices also called Card Acceptor Devices or CAD. However, there is no guarantee that a given card will work in a given device. Why? Because, as in the VCR analogy, the standard doesn't go far enough. It defines the physical dimension of smart cards, the position of the read head and some basic header information but each manufacturer has developed and maintained its own proprietary chip operating system. How can this be after 15+ years of standards meetings? There is no single answer. It's partially because chip for smart cards continues to evolve; partially because smart card manufacturers are trying to protect real or perceived marketing advantages, the "my chip operating system is better than yours" syndrome; and partially because a standard chip operating system will hasten the day smart cards become a commodity product. This last reason may also be one of the most important because lots of new low cost manufacturers will be able to join the chase once a true standard is developed.[6]

FEDERAL AGENCIES INTERESTED IN SMART CARD TECHNOLOGY

There are a number of Federal Agencies in the United States that are particularly interested in the development of smart cards. These agencies monitor and track the progress of smart card applications and influence a number of committees that help determine the standards in their decision process.

The Treasury Department's Technology Transfer branch of the Financial Management Services Agency is monitoring development of smart cards for funds transfer between branches of the government. The quarterly meetings of its smart card user committee are open to all government agencies and their advisors.

The Department of Justice has put owners of automated teller machine networks on notice not to try and stop cardholder's of other networks from using their machines to load value into cards. It will also be concerned with protecting the privacy of the data stored in the cards.

The Office of Technology Assessment, a research arm of Congress, could investigate smart cards from the standpoint of cost, privacy and services to the nation's 25 million participants in electronic benefits programs.

The National Security Agency under the Department of Defense may want to establish guidelines for protecting the privacy of personal data encoded in cards not directly related to banking.

The National Institute of Standards and Technology under the Department of Commerce has been given responsibility by Congress to develop policy and provide technical assistance for security issues related to federal unclassified computer systems. It is researching the cryptographic capabilities of microchips (the Department of Defense does its own research on classified systems).

The Federal Reserve Board is interested in smart cards from the standpoint of prepaid (stored) value that would come under Regulation E of the Electronic Funds Transfer Act. The FBI is also investigating how current rules limiting consumer liability on cards should apply.

The Department of Health and Human Services and the Social Security Administration are interested in how smart cards might be used to make electronic benefits transfers.

Who's Buying What?

The U.S. Department of Agriculture's Food & Consumer Services (FCS) is exploring new technologies for delivering food program benefits to millions of recipients. One approach would use smart cards in an off-line environment at retail merchants. Recipients' benefits would be stored in the card itself. Food purchases would be authorized by an interaction between the card and the food retailer's terminal, with no immediate on-line connection.

A key issue in this off-line approach stems from a tension between two important objectives: maintaining the security and integrity of electronic benefits transfer (EBT) transactions, and allowing EBT to be integrated with the retailers' electronic debit card payment system. In current demonstrations in Ohio and Wyoming, the state's EBT system vendor must control the development and deployment of POS terminals. This helps to meet the security objective, but does nothing to promote the level of integration desired by many retailers.

The current chip operating systems requirement for card acceptor devices to initiate and control each step of the transaction process is magnified even more, from a systems integration point-of-view, because of the incompatibilities between the different manufacturers' chip operating systems mentioned earlier. Not only does it take many commands and responses to complete a task at the micro level, but the commands and responses themselves are different from one smart card to another.

The FCS recently distributed a preliminary functional specification of macro-level smart card commands for electronic benefit transfer (EBT). The implementation of these commands would ensure that EBT related functions could be performed consistently and securely at both off-line and on-line POS devices. Their implementation would also assist in developing a compatible source of smart card acceptor devices. Their implementation would also ensure a compatible source of smart cards and card acceptor devices from multiple vendors. If their implementation is done in compliance withe the EMV specifications, they may also facilitate the integration of commercial payment transactions and government EBT transaction on a shared retail POS infrastructure.[7]

END NOTES

1.   Svigals, Jerome. 1985. *Smart Cards*. New York: MacMillan Publishing Co. p. 114.

2.   Tarbox, Andrew W. May, 1995. *Foundations for a Chip-Based Future*. pp. 11–12.

3.   Tarbox, Andrew W. April, 1995. *Standards Review*, SCAT Presentation.

4.   Tarbox, Andrew W. May, 1995. *Foundations for a Chip-Based Future*. pp. 12–13.

5.   Tarbox, Andrew W. Feb., 1995. *Profile of a Chip Card Transaction*. p. 12.

6.   Schuler, Joe. May, 1995. *Standard Chip Operating System*. Stored Value Systems, Division of National City Processing Co. p. 50.

7.   This chapter was prepared with the assistance of Andrew Tarbox, vice president of Chip Card Implementation for MasterCard International.

9

Protecting Intellectual Property: The Competitive Edge

I was amazed that most smart card patents today are technology driven and do not focus on applications.

—Robert Katz, Esq.
Cooper & Dunham

DOUGLAS TAYLOR—TWENTY-FIRST-CENTURY PATENT

Douglas Taylor, an inventor, filed a patent in December, 1993 and another patent in February, 1995, for a smart card process he believes will be a valuable asset in gaining a competitive edge for the company.

Needing a career opportunity and becoming a partner in a new business venture, he envisioned how a smart card would be used in the twenty-first century.

Initially Mr. Taylor was content as a portfolio manager and looked forward to many years of prosperity. Unfortunately, the business was down-sizing, so Mr. Taylor turned to emerging technology start-ups, which he thought was worth pursuing as a career. It all began when reading the newspaper and eyeing an idea that was applicable to banking invest-ments. He saw an article in the *New York Times*, the Monday section on patents, about how ATM cards are used in a financial transaction envi-ronment. The idea was born of using a "smart card" for multiple applications and interacting the applications and being dynamic. "If I hadn't been exposed to smart cards and read an article on process patents, this never would have happened. Its also important to be in an environment where others will help develop the idea and support it, both from the business side and the funding side." Table 9-1 contains the steps Mr. Taylor followed from idea to patent.[1]

Table 9-1. From Ideas to Patent—Steps to Follow

1. Idea for a smart card opportunity.
2. Write a brief description of the idea.
3. Identify Intellectual Property Firm and visit them for an initial consultation and review of Idea. Initial visit is usually at no charge.
4. Preliminary Research—Either you or your lawyer can do a computer search of patents already issued. If you do not find a patent issued already then you can advance to the next step.
5. Detailed Search—This entails an in-depth review of identifying and reviewing any related patents. This research must be disclosed to the Patent Office. If there are no conflicting patents you can proceed to the next step.
6. Prepare patent application for filing with diagrams and flow charts.
7. File patent—receive filing data from Patent office.
8. WAIT! It takes approximately 9–12 months to get a response from the patent office in the form of an Office Action letter.
9. Respond to the Office Action letter—This is your opportunity of response to any objections or issues the patent office has in regards to your patent.
10. Wait—For the next 4 to 6 months you wait to hear if your patent is accepted or rejected. Maybe only part of your patent will be accepted.
11. Patent acceptance and patent number is issued.

Total time for the above process to occur is about 18 months.

Total legal costs run about $10,000–$20,000, depending on the complexity of the patent.

First Mr. Taylor identified a law firm, then discussed the idea (without a fee) and determined if it made sense to proceed. Second, he asked for a computer search of patent records to see if there are conflicting patents.

After receiving back from the lawyer all relevant patent-related information, it seemed most favorable to proceed. Then prepared an outline and scope of the proposed idea and submitted the document to the law firm in order to then do a much more detailed search at the patent library office in Washington, D.C. This search is important when you file a patent—since you must address prior art in the field and be able to cite examples.

Mr. Taylor then prepared a patent along with preliminary flow charts and describing the process for using smart cards in a multi-application environment. This was then submitted to the law firm to prepare the proper format for filing. It took multiple revisions and many hours of flow chart formatting. After waiting 12 months without any notice of the patent, he received an Office Action letter that identified the examiner objections and issues to the patent that requires further clarification. The guidelines I used to select a firm are described in Table 9-2.

Table 9-2. Guidelines to Selecting an Intellectual Property Firm

1. What are the qualifications of the law firm and the particular individuals who will be handling your proposal?
2. Do they have the experience in computer technology and software-related expertise?
3. What legal opinions have been given by the firm to other companies?
4. What warranties will be provided with what the firm offers and what liabilities do they impose on the company?
5. What potential lawsuits, if any, can be foreseen?
6. What other areas can the lawyer provide assistance in? Examples are:
   - Giving advice and asking questions from both a personal and business viewpoint.
   - Setting up stock options and incentive programs
   - Developing and processing patent applications and later legislation
   - Arranging introductions and business contacts
   - Drafting non-disclosure and non-competition agreements
   - Handling lawsuits
   - Licensing
   - Advising on royalties and agreements

In summary, it was important for Mr. Taylor to respond clearly to all the examiners' questions and overcome objections and provide additional materials required by the patent office. Objections that are overcome strengthen your patent as it is harder for someone later to raise an objection when the patent office has already reviewed and decided upon the issue.

On October 30, 1995, Mr. Taylor finally received official notice from the patent office that his first patent application had been allowed and would be issued within several months.

PROTECTING PROPRIETARY RIGHTS

by Robert Katz, Partner
Cooper and Dunham, New York, NY

The effective protection of intellectual property can make the difference between success and failure for a business by protecting its innovations and ideas from unscrupulous competitors and gain a competitive edge in the marketplace. Protection of intellectual property may include trade secrets, patents, trademarks and copyrights. Each form of protection has advantages and disadvantages, and proper protection often includes some combination of these forms, particularly for computer-related products such as Smart Cards and their applications. For a successful business the importance of intellectual property rights should not be overlooked or underestimated. Let us look briefly at each form of protection, and see how it can work to give your business a competitive edge.

Trade Secrets and Their Protection

A trade secret may be any information not generally known to others outside the business which gives a person in business an advantage over his or her competitors. It spans subject matter as mundane as customer preferences or as sophisticated as computer programs for interest-rate swaps or commodity trades. Its use in the smart card area mostly pertains to computer programs. Trade secrets have several important advantages, particularly for start-ups. First, creation of a protectable trade secret does not involve registration with any state or federal agency—a big savings to cash-starved entrepreneurs. It merely involves the mental recognition of the existence of a trade secret, followed by appropriate steps to protect its confidentiality. This may involve having employees sign an employment agreement; restricting access to and copying of important business documents; and keeping the public off the premises or away from an area where the secret may be exposed, to the extent possible. Second, a trade secret remains your property for as long as you can keep it secret; a trade secret may last almost indefinitely under the right circumstances, and certainly may last longer than the term of a patent or copyright, as the more than 100 year-old secret formula for Coca-Cola demonstrates.

The main disadvantage of trade-secret protection derives from the ephemeral nature of the property. If a third party independently discovers the secret, that individual has an absolute right to use it. So, for example, independent development of a computer program—the so called "clean room" development—is an absolutely legitimate endeavor, and a complete defense to a charge of trade-secret misappropriation, if it can be adequately proved.[2] Indeed, any form of independent discovery, accidental or intentional, as long as it is truly independent, deprives the trade secret holder of the exclusivity of his property. So too would "reverse engineering," the systematic dismantling and study of a competitor's product to help understand its constituent parts. Trade-secret status, therefore, becomes lost if a competitor independently discovers the secret (without wrongdoing) or if he learns from an authorized examination of the product. The cost of protecting a trade-secret can run quite high, another disadvantage of trade-secret protection. Plant or building security has costs, as do other protective measures such as encoding programs or encasing chips. In some instances, the product (and therefore the secret) is so freely available that trade secret protection becomes nearly impossible. In these instances, where no effective way exists to protect a secret, patent protection presents the most attractive way to protect and important invention.

Elements of Patent Protection

The Patent

A patent is a U.S. government grant giving its holder the right to exclude others from making, using, or selling a particular invention for the non-renewable period of 17 years. The rights granted by the government end at the United States' border, so in some instances patents must also be sought in foreign countries for a product sold internationally. Many smart card related inventions qualify for patent protection, including hardware, software, process for manufacture, and application methods. Several examples of smart card related patents, some older, some more recent, may be found in Table 9-3.

Table 9-3. Significant Chip Card Patents

Moreno	France 1975—covering PIN and PIN comporator within chip. Patent assigned to Innovatron: U.S. patent Nos. 3,971,916; 4,007,355; 4,102,493; and 4,092,524.
Ugon	France 1978—covering automatic programming of micro-processor. U.S. Patent No.: 4,382,279.
Billings	France 1987—covering flexible inductor for contactless smart cards used by AT&T. U.S. Patent No.: 4,692,604.
LeRoux	France 1989—covering a system of payment on information transfer by money card with an electronic memory. U.S. Patent No.: 5,191,193 is assigned to Gemplus Card International.
Hennige	Germany 1989—covering method and device for simplifying the use of a plurality of credit cards, or the like. U.S. Patent No.: 5,220,501.
Lawlor	USA 1993—covering method and system for remote delivery of retail banking services U.S. Patent No.: 5,220,501.

The patent laws require the U.S. Patent and Trademark Office (PTO) to grant a patent to any applicant who files a properly prepared patent application including a complete written description of the how to make and use the invention, which upon examination by an examiner, appears to meet the three statutory criteria for an award of a patent: utility, novelty, and non-obviousness.

Briefly, the utility and novelty requirements devolve from the constitutional mandate "to promote the progress of Science and the Useful Arts" (Art I, Section, cl. 8). Utility, as set forth in the patent statute applies to any "new and useful machine (etc.)" 35 U.S.C. §101. Courts have interpreted this phrase broadly, and the Supreme Court has noted it includes "anything under the sun made by man."[3] For smart card and computer-related inventions, utility is not usually a problem unless the inventor tries to claim a "method of doing business" or "mathematical algorithm," as opposed to an article of manufacture, such as a computer capable of carrying out a process. The line between useful, a patentable subject matter and unpatentable mathematical algorithm is often difficult to draw, and may be a matter of semantics. Nevertheless, the courts facing the issue have looked at several factors, including computer-performed calculations that may be patentable subject matter. A capable, experienced patent attorney should be able to navigate this shoal without too much difficulty.

Assuming that we have cleared the "utility" hurdle, we must next ascertain (as best we can) that the invention is both novel and non-obvious. The PTO will not issue a patent for an invention which its examiner believes is a novelty or lacked detailed subject matter. Therefore, before going to the expense of preparing and filing a patent application which can cost as much as $6,000 or more depending upon complexity, one should make sure that it can be patented. This can be done in one of two ways: (1) by a search of the patent literature in the public search room at the PTO, in Arlington, VA, or (2) by use of computer databases available on DIALOG and LEXPAT. For a relatively small sum (on the order of $500–$1,000), compared to the rather hefty expense of preparing a patent application, an inventor or his employer can learn whether the invention has been patented or described in a printed publication, such as a trade journal. The patent statute precludes the grant of a patent for an invention which has been previously published or patented, by a third party as well as for an invention which has been used by others more than a year before filing a patent application. These measures seek to avoid extended protection of an invention as a trade secret, followed by an improper attempt to secure further patent protection following discovery or dissemination of the trade secret for the entrepreneur. In other words, one cannot choose to protect an invention by keeping it confidential and then seek patent protection once secrecy evaporates. This requires an early election to seek or forego patent protection, which in turn involves early consultation with a patent attorney. This consultation should take place, if at all possible, before the public announcement of the product.[4] In deciding between trade secret or patent protection, a good rule of thumb suggests patenting any product which a competitor can obtain, disassemble, study, and copy. In such a case, many secrets about the product itself, and sometimes aspects of the method of manufacturing, can be learned by careful study of a product. In the case of smart cards, the software, and operating systems on the chip that is stored in memory can be downloaded, analyzed, and copied, and even the chip architecture can be analyzed, but probably at a rather large expense.

The Application Process

Assuming you have decided to go ahead with trying to obtain patent protection, you should provide your attorney with the necessary information to allow preparation of the application. The patents give some idea of what goes into the application: (1) a discussion of the background of the invention, which includes a summary of the particular technological problem to be solved and prior attempts to solve it; (2) a summary of the invention, a brief discussion of the apparatus or method developed by the inventor to solve the problems identified in the background; (3) a brief description of the drawings accompanying the written disclosure which aid in understanding the invention (for example, schematic or mechanical illustrative drawings, flow charts, or perhaps program listings); (4) a detailed description of the preferred embodiment, which discusses how to make and use the invention (with reference to the drawings) and discloses the "best mode" for carrying out the invention which is known to the inventor of the time of filing the patent application; and (5) the claims, the legal description of the boundaries of the invention sought to be protected, akin to the description of the meter and bounds of a property deed in a real estate transaction. Some attorneys use an inventor application form to help inventors provide the necessary information for drafting the patent application.

Each of these parts plays an important role in the patent document issued. The written description and disclosure application help readers to understand the invention and its potential use. It can be a launching point for further research, and future improvements. Once the patent expires, the description should enable one to practice the invention, which upon expiration of the patent is "dedicated" to the public or in the "public domain." The claims in the patent define the boundaries of the invention, which the inventor claims to be his invention and gives notice to potential competitors about trespassing, and using a similar invention.

The application gets prepared by or drafted by the attorney, usually in consultation with the inventor, who in any event reviews the application and signs the declaration before filing. The declaration, required by the Patent Office, contains the applicant's oath (under penalty of perjury) that states the inventor is original and is the first inventor of the invention claimed in the patent application. The attorney files the application, the drawings, an assignment (if the employer of the inventor owns the rights to the inventor), and the filing fee ($730 for a large company, $365 for a company with fewer than 500 employees) in the PTO.

The application, once filed, gets assigned according to its subject matter to an examiner, who examines applications relating only to a particular technology. This examiner has responsibility for examining the application. Typically, the examiner will review the application and perform a search to determine whether the application claims novel and non-obvious subject matter. If the examiner concludes that it does not, he may reject the application, providing a written statement of the reasons for his conclusion. The written statement, known as an Office Action, usually includes copies of prior patent or publications which the examiner believes tends to demonstrate that the invention or something quite similar has been patented or published before. The applicant's attorney may respond by asking for reconsideration. The attorney may amend the application to narrow the claims, and may point out why the attorney believes the invention to be patentable. Sometimes the attorney may present evidence tending to show how the invention is significant, including its commercial success or unexpected results. The examiner will then reexamine the application, including the amendments, evidence (if any), and arguments presented by the patent attorney. This give and take generally leads to an agreement by the examiner that the claims, perhaps in amended form, are allowable. Upon payment of an issue fee the patent can be issued for the invention.[5] Failure to secure allowance of the application the first time around often occurs, but the rejected applications can be refiled for continuing prosecution or appealed either to a Patent Office Board of Appeals, or to the Federal Court. The PTO guidelines suggest that the time from filing to issuance usually is about 18 months.

Patent Infringement

Once issued, the patent gives its owner the right exclude others from making, using or selling the claimed invention in the U.S. for 17 years, a nonrenewable right. These rights have the attributes of personal property, and may be bought, sold, transferred, traded or licensed. A license gives the licensee permission to use the patented invention, usually for a fee, and may include a geographical area like the United States in whole or in part. Also the use of the application for some specified market area (e.g., medical history, retailing), and the term of the patent (for example, 5 years).

A party who attempts to use an invention claimed in a patent without permission from its owner may be sued for infringement, which leads to our next topic. One determines infringement by comparing the claims of the patent (its legal boundaries) against the device in question, to see if each element recited in the claims may be found in the device.[6] Interpreting issued patent claims is usually a matter for experienced patent counsel. If the device appears to be covered, the purveyor of the device runs the risk of being sued as an infringer, so some mitigating steps should be taken. A party may approach the patentee for a license (a payment of a royalty fee for the right to use the invention), the party may redesign the product to avoid using the claimed invention, or may investigate the validity of the patent by having a search performed to determine whether the invention is truly the first and whether the invention is sufficiently different from earlier inventions to be non-obvious. Approaching a patentee for a license involves risk because it may awaken the patent holder to a potential infringer of which they may otherwise be unaware.

Generally, before launching an important and visible product, a business will ask its patent attorney to make sure the product does not infringe upon any issued unexpired patents. The attorney performs a search of unexpired patents in the same area of technology, and carefully reviews the claims of those patents to see if any claim covers the product. The attorney is thus able to "clear" the product so that the manufacturer can market without substantial fear of a patent infringement suit. In the event that one or more patents cover the product, steps may be taken to obtain a license [to] modify the product to avoid the patent, or determine the validity of the patent.

Trademark

Trademarks (and service marks) protection helps protect the integrity of the marketplace in quite a different way from patents or trade secrets. If a product, even one commonly available through several different sources, acquires a reputation for consistently high quality, value, or other salutary attributes, the producer will want to protect this franchise so carefully nurtured by preventing others from trading on the goodwill established for the product. The producer will seek to protect consumers from inadvertently purchasing a product from a different source, or from being duped into purchasing the wrong brand of product because of another producer's intentional attempt to use a similar brand. In other words, the manufacturer will want to give satisfied customers a fairly simple way to identify its product as a way of assuring them that they can count on the same quality in their next purchases of the same or a related product offered by the same manufacturer. These are the primary goals of trademark protection.

Unlike patents, trademark rights develop through use of the mark in commerce. The producer of a product, by associating a particular trademark or brand name with the product, gradually develops an association in the mind of purchasers between the product and the mark. Advertising helps reinforce this relationship; advertising of course consumes precious funds quickly, so selection of a strong, protectable trademark will assure that this investment will bring customers to the right source the first time and each time thereafter.

How, then, should one go about picking a trademark? The mark can be chosen to convey whatever impression or image one seeks, with imagination and the operation of the trademark law the only real constraints on selection of a mark. Let us look then at several principles of trademark law which will help to avoid mistakes in selecting a suitable and protectable mark.

Trademarks, at least in the eyes of the law, span a continuum which helps determine their "strength" or relative protect ability. The different types of marks, in descending order of strength, include the following:

- Coined word or term

- Arbitrary

- Suggestive

- Descriptive

- Generic

A "coined term or word," such as Xerox, Kodak, or Univac, or an "arbitrary term or word," such as "Old Crow" for Scotch whiskey, or "Blue Bonnet" for margarine has the potential to be the strongest of trademarks, because they do not in any way describe the product. They therefore have the greatest source-identifying potential, assuming no one else on the market has used the same mark (or one that is even similar) for a similar product. These marks when mentioned do not call to mind the type of product they represent. Entrepreneurs are often reluctant to use these types of marks, however, because they want their mark to identify the brand or source and the type of product goods. Here they are mistaken because of their lack of understanding of trademark law. Given sufficient advertising to create awareness of the mark as representing the source of a product, the mark can continue to gain strength as long as the product continues to thrive, and a definite association between the goods and the source will eventuate. The "coined" or "arbitrary" mark, then, is among the most desirable types of trademarks from the point of view of the trademark law.

The next point on the spectrum of trademark protection is the "suggestive" mark. Like its stronger counterparts, the suggestive term does not conjure up a specific product or even a specific type of product, but instead merely suggests some attribute of a product. Examples abound for this type of mark—"Downy" for a fabric softener or "smart card" for a microprocessor that calculates and processes data on a card. This type of mark has considerable strength and protection, since it can function as a strong source on the mark.

Two types of trademarks one should try to avoid, if possible. The "descriptive" mark, which serves more to describe a product than to identify a source, does little to help build brand recognition, and does so usually only at a significant and unnecessary cost. Examples of such marks saturate commerce, particularly in the computer field—"Digital Equipment" for computers, "Advanced Micro Devices" for semiconductor chips. The news about descriptive names is not all bad, however, because these marks, with enough use and advertising can begin to represent a source, as the two examples chosen clearly do. Early on, however, the entrepreneur runs the risk that the trademark will not help identify his product, or will not be distinctive enough to stop an imitator from choosing a similar mark. Also, the U.S. Patent and Trademark Office may deny them registration on the Primary Register of Trademarks until the owner can show 5 years use.

The "generic" trademark is really not a trademark at all. It is rather the final stop on the trademark spectrum, and includes the group of terms unprotectable as trademarks. These terms come to represent solely a type of product rather than a source of a product, and so do not serve any source identifying or trademark function at all. Significantly, even an arbitrary or a coined term can become generic with continued misuse by the consuming public, usually in conjunction with improper policing and supervision by its owner. Xerox came dangerously close to becoming a generic term for photocopiers rather than a brand of photocopying equipment, until the firm launched a campaign to correct the misuse of its trademark. You cannot make a Xerox copy on a Kodak, Minolta, or other brand of copier, just as you cannot use a photocopier to "Xerox" anything. The term is a brand name, a noun, and its misuse either as a verb or to identify products starts eroding its strength and ability to function as a trademark. The "Formica" brand suffered this fate recently, as did "Singer" sewing machine and "Aspirin" brands earlier in this century. "Smart card" is dangerously close to generic, if not in fact generic. Generic marks can cease to be generic, usually as the result of a corrective advertising campaign, and become strong trademarks once again, as Singer has done. One usually does not start out with a generic mark, but one can soon have one through carelessness.

Trademark Registration

Trademark registration is simpler than obtaining a patent. The trademark application includes an identification and drawing of a mark. The goods or services on which it will be used, and a declaration of the applicant (or any author of the applicant company) asserting that the applicant believes he or she is the owner of and first user of the subject in commerce, and is unaware of any other user of the same mark for similar goods or service which is likely to cause confusion among prospective purchasers or consumers; otherwise, an application may be filed based upon a good faith "intent to use" the mark in conjunction with the specified goods.

Trademark applications usually take about a year to issue. The application itself, if relatively straightforward, and if it contains a drawing of the mark, a specification of the goods or services on which it is used, identifying information about the applicant, and a declaration from the applicant or an authorized officer of the applicant's corporation attesting that applicant owns the mark, has used it in commerce, and is aware of no other prior use of a mark by a third party which would be likely to cause confusion. Once filed, a trademark attorney in the U.S. Patent and Trademark Office examines the application to be sure it complies with the applicable statutes, and identifies any existing registration believed to conflict with the applicant's mark. The trademark attorney may refuse registration where the applicant does not comply with one or more aspects of the trademark laws. For example, registration may be refused if the applicant's mark is deemed to be confusingly similar to an existing registration. Or, for example, registrations may be refused to marks which are " primarily merely a surname," geographically misdescriptive, or descriptive of the goods. In the last case, the mark may be included on the "secondary" register, and after 5 years of continuous use, it may be transferred to the primary trademark register, if applicants can prove that the mark has acquired secondary meaning through use, advertising, and promotion. Just as with patent prosecution, the applicant can file a written response to a rejection, in which he or she seeks to refute the trademark attorney's assertions. If the application is allowed, it gets published in the Trademark Office Gazette for "opposition." Thus, publication lets a member of the public thirty days to file an explanation in writing why he or she would be injured if the registration were issued.

Recently, Congress passed a statute which permits an applicant to apply for a trademark registration for a mark which the applicant has a *bona fide* intention to use.

Trademark Enforcement

The trademark laws are such to prevent consumer confusion or deception arising from use of similar marks or similar goods. The United States District Court will grant injunctive relief against those infringing an existing trademark, even if the mark is not registered. Many states afford similar protection against trademark infringement and unfair competition. The federal action for trademark infringement focuses on whether the coexistence of the two marks in the marketplace is likely to cause confusion, mistake, or deception concerning the source of the respective parties' goods, based upon an evaluation of the following factors:

1. The strength of the first user's mark;

2. The similarity (or lack of similarity) of the marks;

3. The similarity of the goods or services associated with the marks;

4. The channels of trade in which the products or services are sold;

5. Any evidence of intent to trade or the goodwill of the mark's first user;

6. Evidence of actual confusion by customers or prospective customers;

7. The sophistication of the buyers of the goods or services; and

8. The degree of care demonstrated by the purchasers or users of the goods or services.

Each of these factors helps the trier of fact (the judge or the jury) to determine whether the consumer is likely to be confused. No one factor controls, although evidence of actual confusion carries special persuasiveness. A party found liable for trademark infringement may have to pay the trademark owner for the losses attributable to the infringement or to surrender his profits from the infringement, as a measure of damages for the infringement, and may also be liable for the attorney's fees where the infringer was willful. The infringer may be ordered by the court not to use the mark any longer, requiring him to change label, packaging, catalogs, and the like.

Copyright Protection

We have reached copyright, the final form of intellectual property protection useful to the smart card entrepreneur. Copyright protects a wide variety of creative expressions, including musical, literary, and artistic works. But it also affords protection to original works of authorship, including computer programs and instruction manuals.

In 1976, after much study and numerous hearings, Congress enacted the 1976 Copyright Act, which took effect in 1978. The new copyright act completely replaced the old one, and even displaced state causes of action for copyright. The new act extended copyright protection to "original works of authorship fixed in any tangible medium of expression, now known or later developed, from which they can be perceived, reproduced, or otherwise communicated, either directly or with the aid of a machine or device" (17 U.S.C. § 102). This expanded definition afforded protection to a work as soon as it became "fixed," rather than published. Even though computer programs spurred the enactment of the statute, Congress tabled for a time the attempt at a definition of a computer program which could be copyrighted. A legislative definition would have to wait until after submission of a report by the Commission of New Technological Uses of Copyright Works (CONTU), authorized by Congress to study the field and make recommendation for a legislative solution.

Copyright protection under the 1976 Act, just as under previous statutes, extended only to expression of an idea, but not to the idea itself. A mere idea, such as a particular use for a smart card, cannot be copyrighted, whereas a computer program for achieving such a use can. Importantly, copyright protection attached as soon as a work was fixed in a tangible medium, as opposed to published with copyright notice, as the 1909 Act required. In fact, under recent amendments, any work published after March 1, 1989, need not bear any copyright notice, although in all cases it still would be advisable. Moreover, because a work may be both unpublished and copyrighted, it need not be registered with the Copyright Office for a copyright to be effective.

In 1980, Congress enacted a major amendment to include a definition of computer programs:

> A "computer program" is a set of statements to be used directly or indirectly in a computer in order to bring about a certain result.

Additionally, Congress added a provision which limited the ability of even lawful users to copy and use a computer program. After the amendment, copies can be created: (1) as an essential step in the utilization of the computer programs; or (2) for archival purposes only.

As with many statutes, not every issue could be anticipated, and the courts had to decide whether certain types of computer programs or uses received copyright protection. In a case involving video games, the court held that the visual images on a screen were protected by copyright.[7] A later decision extended this protection to both the video images and to the program itself,[8] even though the video images were transient. In other words, the video images resulting from the computer program were sufficiently permanent to merit copyright protection. In another seminal decision, one court presented with an unauthorized attempt to clone the proprietary Apple II computer, agreed that computer programs written in object code could be protected,[9] even if it were embedded in a ROM chip. In its ruling, the court addressed and rejected an argument that an operation system was an idea unprotectable, not a protectable expression. A later court held the microcode embedded in an Intel chip protectable in the face of an attack by NEC Corporation asserting the microcode lacked originality.[10]

An important aspect of software involves ownership of computer programs made by an employee or a consultant. Programs created by an employee within the scope of his or her employment belong to the employer.[11] The work-for-hire doctrine, which gives a commissioning party copyright ownership of a work created by an independent contractor, does not apply to computer software.[12] Care should be taken, therefore, to obtain exclusive rights ordinarily by a written license agreement.[13]

Copyright Registration

Registration of a computer program or an instruction manual is much simpler than either trademark registration or patent solicitation. One files an application, supplies a specimen, pays a fee of $20 and usually within several months to a year receives a copyright registration in the mail. The Copyright Office designed the application to be "user friendly" and offers clear, simple instructions to permit the applicant to apply for registration without consulting an attorney,[14] although for important works, it may be well worth the fee involved to get the assistance of an experienced copyright attorney. Expedited consideration of the application (sometimes resulting in an issued registration within a week) may be obtained for an extra fee (37 C.F.R. § 202.03).

Enforcement of Copyrights for Computer-Related Works

A copyright owner has the exclusive right to "do and to authorize" the following: (1) copy the work; (2) to prepare derivative works; (3) to distribute copies of the work to the public by sale, lease, or rental; and (4) to display the work publicly. Anyone in violation of one or more of the foregoing exclusive rights infringes the copyrights, unless he or she can prove one or more defenses (17 U.S.C. §§106 and 107-18).

Copyright infringement requires copying The Courts have construed this to mean proof of access to the accused work coupled with substantial similarity between the original and the copy. Substantial similarity is judged by an objective test: whether the average lay observers "would recognize the alleged copy as having been appropriated from the copyrighted work."[15] Copyright protection extends only to the expression of the idea, which is a rather difficult issue to resolve. The copyright law provides important and formidable remedies including summary seizure and impoundment,[16] restraining orders, injunctive relief and recovery of attorney fees.

CONCLUSION

The intellectual property laws provide a variety of tools to businesses and individuals to help protect their proprietary rights. Early consultation with an attorney who specializes in this field may help avoid inadvertent forfeiture or theft of invaluable rights, indeed of the crown jewels. Often patents, trademarks and copyrights are the only weapons that innovators have to insure respect and fair competition by their competitors, who may be much larger enterprises. Accordingly, due care must be given right from the beginning by all enterprises to development of a proper and comprehensive program to protect intellectual property.

END NOTES

1. Taylor, Douglas. Preparing a Patent Application. July 1995. Interview.

2. Intel, Advanced Micro Devices, *Wall Street Journal*. May 15, 1995.

3. United States vs. Chrakrabarty, U.S. (1980)

4. A patent application must be filed even sooner—before any commercial announcement, demonstration or sale—if the inventor will seek foreign patent protection. Most foreign countries require this "absolute novelty," no disclosures before filing requirement.

5. Refusal to allow the application may be appealed to the Patent Office Board of Appeals or challenged in Federal Court.

6. Another test for information may be invoked if one or more elements appears to be missing: infringement by equivalence. Infringement may still exist, despite this difference if the device accused of infringement performs the same function, in the way, to achieve the same result.

7. Williams Electronics, Inc. Arctic International, Inc. 685 F 2d 870 (3d Cir. 1982).

8. Stern Electronics, Inc. v. Kaufman, 669 F.d 852 (2d Cir. 1982).

9. Apple Computer, Inc. v. Franklin Computer Corp., 714 F. 2D, 1240 (3d Cir. 1983).

10. Intel Corp. v. NEC Corp. [Cite].

11. 17 U.S.C. § 101(1), 210(b).

12. 17 U.S.C. § 101(2), 201(b).

13. 17 U.S.C. § 203.

14. These instructions and a packet of applications can be obtained from the Register of Copyrights, Library of Congress, Washington, D.C.

15. Novelty Textile Mills, Inc. v. Joan Fabrics Corp., 558 F. 2D 1090 (2d Cir. 1977).

16. 17 U.S.C. § 503(b). This may include seizure of the pirated articles, and in some instances related business records.

10

Smart Cards Are Here to Stay

INTRODUCTION

Twenty years ago visionaries from the banking industry forecasted that the smart card would lead to a cashless and checkless society. With its self-contained computer capabilities its features and data storage capacity, the prediction is beginning to happen. But, despite the clear technical superiority of the smart card, its high cost (up to $10 per card) is a primary factor in keeping U.S. financial institutions and other card-issuing businesses in the magnetic stripe camp. Even as smart cards gain acceptance in other parts of the world, particularly Europe and Asia, smart card programs in the U.S. are still limited to small-scale pilots. However, this is now changing.[1]

Today, smart card programs are springing up throughout the U.S. True, many are still pilots, but the size and scope of the programs are a clear sign that the visionaries of the past decades were correct—smart cards will become the dominant technology choice for card-based systems. However, there are still refinements that should be considered when examining the outcomes of the technology.

- First, although smart cards will eventually displace a large number of cash and check transactions, it's no longer expected that they'll create a totally cashless or checkless society.

- Second, with more than 800 million magnetic-stripe-cards in the U.S. and millions of magnetic stripe reading terminals, the transition to an all smart card environment will be evolutionary, not revolutionary. And, its quite likely that magnetic stripe and smart card technology will operate side by side well into the 21st century.

- Third, smart cards will go far beyond the original financial applications envisioned during the 1970s. Today, the smart card is viewed as a vehicle to add convenience and service to virtually every aspect of day-to-day living.

THE UNITED STATES: THE SLEEPING GIANT OF SMART CARDS

As one of the most technologically advanced countries in the world, why has it taken the United States so long to adopt smart card technology? As mentioned earlier, card cost and replacing mag stripe terminals are high on the list. But there are other reasons as well, including:

- Reliable and inexpensive telecommunications that reduced the need for a sophisticated off-line storage and authorization system, such as the smart card.

- Huge existing investment in magnetic stripe cards, ATMs, and other magnetic stripe reading terminals—all of which would require replacement or upgrading in a smart card environment.

- Decentralized banking and business operations that would make it difficult and expensive to adopt new technologies on a widespread basis.[2]

Today, however, these views are being offset by the recognition that the unique benefits of the smart card offer unique opportunities. According to Faraday Corporation, a division of DelaRue Inc., president, Dr. Steven Schulman, "The first significant smart card applications in the U.S. are likely to be those for which the smart card provides a unique solution to a specific problem or those that present the opportunity to offer a unique solution to a specific problem or those that present the opportunity to offer a totally new product or service." He cites the examples of using the smart card as a portable security device to secure cellular telephone or satellite TV services. He believes that applications such as these, for which the smart card is especially well-suited, will lead the way for acceptance in other areas, such as traditional banking functions, where the smart card will eventually replace existing technologies.

Dr. Schulman also points to the recognition of the security advantages of the smart card as a key factor in its growing acceptance. "There's no way of accurately determining the level of present card-based systems," he says. "We do know, however, that the smart card is a much more secure device than the magnetic stripe card and has the potential to have a major positive affect on fraud."

And, finally, he notes, "The simple fact is that if the U.S. sticks with magnetic stripe technology when a large part of the world has moved or is moving toward the smart card, we'll be isolating ourselves in significant ways—both economically and technologically."

Clearly, the U.S. is on an irrevocable course that is moving in the direction of the smart card. The issue is no longer if the smart card will make it in the U.S., but when. While acknowledging the many factors that will affect the speed of adoption of the smart card in the U.S., Dr. Schulman predicts that within two years, smart cards will find their way into the wallets of the early-adopter group, likely upscale business travelers. And within the next several years, "average" Americans also will become owners of smart cards.[3]

TECHNICAL STANDARDS: A MAJOR STEP FORWARD

A major event supporting the U.S.'s move toward the introduction of the smart card is the recent agreement on international smart card technical standards. One of the primary purposes of the standards is to address the critical issue of inoperability.

Currently, even in Europe, one of the most advanced smart card markets, there is no full smart card compatibility across national borders.

And, even within one country, smart cards may not be usable across industry lines. To promote global smart card compatibility, Visa, MasterCard, and Europay worked cooperatively to develop technical standards for worldwide use. These standards will allow issuers, manufacturers, and terminal vendors to proceed with smart card programs with confidence.

And the implicit endorsement of smart card technology by Visa and MasterCard is essential to pave the way for future development.

GEMPLUS: PROFILE OF A SMART CARD MANUFACTURER

Gemplus believes that use of smart cards in the U.S. will be widespread soon. Having broken down the technological barrier, Dan Cunningham, president of Gemplus USA. It will come down to coordinating all of the systems to function in an efficient manner.[4]

Gemplus in the U.S. is controlled by Gemplus Group of Gamenos, France, a six-year-old organization that has claimed the number-one market share in Europe. The company and the industry as a whole is beginning to see momentum build among telephone companies, which may be capable of establishing a new payment service ahead of banks, which replaces cash.

Since Chemical, Citibank, Bank of America, Nations Bank, and Wells Fargo are now part of the Smart Card Forum and also board members, this makes banks in major cities a major issue related to smart cards.

But the banks' and related entities' growing interest and activity may be only the tip of the iceberg, based on Gemplus' performance and what Mr. Cunningham sees from an industry leadership position.

"This year we are going to make about 150 million smart cards. Last year we made about 103 million of the 310 million worldwide. The U.S. will be led into chip [cards] by one of these two industries, banking or telecommunications. It's really up for grabs; 1995 will be a start-up year for both industries, and we'll see significant quantities in 1996."[5]

Telephone companies in the Bahamas and Bermuda are issuing stored value telephone cards in the hundreds of thousands. Among the many

U.S. telecommunications groups marketing prepaid card services, US WEST recently became the first to test a chip-based card, with an initial issue of 140,000 units from Gemplus.

The company also has worked on an electronic payment system for parking meters at a mass transit station in the Washington D.C. area, and on the Laundromat system installed by a Maytag distributor in Florida that uses smart cards in place of coins.

Unit costs for high-volume chip card production are falling below the $1 threshold, making them competitive with magnetic stripe cards. With anticipated technological advances "we could go farther in the next 2 to 4 years than in the past 10," Mr. Cunningham added.[6]

The economics and perceived market opportunities have created a crowded market. France's big three and their chip suppliers are running up against world-class technology players such as Toshiba and Hitachi from Japan, Philips and Siemens from Europe, and AT&T from the U.S., with its competing "contactless" technology that does not require the traditional type of transaction terminal.

Among others coveting the U.S. market are the two German companies; Giesecke & Devrient has set up shop in Reston, VA, and Orga Card Systems has established a beachhead by taking over ADE Applied Digital Electronics of Paoli, PA.

Both companies are strong in the European prepaid phone card market and in cards associated with the burgeoning wireless communications networks. There are 16 million U.S. mobile-cellular subscribers projected by 2000, and they will need the access, authentication, and payment security that a chip card can ensure.

Because of their familiarity with the technical standard, global systems for mobile communications (GSM) European card companies are jockeying for position in the U.S., and that can only accelerate the chip market's growth.

"This will be a billion-card industry, in terms of chip cards worldwide, by 2000, but that is a conservative estimate," Mr Cunningham said. "If we keep up the current rate of 40 percent to 50 percent a year, we'll get there by 1996 or 1997."[7]

WHO ARE THE PLAYERS?

Table 10-1. Chip Manufacturers

Atmel	719-540-1834
Catalyst	408-748-7700
Hitachi Europe	44-628-585-000
Motorola	512-891-3559
Oki Semiconductor	408-737-6445
Philips Semiconductor	408-991-2557
SGS/Thomson	617-259-0300
Siemens Components	408-777-4960
Texas Instruments	214-997-6239
Toshiba America	214-746-5595

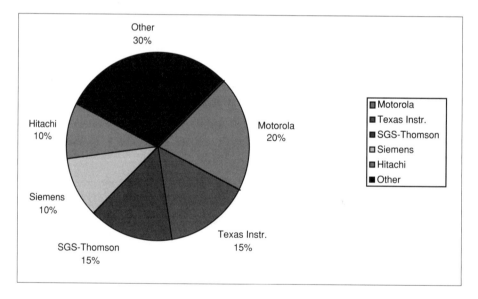

Figure 10-1. Chip manufacturers.

Table 10-2. Manufacturers of Smart Cards

Ammi	408-986-1122
Cardcorp	61-2-898-0922
CP8 Oberthur	33-1-412-52828
Data Card	215-654-8900
De La Rue Card Tech.	44-684-290-290
Digicard	43-1-250-950
Gemplus	301-990-8800
Giesecke & Devrient	703-709-2880
IBM	704-594-2041
MicroCard (Bull)	703-847-3672
ODS Oldenbourg	49-89-450-19301
ORGA Card Systems	610-993-9810
Philips Comm. Systems	33-1-412-87270
Schlumberger	804-366-0593
SOLAIC	408-879-4039
Toshiba America	214-746-5595
US[3]	408-748-7725

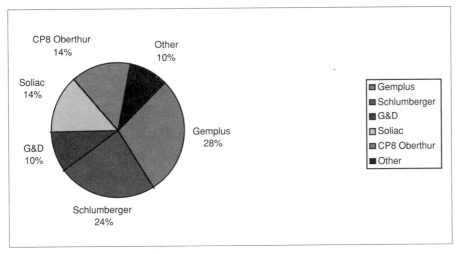

Figure 10-2. Smart cards.

Table 10-3. Manufacturers of Terminals

American Magnetics	213-775-8651
Dassault Electronique	212-909-0550
Data Card	612-938-3500
Diebold/Schlumberger	216-490-5710
Direct Data/SOLAIC	414-367-5120
Fortronic (De La Rue)	44-31-459-8800
Fujitsu ICL Systems	619-458-5434
Gemplus	301-990-8800
Hypercom	602-866-5399
IBM	704-594-2041
Ingenico	33-1-46258262
Innovatron Data Sys.	310-208-0850
International Verifact	602-866-5399
MicroCard (Bull)	704-594-2041
NBS Technologies	310-208-0850
Oki Advanced Products	602-596-6600
Omron Electronics	708-843-7900
Philips Comm. Systems	33-1-412-87270
Schlumberger	804-366-0593
Telxon	703-450-2700
US[3]	408-748-7725
Verifone	415-598-5538

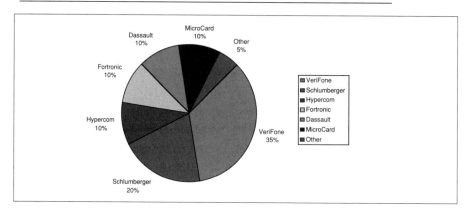

Figure 10-3. Terminals.

Table 10-4. Smart Card Consultants

Anderson Consulting	212-708-8153
Applied Systems Inst.	202-371-1600
Arlen R. Lessin	717-831-4590
Arthur D. Little	617-498-6047
Battelle	614-424-4943
Booz Allen	212-551-6661
Cardinal	44-442-236-665
Carmody & Bloom	201-670-1700
Datamark	212-736-2838
Jerome Svigals	415-365-5920
Larry Linden	301-854-6637
Price Waterhouse	415-322-0606

Table 10-5. System Integrators

Applied Systems Inst.	202-371-1600
Banksys	32-2-727-6428
Cardinal	44-442-236-665
Datamark	212-736-2838
DelaRue Fortronic	44-31-459-8800
Giesecke & Devrient	703-709-2880
Gemplus	301-990-8800
IBM	704-594-2041
Innovatron Data System	310-208-0850
International Verifact	602-596-6600
Philips Comm. Systems	33-1-412-87270
Schlumberger	804-366-0593
Security Domain	61-2-954-5747
Stored Value System	502-423-3800
US[3]	408-748-7725

AMERICAN EXPRESS'S SMART CARD VISION

by Robert Wesley

Robert (Bob) Wesley has over 14 years experience in developing travel related and financial service businesses. He has also been involved in building travel and tourism in various parts of the globe. For efforts in promoting tourism, he was presented with an award by the Government of New Zealand and Queen Elizabeth in 1990. Today he is a Vice President of International Business Development for American Express Travel Related Services in their New York Headquarters, responsible for leading the company's worldwide smart card strategy and other advanced payment platforms. Bob has been with American Express for over 16 years, 14 of which were spent in international business. Prior to American Express, he was a Certified Public Accountant with Coopers & Lybrand in New York.

In March 1994, Bob was named Vice President of the International Business Development Group (IBDG), with focus on developing an international strategy for EDC/POS deployment, and international ATM network development. Within a few months of this new appointment, the role was expanded to include worldwide smart card research, development and strategy deployment for American Express, International telecommunications strategies was subsequently added to his responsibilities. The addition of these roles helped to evolve the department to become a key part of the Advanced Payment Business Development Task Force. Advanced Payments will deal primarily with worldwide smart card strategy development and implementation, international telecommunications strategies and deployment, as well as maintaining responsibility for expanding the Amex International ATM network.

American Express's approach to smart cards is to promote inter-operability on a global basis while developing locally targeted product offerings in accordance with the unique environmental factors, especially consumer driven factors.

Smart cards will be one of the catalysts which will change the way financial products are delivered. They will have a profound impact on alliances within the financial services industry and facilitate alliances between other industries. These alliances will be initiated by the need to restructure existing payment infrastructures, but will ultimately be driven by consumer demand for convenience, security and recognition.

The evolution of smart cards will vary around the globe. Market factors impacting the evolution will be: existing telecommunications structures; banking industry needs and structure; point-of-sale infrastructure; emergence of other delivery platforms, such as the Internet; consumer needs; and regional cultures. Basic smart card solutions such as credit cards and stored value applications will represent initial product offerings. These offerings will increase consumer demand, particularly in countries where magnetic stripe systems are reliant on poor telecommunications. Smart card applications used in mass transit and telephony will continue to raise consumer awareness and appreciation for these products.

Consumer interest will be heightened with the introduction of multi-application smart cards. These cards will allow financial companies to bundle products and services tailored to the needs of multiple niche consumer segments. Only at this point will consumers be willing to pay additional fees for these value-added services which will provide the shareholder returns required to support smart card growth. At that point smart cards will prove to have a competitive advantage.

INTEROPERABILITY

The industry's ability to develop interoperability is the major factor impacting the potential smart card evolution. The merchant cannot be expected to accommodate multiple terminals and different acceptance procedures for each card issuer. To maximize the benefits of this technology for the consumer, critical systems features must be standardized to assure broad access, rather than be allowed to become mechanisms of competition. In the magnetic stripe world the financial services industry wisely decided to maintain common standards, as relates to software deployed at the point-of-sale. Many of the card issuers today have unique software applications for credit, debit and other charge applications. They all fit into one terminal requiring little or no memory.

There will be a major paradigm shift in the smart card world. Software requirements are far more demanding and product offerings will proliferate. If we use the magnetic stripe model, the point-of-sale infrastructure will become cumbersome and expensive to install and maintain. Issuers could potentially be forced to install large and inefficient independent software, requiring massive processing time and expensive memory upgrades. This, in turn, will result in additional costs to consumers. To avoid this result, industry cooperation on point-of-sale access will be critical. The exact sharing process still needs to be defined beyond the scope of the standards being developed by Europay, MasterCard and Visa (EMV). Furthermore, the definitions cannot be made in isolation by the card associations, but must be done through cooperative ventures involving all substantial global and regional card issuers.

American Express is facilitating the global development of interoperability standards with institutions responsible for funding the point-of-sale infrastructure. The Company has made, and continues to make, global investments in its merchant point-of-sale network. A large portion of this network is positioned to migrate with relatively simple modification to accept smart cards. As a result, American Express is ready to support the introduction of a smart card-based open payment environment through leveraging its global network. The traditional card associations as well as new and evolving franchises should all participate. American Express aggressively opposes attempts by any organization to limit payment options at the point-of-sale by creating unnecessary technical or financial barriers. At the same time, American Express will continue to support and encourage non-partisan organizations whose primary mission is to facilitate interoperability, for example, the Smart Card

Forum of North American and various smart card forums emerging in Europe.

Developing Products

American Express is concentrating on the development of smart card products which will enhance and deepen its relationships with travel and financial service customers. These products could be classified briefly as follows:

Credit/ Charge Card Products

These products will contain the same functionality as magnetic stripe cards. The major variation will be in the method used for authorization and authentication. American Express has numerous programs and processes to manage credit and fraud. Our objective is 100 percent on-line authorizations in a magnetic stripe environment. While this is achievable in countries with efficient and low cost telecommunication infrastructures—such as the United States—it is more difficult in countries without a comparable infrastructure or costlier telecommunications.

Some countries in Asia, Africa and Eastern Europe have an extremely limited telecommunications infrastructure. In those countries, smart cards operating off-line are becoming an attractive business option for locally issued cards. However, this option will not accommodate magnetic stripe cards issued in other countries. Over the long-term, a wireless communication platform may be the answer.

Smart credit/charge card products can also be made more attractive by allowing the consumer more control over his or her credit account. One example would be a scenario in which parents can allow their children to have a card on the same account, but which holds internal controls on spending and usage type (to prevent excessive purchasing).

Electronic Purse/Stored Value

Card associations claim this is an $8.1 trillion industry worldwide, with cash expenditures under $10 alone representing $1.8 trillion. Telephone and transit industries have been early pioneers for stored value/electronic purse products, using closed end systems to facilitate the transactions. The development of this industry will require major investments to deploy the point-of-sale devices for large, open, universal systems. American Express has the ability to play several different roles in this industry. For closed-end systems, especially those that are campus oriented, American Express has a leading product offered by American Express Special Teams. This system can manage stored value and other information; currently it uses magnetic stripe technology, but it has the ability to be upgrade to a smart card system. With respect to national purse schemes, American Express could consider offering stored value products as part of the normal Card offer, possibly in partnership with other financial institutions.

Loyalty

Loyalty schemes are products in which American Express excels. Our position as developer of one of the leading global programs (Membership Rewards) will provide the basis upon which these loyalty programs could be developed. In a smart card scenario, loyalty will mean much more than point accumulation to consumers. It will also provide them with special recognition wherever they shop or travel by maintaining important customer profile information on the chip. American Express anticipates that consumers will demand attractive product offerings for the travel, entertainment and retail industries.

Ticketless Travel

Smart card ticketless travel will provide the airline industry with major cost reductions while at the same time allowing for enhanced customer servicing. Some have speculated that airlines will use ticketless travel as a way to reduce travel agent commissions. Ticketless travel, however, represents a major opportunity for travel agents themselves to reduce costs. While it might be perceived as reducing a consumer's reliance on travel agents, business and vacation travelers indicate that they still rely on a travel agent's consultation in making trip arrangements. Ticketless travel, which eliminates much of the costly paperwork in processing tickets, should result in lowered costs and speedier service delivery. As smart card tickets integrate loyalty and payment products onto one card, the consumer demand for this product will build rapidly. The clearest challenge is creating interoperability for ticketless programs within the travel industry, and overcoming the airlines' reluctance to allow card companies greater access to their passenger records.

GSM Cellular Systems

The demand for wireless telephone systems is expanding quickly worldwide, but is building for different reasons in different places. In some parts of the world where there are structural problems with the fixed wire network, cellular devices will become the gateway to dependable telecommunications services. In more developed countries, the demand for cellular is mounting as consumers demand increased convenience. Over time, the development of digital networks will help cellular phones become more commonplace. Smart card-enabled cellular phones (GSM standard) have the potential to transform the payment industry from a specific point-of-sale terminal market to an "anytime, anywhere financial transaction" environment. For example, it is possible to envision GSM phones becoming: portable ATMs which load value onto electronic purses; authorization terminals; and, electronic data capture credit card terminals. The GSM phone could be the first successful prototype of the fully integrated personal digital assistant.

Internet Access Cards

The possibility of using smart cards in conjunction with the evolving Internet marketplace may be a unique opportunity. As card companies develop safer methods of conducting commerce over the Internet utilizing stationary smart terminals (personal computers), smart cards may evolve as one of the required access enablers. Smart cards could store encrypted passwords required for secure purchase transactions over the Internet. It could also potentially serve as a convenient navigator for cardholders to locate frequently used Web pages. Smart cards could provide the cardholder with such flexibility that, while traveling, one could access a personal computer with a standard Web browser while maintaining adequate levels of security for executing personal and business transactions via the Internet.

Multi-Application Cards

Multi-application smart cards will provide the financial services industry with the opportunity to bundle products and services on one piece of plastic in a variety of combinations. The classic multi-application financial services products will combine credit, charge, debit and electronic purse on one card. They promise to provide the consumer with ultimate flexibility at the point of transaction without the inconvenience of having to carry multiple plastic cards. However, with respect to multi-application cards, the major opportunities seem to exist beyond the financial services product range. Coupling charge cards with loyalty products and/or other information services can provide opportunities to meet customer needs on a totally new level. The development of these products will be primarily driven by customer requirements and viable shareholder returns. The product possibilities are endless and will provide major customer-driven opportunities.

Opportunity for New Alliances

American Express is unique in the credit card industry. Globally, it is an issuer of cards, an acquirer of merchants, and a transaction processor all in one. This closed loop brings significant competitive advantage. In addition, American Express has developed many successful alliances to meet various customer needs. Working closely with selected business partners, the Company has been able to tailor and develop products and services which meet specific customer needs. By taking this approach, American Express is able to create increased share shift in its consumers' preferences for products and services of its alliance partners. Furthermore, by utilizing its marketing expertise and resources, American Express is able to stimulate use of these services and retain valuable customers. With its worldwide network, these resources can be provided in many countries around the world, in the currency and language of the customer.

Smart cards enable American Express to offer a unique opportunity to new and existing alliance partners. To the customer's benefit, the technology also presents an opportunity to unite with companies which may have in the past considered American Express a competitor. American Express expects to continue to forge partnerships with a variety of organizations, including banks, airlines, hotels, car rental agencies, telecommunication companies and retail concerns.

Summary

American Express is well positioned to actively participate in the smart card payment industry evolution. Quite clearly, its smart card activities will accelerate over the short term. The level of activity will, however, be targeted to meet evolving customer needs and generate returns on investments. American Express will also continue to develop the capabilities to deliver products and services in other emerging payment platforms. Smart cards will have a key role in this evolution. The real opportunity may, nonetheless, exist in linking the capabilities of this new technology with other evolving platforms.

> *Thanks to Joseph K. Clarke from American Express Travel Related Services Company, Inc. for his contribution in editing American Express Vision.*

THE IBM VIEW OF SMART CARDS

by Jerry Smith

Jerry Smith is Market Opportunity Manager in IBM's Financial Services Industries Solutions Unit which provides management and technology solutions to banks, securities, and other financial institutions in North America. He is responsible for identification and development of new strategic solutions evolving around the use of smart cards. This includes analyzing and forecasting trends, evaluating the impact of emerging technologies, competitive analysis, business case development and validating engagement opportunities with external clients and IBM business managers for all industries.

Mr. Smith has spent 28 years with IBM in technical and marketing support in various professional and management positions directing projects related to information systems planning, solution conceptualization, project definition and design, application design and development, and project implementation management for numerous institutions in the U.S. and western Europe.

Within IBM, his responsibilities have included managing the introduction of advanced technology products, creating and implementing marketing strategies and programs, developing and executing customer service delivery and support methods, developing and evaluating product requirements and business cases.

His current assignment involves working with external clients and IBM client personnel to evaluate needs and requirements related to smart card based solutions, assessing market opportunity and timing for IBM solutions, exchanging concepts and experience with industry leaders and suppliers while responding to customer interest in smart card solutions. Mr. Smith regularly speaks with executives from a variety of industry institutions and with IBM peers in other parts of the world to develop strategic business and solution plans for smart card based consumer services across all industry segments.[9]

Where are smart cards today? Institutions in the public and private sectors have only begun to take smart card technology seriously. Currently, there is a small number of knowledgeable people on the subject and many of these tend to be technologists. Business people, those responsible for returning a profit or managing expenditures of public funds remain skeptical about the future of smart cards. There are, however, recent trends pointing to potential rapid expansion of investments in smart card based solutions. But, virtually no one issues a smart card in North America today and if they did, there is nowhere to use them.

The average American today carries seven credit cards. Magnetic striped cards have become prevalent for numerous other uses such as identity cards, affinity cards or frequent shopper programs, room keys, metro passes, campus multi-purpose cards and electronic cash. Carrying a card is a very natural thing to do. In Europe, where chip-cards have been in use for several years, it is common to find a frequent traveler with four or five, even six or seven chip cards. The fact is smart cards are only a stranger in North America.

Europe, Asia, and increasingly South America are accepting smart cards as an everyday part of their relationships with service providers. Smart cards are even viewed as a part of the solution to securing the Internet for electronic commerce and payment.

So, what will it take for consumers to accept smart cards as a replacement for, or expansion of, today's magnetic striped cards. This brings us to the question: What is important to the consumer?

First and foremost, privacy. The American priorities on personal rights and freedom demand privacy and security be guaranteed at no extra cost to the consumer. One critical difference between magnetic striped cards and smart cards is the improved security available on smart cards. It is insufficient to say this, however. It must be shown, through example, careful advertising, and offering the opportunity to the opportunity to get your "hands on" using the cards.

Critical to the acceptance of smart cards is realizing they are a consumer-based tool. That is, the consumer will be the ultimate decision maker on whether smart cards will be accepted. Further, consumers will make this decision on the basis of how it affects their lives and interactions. Many experts involved in smart cards for several years have visions of a wide range of applications made simple by smart cards, but these applications must be related to what consumers view as being of value.

Many have said smart cards must cost between $1 and $3 to be economically feasible. Several card-based schemes exist that challenge this notion:

- Rental car agencies charge $50 and more per year for VIP services

- Airlines charge $50 and more per year for VIP lounge services

- Gold level credit cards are issued with annual fees of $50 and more.

And the list could go on. It is not inconceivable to be spending over $100 each year for what, by comparison, are limited function cards. So, what is important is not what the card costs, but what the card entitles the end-user to receive.

We must keep the following in mind:

- It took 25 years to get where we are today with magnetic cards.

- My 67-year-old mother has never used an ATM and doesn't plan to.

- Only 25% to 30% of American homes have PCs after 15 years.

- Nearly 60% of VCR owners have never taped a program, even after owning a VCR an average of 7 years.

- Nearly 60% of cable users buy it to improve commercial TV reception.

What are the future scenarios in this area (end-user empowerment)?

A discussion of scenarios dealing with consumer acceptance must focus on what is of value to the end-user or the carrier of the card. There are numerous ideas of using smart cards for maintenance records for automobiles and machinery, as secured portable databases, electronic coupons, and so forth. However, the real opportunity in the near term is in applications that enhance consumer services. Therefore, improving and expanding card services will be necessary to lure consumers away from their magnetic stripe and onto the chip.

These cards will become available in a variety of flavors related to the application suite they offer. They can be grouped into categories as follows:

1. Inexpensive, limited function, disposable cards.

2. Multiple application cards.

3. Multiple application card schemes.

In category 1, the future is more of the past. Hundreds of millions of cards today are used for a single purpose—for example, telephone calls only and then discarded. The stored value card planned for use at the Atlanta Olympics assumes most will be disposable. Many of the several pilots in the U.S. currently planned or underway are beginning with disposable or very inexpensive, low function cards. This scenario assumes microprocessor cards are too expensive to justify enhanced security or economical market acceptance. They may, however, improve convenience and reduce operating costs for card issuers and service providers.

The category 2 scenario represents the greatest promise in exploiting the potential of smart cards to the consumer. In the ideal sense, one simply empties their purse or wallet onto their smart card and away they go. No more fumbling for the correct card or exact change. Get cash at home, electronically, rather than at an ATM. Collect your payment transactions and dump them to your PC when it is convenient, no more receipts and keying on weekends or evenings. One simple card does it all.

But wait! How is anyone going to know just which functions I wish to have enabled on my card? Category 3 addresses this issue. Not that your exact wishes are enabled, but certainly that it is possible to target consumer buying habits and trends, couple them with geographic preferences and come up with a variety of "schemes" enabled on a single card or group of cards offering very similar functions. These schemes will evolve around relationships that exist today between those same consumers and banks, merchants, government agencies, travel and entertainment services and so on. By forming alliances around the concept of co-branded cards and affinity services, many private and some public institutions will unite to deliver a suite of applications certain segments of consumers will find appealing and be willing to pay for. These services will be enabled using the card, will include varying fees associated with the card's utility, and service fees associated with selected transactions.

Cards issued under any of these categories will relate directly to a relationship or group of relationships. For example, payment cards or bank cards will enable payment using credit or debit transactions, stored value or electronic purse, frequent buyer points, coupons, or other forms of value associated with the purchase of goods and services. Identification cards, campus or community cards, electronic benefits cards, and health cards are just other examples of cards enabling multiple functions.

Multi-application or scheme cards may have a single issuer or may be issued by several institutions. A bank or a state, for example, could issue an electronic benefits card for a given area as a benefits agent. The card could enable several government benefits, Federal, State, and Local. Postal kiosks across the country could provide access to benefit services. In addition to benefits, these cards could also replace a voter registration card, library card, drivers license or other similar forms of identification we carry today. Issued only by the single bank or state, the services enabled could be available at numerous locations around the area, across the country or around the world. The services enabled on the card are delivered directly by service providers or government agencies, without regard for who issues the card; much like Visa and MasterCard do today for credit transactions.

An alternative scenario is a consortium of multiple issuers and service providers. Issuers of cards select from a consortium library of available services that may be enabled on a card. This allows issuers to maintain existing "card" based relationships while providing the ability to improve the services offering in migrating to smart cards. The library of applications comes from alliance members joining together to service a given consumer group.

In considering various scenarios, the issue of open versus closed systems must be considered. Open systems will require a high degree of interoperability between cards, readers and service providers. This will require cooperative efforts among the public and private sectors to devise standards to support inter-operability. And, it will require agreement across industries in such areas as electronic payment, electronic shopping and electronic benefits to ensure broad geographic card scheme acceptance.

Closed systems, on the other hand, limit the number of participants sponsoring the card and the services it enables. These systems may be easier to implement, however, they also limit the utility of the card to the consumer. For many consumers, this may be acceptable. For increasingly mobile and electronic consumer groups, closed implementations may be too limited, thus unacceptable.

This brings us to the question of what scenario would your stakeholders group like to see?

Disposable, single-function chip cards benefit a few suppliers. There is minimal impact on existing systems and likewise, minimal advantage to consumers. The multiple application scheme scenario offers the greatest promise to industry and to the consumer. Improved secure consumer services enabled by sound end-to-end service networks represent a significant opportunity for providers of technology-related products and services. Whether moving transactions, building hardware and software, designing new business processes or delivering whole new consumer services, the opportunities associated with the evolution of electronic commerce and services represents significant opportunities for us all.

The smart card, implemented in an open system scenario provides the greatest degree of selection to the consumer. This, in turn, will provide the greatest amount of competition and thus, a great deal of creativity as business and government work to meet the demands of their customers. All of this represents opportunity for suppliers. Estimates range as high as $25 billion to replace the current magnetic striped infrastructure. And that's just the beginning.

While smart cards have users across a wide spectrum of industry, it appears that early industry interests center around finance, health, retail, government and education. The following is a brief look at each industry and applications being considered today in pilots being implemented around the U.S.

Finance Industry

Credit cards have become widely used around the world as a form of payment and payment authorization. Debit cards, slow to evolve in widespread use, have begun to see significant growth as more merchants accept magnetic striped cards. Smart cards represent a logical growth path for credit/debit cards since the form factor allows for a gradual migration from embossing and magnetic stripe to chip. A smart card with a modest memory size and limited processing capability will be able to combine current card functions along with a pre-paid cash purse and integrated off-line card authentication and cardholder verification. Cards with greater memory and processing capacity will be able to improve current PIN verification with on-card biometric verification. Smart cards would also be capable of combining what, today, are several cards into a single card for selection at the time and point of use. Imagine Visa, MasterCard and American Express residing on a single card and the customer deciding which to use.

Health Industry

With ever-increasing potential for a national health care card, many providers of payment systems services are working to position themselves for the potential business opportunities from processing health care payment transactions. Smart cards are also being piloted as portable databases for emergency medical information such as allergies or illnesses (i.e., diabetes) that require specialized treatment and consideration, insurance authorization and coverage, drug prescriptions and medical diagnosis. The security processing enhanced by a smart card provides a level of privacy protection not available with magnetic stripe and without the need for a large computer-based information infrastructure required to provide this level of service today. In delivering the information and security needed in health industry applications, clearly a limited storage capacity card would be inadequate to serve the needs of patients and care providers.

Government Industry

The "one card" concept for government has been getting a lot of press of late. Why does one need a separate drivers license, passport, benefits card, automobile registration, and voter registration card? One miniature portable processor could eliminate all of these devices as well as serve as a way to electronically sign a document with a so-called electronic signature. Smart cards can also provide the functions of food stamps and other forms of social service payments with a greater degree of security, fraud detection and controlled use. The capability of the smart card to provide a digitized photo, fingerprint identification, signature biometrics or other forms of positive identification and authentication can be combined to eliminate duplication as well.

Retail Industry

Aside from a form of payment (credit/debit or electronic purse), smart cards offer tremendous opportunities for market data capture and loyalty incentive programs. And, free from ties to the few card issuers of today, major brands of any variety could market "real-estate" on cards carrying these high profile and popular names for brand association. Special promotions and frequent buyer points can accumulate on the card enhancing the value and convenience consumers so often desire, but are simply not possible today without a staffed customer service operation or multiple scraps of paper. The smart card has high cost savings potential in cash-and-carry operations as a way to reduce or eliminate cash and the expenses associated with counting, handling, and other inherent costs.

Education Industry

It is estimated as many as 2000 university campuses in the U.S. now use a card-based system for multiple purposes. All are based on magnetic stripe and can be used for many applications on and off campus. The card serves as identification, access, payment, and more. Many of the uses require on-line authentication due to the security limitations of magnetic stripe cards and readers. With smart cards, off-line use could now further reduce the cost of implementing these new applications while offering additional new services.

Multiple Functions Across Industries

As semiconductor technology advances, one could conceivably include all the above industry-unique applications on a single device. That device could be a single chip micro-computer with integrated security. An individual could buy the device from multiple manufacturers or distributors, as one buys a personal computer today. Devices with many different form factors meeting the user's preference will be offered. The individual could then accept service providers and buy the services needed or desired (e.g., drivers license, multi-use personal electronic key, credit functions, electronic purse, health database, electronic checkbook, etc.) and have the required application programs and data loaded on the device.

Imagine the convenience of carrying a single multi-purpose card in your wallet. Consider also, this card could replace your wallet, cash, keys, coupons, tokens, credit/debit cards, or other similar items. All of these are being seriously evaluated as "smart cards" are increasingly recognized as a powerful emerging technology. The size of a credit card with an integrated circuit chip, smart cards represent new opportunities for reducing fraud, eliminating cash, gaining customer loyalty, and assuring privacy. Applications for smart cards have the potential to dramatically change the way we work, shop, and communicate whether at home, in the office, or in between.

MICROSOFT'S ENTRY INTO THE ELECTRONIC CASH CARD MARKET

Microsoft is developing a plan to offer plastic cards embedded with microchips that can be used to make cash payments. The company hopes to be testing a stored value card within the next year. The company is working with chip manufacturers to develop the specifications of its card and then expects to approach banks that would stand behind the payments on the card.

Microsoft is entering a rapidly crowded field of companies who plan to offer electronic money. The difficulty, however, may well be in finding a strategic partner. It is no secret that Microsoft irked many bankers with its aborted plan to acquire Intuit Inc., the provider of personal finance software. Some bankers perceived such a move as an attempt to dominate the market known as electronic commerce.

Bill Gates, founder and chairman of Microsoft, is making a strong effort to allay the banks' fears. At a convention with 100 top executives of the world's largest banks, he announced, "In no way will we be competition to banks in what we're doing. We're coming up with ways for banks to use our technology. We'll never be in the business of doing what banks do."[10]

SMART CARDS GAINING ACCEPTANCE AMONG CONSUMERS

The Smart Card Forum, an organization comprised of corporations involved in smart card technology, conducted a study of 1000 consumers entitled "Reaction to Smart Card Technology." The study indicated that two-thirds of consumers perceive smart cards as a viable option for carrying information about medical and insurance data. It also suggested that 40 percent of consumers would prefer to use smart cards for daily purchases instead of carrying cash. The major benefits that most consumers included were the convenience and security of not carrying cash, the ability to control expenditures more effectively, and the reduction of paperwork. Another major benefit cited was using one card for multiple services, thus eliminating the need for multiple cards.

Consumers indicated several potential drawbacks to using smart cards, however. For example, although they liked the idea of carrying emergency medical and insurance data, they were somewhat skeptical at having this data available on a personal basis. In fact, the issue of privacy and hackers "breaking the code" to access data was a concern to over 70 percent of respondents to the study. Yet the single most important issue on consumers' minds was what might happen to stored cash on the card if it was lost or stolen.

Practical considerations were foremost on consumers' minds. They wondered if the new technology would spread wide enough to be used on a regular basis. They also wondered how information would be updated, deleted, and downloaded and by what means their cards would be refreshed with cash.[11]

END NOTES

1. Schulman, Steven. *Smart Money Says Smart Cards are Here to Stay*. Faraday. Sept.,1994. pp. 1

2. Ibid. p. 2

3. Ibid. p.3

4. Kutler, Jeffrey. *Running Start in Smart Cards*. American Banker. Nov., 1994. pp. 1–2.

5. Ibid. p.7

6. Ibid. p. 8

7. Ibid. p. 8.

8. Wesley, Robert. American Express. *Vision on Smart Cards*. Oct., 1995.

9. Smith, Jerry. IBM Vision on Smart Cards. IBM. April 1995. pp. 1–6.

10. *New York Times*. "Microsoft Introduces Smart Cards." Sept. 10, 1995.

11. Smart Card Forum. "Reaction to Smart Card Technology." Sept., 1995.

Part 3

Special Information for a Smart Card Start-up and Fledgling Companies

11

How to Start Your Company's Smart Card Operation

INTRODUCTION

There are several paths for a company to follow for starting and financing a smart card business. What are the steps through which a business should succeed? Is there a typical sequence? Is each highly specialized? What are the barriers for a smart card business and what are the possibilities of success?

This chapter is designed to help you start thinking and acting in a manner that improves your chances for success. It will guide you through the process and identify the seemingly hidden traps of failure and the ingredients for success.

EVALUATION PROCESS: DUE DILIGENCE

Starting the business can be personally and financially rewarding if you plan ahead for the inevitable pitfalls and problems that can occur. Over one million new businesses are formed each year, but a high percentage fail within five years. The reasons for these failures vary. Insufficient start-up capital and poor business planning are frequent causes of business failure, together with poor business performance, lack of management expertise and inadequate cost control.

A hasty start can lead to the untimely end of a business. Six months to one year is not an unreasonable estimate of the time it may take to get ready to open your doors for a smart card business. Myriad issues should be addressed during the start-up period to improve probability of success.

A critical task in starting a new business is to determine the feasibility of the smart card product or service idea. You should first put your ideas through the following evaluation analysis to discover if they contain any fatal flaws. Figure 11-1 highlights the appropriate evaluation activities for each phase. Detailed guidelines for each heading are given in the following sections.

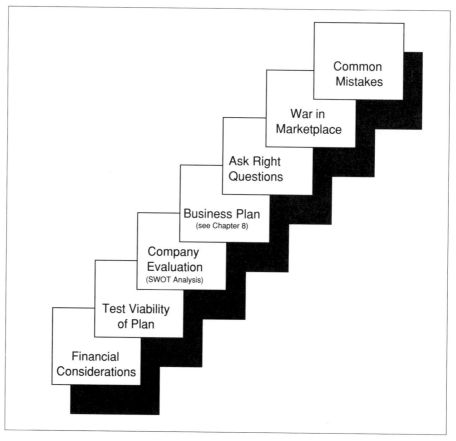

Figure 11-1. Evaluation process.

COMMON MISTAKES

From smart card manufacturing to finding the product or service that is right for you, no matter the product, there always is a series of common mistakes that you should be aware of and avoid at all costs.

Primary Mistakes

- Trying to make the business appeal to everyone
- Starting out with too little cash
- Failing to detect bad credit risks early
- Setting the wrong price
- Not listening to customers
- Grossly inaccurate sales projections
- Not piloting/testing your ideas or products
- Management experience does not match industry experience
- Not understanding your competition
- No niche strategy
- No competitive advantage

Secondary Mistakes

- Mistaking a hobby for a business
- Bleeding the business
- Inability to recognize and react to the unpredictable
- Not using enough managerial sense to plan and anticipate
- Acting on blind faith
- Not calculating potential sponsors or customers
- Unrealistic time horizons

WAR IN THE MARKETPLACE

Developing and maintaining a successful business requires planning. The business environment has undergone great change during the past decade. Changes will continue to accelerate due in part to rapidly advancing technology, increased foreign competition, continuing tax reform, and government regulations. As companies in all industries and at all stages of growth endeavor to cope with these changes and outperform the competition, the need for effective planning increases.

Market Analysis

An understanding of the market and the competition's relative position in it is part of the planning process. Focus on understanding customer needs, competitor strengths and weaknesses, and the industry structure.

- **Customer Analysis.** Customer analysis includes identifying the company's customer segments and their motivation, and determining how well customers' needs are being met. This can be done through customer interviews performed by mail or telephone.

- **Competitor Analysis.** Analysis of competitor strengths and weaknesses helps guide strategy development to match the organization's strengths against competitor weaknesses. Information about competitors is usually available from a variety of sources, including competitors' customers, distributors, annual reports, advertising, and trade shows.

- **Industry Analysis.** Questions to be answered include: Who makes up the industry? What are the industry's characteristics? What is the industry's rate of growth? What are key success factors for the industry?

Assembling and analyzing detailed information about the marketability of your business is vital in judging its potential success. I call this "war in the marketplace," which means becoming proactive and following a clear path to exploit the potential market and opportunities. Know and understand the following maxims on the road to your success:

- Find your market segment or niche and dominate it

- Create your reputation and identity

- Stay in touch with your customers

- Marketing means build relationships with customers; it is not just statistics

- The key to marketing is to understand a highly targeted niche customer

- Incorporate the customer into product design

- Invite customers to sit in on your internal meetings

- Develop product positioning, market positioning and corporate positioning

- Defeat the competition

- Selling to your existing customer is easier than selling to competitors' customers

ASKING THE RIGHT QUESTIONS

There are many important evaluation-related questions that should be asked. Here are 10 sets of preliminary questions that can be used to screen your business application.[1]

1. Is your smart card a new product or service idea? Is it proprietary? Can it be patented or copyrighted? Is it unique enough to get a significant head start on the competition? Can the process be easily copied?

2. Has a prototype been tested by independent testers who try to debug the system or rip the product to shreds? What are its weak points? Will it stand up? What level of research and development should it receive over the next five years? If it is a service, has it been tested on customers? Will customers pay for this service?

3. Has the smart card system been taken to trade shows? If so, what reactions did it receive? Were any sales made? Has it been taken to distributors? Have they placed any orders?

4. Is the smart card product or service easily understood by customers, venture capitalists, or your strategic partners?

5. What is the overall market for the smart card business? What are the market segments? Can the product penetrate these segments? Are there special niches that can be exploited?

6. Has market research been conducted? Who else comprises the market? How big is the market? How fast is it growing? What are the trends? What is the projected life cycle of the product or service? What degree of penetration can be achieved? Are there any testimonials from customers and purchasing agents? What type of advertising and promotion plans will be used?

7. What distribution and sales methods will be used—jobbers, independent sales representatives, company sales force, direct mail, door-to-door sales, supermarkets, service stations, company-owned stores? How will the product be transported: company-owned trucks, common carriers, postal service, or air freight?

8. How will the product be made? How much will it cost? For example, will it be produced in-house or by others? Will production be by job shop or continuous process? What is the present capacity of company facilities? What is the break-even point?

9. Will the business concept be developed and licensed to others, or developed and sold away?

10. Can the company get, or has it already lined up, the necessary skills to operate the business venture? Who are the workers? Are they dependable and competent? How much capital will be needed now? How much more in the future?

TESTING THE VIABILITY OF THE BUSINESS

One single test rarely determines the ultimate success or failure for starting a smart card business. In most situations a combination of ingredients influence the outcome. Therefore, it is important that these variables be identified and investigated before the business is put into practice. The results of a test viability approach enable you to judge the business's potential.[2]

The viability criteria test, to help you gain insights into the business, is based on the following questions.

Is your service proprietary? The product does not have to be patented, but it should be sufficiently proprietary to permit a long head-start against competitors and a period of extraordinary profits early in the venture to offset start-up costs.

Are the initial production costs realistic? Most estimates are too low. A careful, detailed analysis should be made so that there are no large unexpected expenses.

Are the initial marketing costs realistic? The answer requires you to identify target markets, market channels, and promotion strategy.

Does the product have potential for very high margins? This is almost a necessity for a fledgling company. The financial community understands gross margins, and without high margins, funding can be difficult.

Is the time required to get to market and to reach break-even realistic? In most cases faster is better. In all cases the business plan is tied to this answer.

Is the potential market large? In determining the potential market, look three to five years into the future, because some markets take this long to emerge.

Is the product the first of a growing family? If it is, the venture is more attractive to investors because if a large return is not made on the first product, it might be made on the second, third, or fourth product.

Is There an initial customer? Financial backers are impressed when a venture can list its first 10 customers by name. This speeds demand and also means that the first-quarter's results are likely to be good, and the focus of attention can be directed to later quarters.

Are development costs and calendar time realistic? Preferably, they are zero. A ready-to-go product gives the venture a big advantage over competitors. If there are costs, they should be complete and detailed and tied to a month-by-month schedule.

Is this a growing industry? This is not absolutely essential if profits and company growth are evident, but there is less room for mistakes. In a growing industry, good companies do even better.

Is the product and the need for it understood? If companies and customers can grasp the concept and its value, chances for funding will increase.

This criteria selection approach provides a means of analyzing the internal strengths and weaknesses that exist in a new business by focusing on the marketing and industry potential that is critical to assessment. If the business meets fewer than five of these criteria, it typically lacks feasibility for funding. If you can meet seven or more, it may stand a good chance of being funded.

FIVE KEY INGREDIENTS FOR START-UP

Evident as these five key ingredients may seem, it often happens that some concentrate on a few and ignore others, resulting in serious problems or failure for the venture. Investors—entrepreneurs, for instance—sometimes focus on the idea to the exclusion of contacts and orders. Promoters may, on the other hand, emphasize obtaining resources with insufficient attention to know how.[3]

Strong Expertise

Someone in the business must possess the professional skill and knowledge to generate the company's product or service.

Product or Service Offering

The concept for what the product or service the company will offer must become clear before the venture can succeed. This does not rule out the possibility that a venture may start with one idea and then succeed not with that idea but another.

Personal Contacts

Although some would prefer it that way, ventures are not started by people in isolation. History indicates that vital roles are played by connections with other people with regard to virtually all requisites of start-up and operation, including getting the idea for the venture.

Physical Resources

Physical wherewithal must be obtained for any business. These resources, which can include various kinds of assets and capital, may have to be substantial for some types of manufacturing or can be modest for some types of services. Pulling them together is the main role of entrepreneurs, as viewed by some historians and economists.

Customer Orders

Without orders from customers, obviously no venture can succeed. Hence, seeking these, either personally or through others, must be a vital early activity for the entrepreneur.

HOW LONG DOES IT TAKE?

The question of how long a start-up takes can be as complicated as anyone wishes to make it. Still, it is possible to choose arbitrary points in the sequence and ask how long start-up takes. One study of some 400 start-ups checked the time elapsed between conception of the idea and execution of the first sale and found a range of from less than one month to over five years, with the average between 4 and 7 months for mostly service firms. One-third took longer than a year. When this start-up period was divided into three sub-periods, from idea to start-up decision, decision to formation, and formulation to first sale, it was found to take an average of three months, with 80 percent completing this stage within one year. The second stage, from start-up decision to formation, took an average of less than two months, with 94 percent taking less than one year. From formatting to first sale was the shortest stage, with 98 percent of the firms completing it within one year.

A more interesting question for most companies is how long they can expect to subsist on financial reserves before the new company can support them. Some services may reach break-even within weeks or even days. Others may take months to a year. A buy-out may already be profitable and hence beyond break-even right from the start. New product manufacturing companies typically take the longest. SmartCard International took over three years to break even, and of course some companies never reach it and consequently fail. A new enterprise producing proprietary products is not likely to become profitable in its first year. The fact that break-even time can range so widely depending on the particular enterprise is one of several reasons for preparing careful financial forecasts before plunging into the business.

THREE MAJOR BARRIERS TO STARTING A SMART CARD BUSINESS

The three main barriers are as follows:

1. Sufficient dollar margins

2. Effective sales

3. Sufficient financing

These three are probably in order for a "typical" company, although the order can vary and the three may obviously be interrelated. From interviewing companies who had already dealt with the first of these, three different approaches were found. In one study, financial and marketing problems were found to be equally severe, both trailing "learning how to run a business," according to the companies responding. The most serious problem area during start-up was found to vary. In some it was finance and in others marketing.

These clearly correspond to three of the five start-up essentials discussed previously, but extend them just a bit. It is not sufficient to have a venture idea; the idea must carry an adequate profit margin. It is not sufficient to obtain initial sales orders; a scheme must be introduced that generates continuous orders and reorders. It is not sufficient to provide the seed capital needed to germinate the venture; either the capital must grow fast enough through high initial profits, or it must be augmented with additional injections for longer-term survival. Each of these three main hurdles along the path to start-up deserves a more careful look than any success stories might imply.[4]

High-Margin Venture Idea

It has been said that to achieve more than the barest survival at best, a venture needs the "3M's," and that these stand for one word; margin, margin, margin. First is *margin to make a profit*. Second is *margin to provide for unforeseen problems*, which virtually always arise in any new venture. Third is *margin to keep making a profit, and coping with problems after competitors have entered and attacked or counterattacked with reduced prices*. Although it varies with industry, a rough rule of thumb for any manufactured product is that it must sell to the end-user for at least four to five times the direct costs and labor and materials needed to produce it. If there are any channels downstream from the manufacturer, such as distributors, wholesalers, and retailers, this means that the manufacturer must typically charge as its own selling price at least twice its direct costs for goods picked up at the factory. Without such a margin-generating idea at the core, the profit-making heart of a venture is missing, and so is its justification for existing in the world of business. If the venture idea has only a low margin potential but not a high one (in total, not necessarily per unit), then it will be unlikely either to grow large or to attract outside capital or to provide much income for the entrepreneur (although there have been ventures, unsuccessful in general, that have, nevertheless, accomplished these things).

How many people try to start smart card ventures but fail to get started at all has never been examined. Presumably there is always some reason or combination of them that explains these "nonstarts," and probably the most common reason is failure to identify a high-margin venture idea. There would be some who, although desiring to do so, were unable to identify any venture ideas they considered with serious effort, or who were for some reason disinclined to apply effort to test any ideas. There would be another group, probably smaller in number, who identified one of more ideas and investigated or tried them to some extent but concluded that their ideas were insufficiently promising or were too risky to carry further. There would be still another group whose ideas were proven inadequate by full-scale implementation culminating in venture failure. One survey of would-be entrepreneurs found that fewer than 10 percent felt they had been able to formulate any high-margin potential venture idea.

Effective Sales-Generation Scheme

Once the barrier is passed of locating an idea that appears to have high margin potential, a second major obstacle is that of developing a scheme to generate orders from customers.

It was pointed out that obtaining orders is one of the five key factors in getting started, but it should also be noted that one sale or even a few sales are not enough. Success requires many customers in most ventures and an automatic repeating pattern of ordering. It is vital, however, that a would-be entrepreneur recognize the importance of this hurdle, not just assume it away, and develop plans for coping with it. These must include clear answers to basic questions, such as: Who can be expected to want what it is the company will sell? How much will it be worth and why? How will potential customers become aware of the product? What difficulties may customers have recognizing its value to them, and how can the company solve these?

Failure to obtain orders can result from many causes, including the following:

> *Basic Product Weakness.* Smart Card International engineers who developed a hand-held computer for improving electronic input of data to sell their design-improvement service to companies found that none of them would buy. The purchase decision at those companies was stymied by the size—too small to key in data—and was rejected.

Established Relationships Market. It can be hard to break into markets of high volume where buyers tend to buy from established rather than new companies.

Wrong Channel Choice. New companies often sell through representatives to avoid the expense of setting up their own sales forces. If the choice of representatives is not right, they find that sales do not result, because representatives are pushing other products in their lines, either because they get larger commissions on the other products, because other products are better-established and easier to sell, because they have so many products they cannot really bother with the new one unless they are asked for it by customers, or for some other reason. Other new companies may set up their own sales forces only to find that the product volume is insufficient to support it.

Long Warmup Markets. When smart cards were first introduced, nobody bought them because people were used to magnetic stripe cards. It took years for the manufacturers to convert people to a perfectly good innovation.

Operational Financing

Most would-be ventures can raise capital to go through many of the steps of starting a venture, often to get it actually operating on a small scale. Sources typically begin with personal savings, family members, friends, and other acquaintances, and partners. This may be enough to draw up legal papers, obtain space, perform some market research, and perhaps develop a prototype, packaging, and initial advertising. If the venture is to be a small one, this seeding may be enough to make the venture permanent. If the initial inventory and set-up is high, or if the personal assets of the entrepreneur and his or her associates are small, then it is typically necessary to secure additional external capital beyond personal assets before the venture can truly become operational. This is often the case with smart card ventures, and consequently obtaining operational capital is often a critical hurdle in getting ventures started.

Having solved the hurdle of finding a good margin idea does not necessarily solve the capital problem. A classic example was the Xerox process, which knocked around, unable to find backing, for years before support was found. Ironically, it can happen that the higher margin potential, the bigger the amount of capital needed, and consequently the bigger the problem of obtaining financing. If the margin promises to be very high, then it can be desirable to move on a large-scale fast to stay ahead of competitors, who are bound to be attracted to the high-profit line of business once the new venture exhibits the opportunity.

Margin is obviously only one of the dimensions of interest to venture capitalists. Although typically about 20 to 30 percent of their deals are with start-ups, the remainder are investments in going concerns. Moreover, their industry preferences are about 60 percent aimed toward high-technology start-ups, and they aim at rates of return of around 30 percent annually on investments of $250,000 and up. The total accounts for only a very small fraction of start-up capital.[5]

END NOTES

1. Kurateo, Donald F. 1994. *Entrepreneurial Strategy*. Dryen Press. p. 47.

2. Ibid. p. 53.

3. Ibid. pg. 50.

4. Ibid. p. 51.

5. Ibid. p. 56.

12

Sources of Financing

INTRODUCTION

You do not need a business plan or outside consultants to know that every business needs money to operate. However, the amount needed and the time period for which the funds are required vary for many reasons. Plan ahead and do not let your financial requirements surprise you. Arranging financing takes time, and rushing decisions can be costly.

SOURCES OF FINANCING

Internal

Internally, additional funds can be obtained by accelerating collection of accounts receivable, controlling expenses, leasing instead of purchasing equipment, disposing of an unprofitable product line, and properly planning for federal and state taxes.

External

External financing may be obtained through debt or equity financing. Each potential source has certain criteria for providing financing. Your ability to obtain financing depends on a number of factors, including:

the management team, collateral, cash flow, earnings capacity, and the marketability of the product. The following financial sources are reviewed.

DEBT FINANCING

Banks

Commercial banks are the most common source of debt financing. They offer several types of loans: short-term loans such as lines of credit, inventory financing, commercial loans, and accounts receivable financing; and medium- and long-term loans, such as term loans, equipment loans, real estate financing, and equipment leasing.

SBA Loans

For a smart card business that is looking for start-up funds, applying for an SBA loan is considered an alternative approach. Today the SBA mostly makes loans for start-up businesses to minorities and in special industries. The approach for SBA financing is to first locate a commercial or savings bank that is a certified SBA lender. The SBA does not directly fund the loan; what it does is guarantee up to 80 percent of the loan for the lending institution. The key advantage for you is to repay the note over an extended period of time. The SBA is not in the business of guaranteeing bad loans, once your institution accepts the credit, it recommends your company to the SBA. Another alternative is a Small Business Development Centers (SBDC). These organizations are partially funded by the SBA and by state governments. They offer different kinds of services like education courses, seminars, and also free consulting. To contact your SBDC, check the phone book for U.S. government listings for the office nearest you.

EQUITY INVESTMENTS

How to Get Investors Interested

The role of venture capital is as a fund of money established for the purpose of making an equity investment in a small, high-growth company. Venture capitalists make their money investing other people's money so they must exercise "due diligence" in their research of potential investments. This is why out of one hundred plans submitted for funding, fewer than ten get reviewed, and actually one or two would be funded.[1]

Private Investors

If your smart card business requires only a limited amount of capital, contacting private investors may be the best choice. By contacting individuals, you have a greater chance of structuring the investment more towards your liking. The deal could be structured as debt or equity and you can vary the terms of repayment. Sources of personal investors can include family, friends, lawyers, and even your potential customers.

Investors prefer a structured arrangement which describes the capital requirements of the business and proposes a fair equity agreement. The plan should indicate a specific dollar amount of capital required. Usually, for venture capitalists, the range of $1 million or more is acceptable, due to the cost of investigating the business.

The best plans should have the following features:

- Expected return on deal

- Exit strategy

- Other participating investors

- Deal structure

Expected Return on Deal

Investors usually maintain a time period of five years with in a range of three to seven to realize their return on initial investment. They expect their investment to increase in net value by five-fold to fifteen-fold, considering inflation.[2]

Obtaining Risk Capital

Timing

Timing is critical and it is important that a smart card business not delay looking for capital by waiting until it has a serious cash shortage. For a start-up, especially one with no experience or success in raising money, it is unwise to delay as it is likely to take six months or more to raise capital. In addition to the problems with cash flow, the lack of planning implicit in waiting until there is a cash shortage can undermine the credibility of a management team and negatively impact its ability to negotiate with investors.

On the other hand, if you try to obtain capital too early, the equity position of the founders may be unnecessarily diluted and the discipline instilled by financial leanness may be eroded.

The right investor can add value in a number of ways, such as:

- Identifying and helping recruit key management team members and providing key industry and professional contacts

- Serving as a mentor, confidant, and sounding board for ideas and plans to solve problems or quicken growth

- Helping to establish relationships with key customers or suppliers, or both

- Having "deep pockets" to participate in and syndicate subsequent rounds of financing

Types of Risk Investment

Private Placements

Private placements involve selling securities or stock to investors. Federal and state laws regulate these fund-raising activities and how such offerings are made. Private placements are complex. It is unwise for a new venture to undertake such offerings of securities without the advice of an attorney who is skilled in these matters.

A private placement is subject to intrastate registration and private placement, and certain conditions need to be met to effect the sale of securities to friendly sources, wealthy individuals, or venture capital firms via a private placement. As outlined below, purchasers may be accredited, nonaccredited, and sophisticated investors.

Under the Securities Act of 1933, securities may not be issued unless registered or unless an exemption from registration is available. The typical exemption would be Regulation D, adopted by the SEC on April 15, 1982, which sets forth a means wherein an issuer may issue securities without the need for registering the same.

Rule 504: $1 million limit in 12 months preceding issue (no more then $500,000 of which may be sold in a state which does not require state registration); there is no requirement of disclosure (caveat: fraud rules are still applicable); there are no advertising restrictions on resale.

Rule 505: $5 million limit in 12 months preceding issue, no more than 35 unaccredited purchasers, no requirement of disclosure to accredited investors; but if to nonaccredited investors, complete Part III of Form -A, if less than $2 million, and complete Part 1 of 5-18, if less than $5 million, with no advertising, restrictions on resale.

Rule 506: No limit as to dollar size, no more than 35 nonaccredited investors (nonaccredited investor must be able to evaluate merit and risks), no requirement of disclosure to accredited investors; but complete disclosure information on Part 1 of Form S-18 if nonaccredited and less than $7.5 million, and Part 1 of registration statement if over $7.5 million, with no advertising, restrictions on resale. The issuer must complete and file form D with SEC with 15 days of first sale.

Rule 701: Securities issued to employees, directors, consultants, or advisors pursuant to written compulsory plan or agreement, shall not exceed in 12 months the greater of $500,000 or 15 percent of total assets or outstanding securities. Form 701 must be filed within 30 days after sales of such securities exceed $100,000 and annually thereafter.

The SCOR Solution

The Small Corporate Offering Registration (SCOR) is a stock offering that is administered on the state rather than the federal level. Currently, 26 states permit SCOR offerings and another 11 give unofficial recognition, according to the North American Securities Administrators Association. SCORs allow companies to sell stock to all comers.

There are other advantages for smaller companies. A SCOR offering is far less expensive than a regular initial private offering (IPO), and you don't need a high-paid underwriter. Its forms are relatively jargon-free.

However, there are two catches. The size of the offering is small—a company can raise only $1 million in a given year, although it can do multiple offerings. The company selling the stock must also be small: $25 million or less in annual revenues. Companies must also register in each state they want to offer stock.[2]

Bridge Capital

This alternative is used by growing firms, typically those with sales in the $5 million to $100 million range, which anticipate a public offering or private sale of the firm in the next 6 to 36 months.

Public Stock Offerings

There is a season for every type of financing, and that includes the public stock markets. Your company is ripe for an IPO if it is past the start-up phase, has exhausted other venues, has growth potential to attract investors, and needs enough capital to warrant such a pricey move. Of course, a stock market that has been roaring ahead for the past year is another enticement; IPOs raised a record $25 billion in the first half of 1994.

The more mature a company is when it makes a public offering, the better the terms of the offering, that is, a higher valuation can be placed on the company and less equity will be given up by the founders for the required capital.

There are two main reasons why a new or young company might want to go public. First, in the right times, the company will get a higher stock price from an IPO than from a venture capital investor. Second, an IPO establishes a public price for the stock and gives a company a sense of wealth, at least on paper. (However, the sale of the stock will have certain restrictions on it.)

Notwithstanding above, there are a number of reasons why IPO's can be disadvantageous. Principal among these are:

- The legal, accounting and administrative costs of raising money via public offerings are more disadvantageous than other ways of raising money.

- A large amount of effort and expense on the part of management are required to comply with SEC regulations and reporting requirements and to maintain the status of a public company. This diversion of management's time and energy from the tasks of running the company can adversely affect its performance and growth.

- The required disclosures to stockholders and, through them, to outsiders can make known information about a company's products, performance, and financial condition that would be better kept secret.

- Management can become more interested in maintaining the price of the company's stock and computing capital gains than in running the company. Short-term activities to maintain or increase a current year's earnings can take precedence over longer-term programs to build the company and increase its earnings.

- The liquidity of a company's stock achieved through a public offering may be more apparent than real. Without a sufficient number of shares outstanding and a strong "market maker," there may be no real market for the stock and, thus, no liquidity.

- The investment banking firms willing to take a new or unseasoned company public may not be the ones with whom the company would like to do business and establish a long-term relationship.

There are a number of financial consideration questions that can be asked. Use this set to guide you in preparing the financial measurements for your plan.

1. How much will be needed for development of the product or service?

2. How much will be needed for setting up operations?

3. How much will be needed for working capital?

4. Where will the money come from? What if more is needed?

5. Which assumptions in the financial forecasts are most uncertain?

6. What will be the return on equity, or sales, and how does it compare with the other similar companies?

7. When and how will investors get their money back?

Also you should be cautious about the following issues:

- When revenues are recognized

- Costs of goods sold

- Inventory valuation

- Timing differences

END NOTES

1.   Tarrazo, Manuel. 1994. "Winning Business Plan." Southwestern Publishing, pp. 6–130

2.   *INC.* March 1994. "Steps to a Start-up: Investors Will Buy." pp. 72–75.

3.   Ibid.

Appendix A

Guidelines for a Successful Consulting Smart Card Program

For a smart card project to be successful, the management consultant and the client must understand their roles and responsibilities and work as a team.

MANAGEMENT CONSULTANT'S ROLE

Management consultants solve problems by analysis and synthesis. They seek relevant facts about the problem to determine its causes, then fit all parts of the problem into a whole for synthesis. Once this is done, the management consultants can determine the end results that can be achieved, then develop and consider alternative solutions and recommend the best one.[1]

In some situations, the management consultant guides an internal task force of client personnel. The consultant's essential function in this situation is to work with and motivate the task force, and the consultant remains accountable for results.

The participation of the client's staff members will help the management consultant to better understand the problem and its implications and will speed the project.

CONSULTANT'S FOUR STEPS IN PLANNING

For most engagements, the management consultant will ordinarily follow four distinct steps in planning the engagement: research, analysis, solution, and implementation.

Research Stage

The research phase includes planning the engagement and gathering facts. Typically, four main steps are involved:

1. Define the engagement and purpose.

2. Determine the approach to the engagement.

3. Determine the end results or deliverables.

4. Estimate the amount of fact-finding required.

Analysis Phase

The analysis phase also involves four distinct steps:

1. Define the problem or opportunities for improvement in precise terms.

2. Determine the conditions that have created and are sustaining the problem.

3. Determine the objectives of the engagement.

4. Develop alternative solutions that may provide answers to the problems.

Solution Phase

At this point, the management consultant must select the most timely, practical, and acceptable solution. To help you solve your problem, the management consultant must make certain that the solution makes sense to you so you will implement the recommendations. Therefore, before working out the solution in detail, the management consultant should try to reach an agreement with you on the acceptability of the solution. The consultant should provide a blueprint of what needs to be done, by whom, and in what sequence so that the recommended solution will be understandable to all.

Implementation Phase

Once recommendations have been accepted, they must be implemented. Some consultants have technical/specialist capabilities that can contribute substantially, as part of a team effort with client personnel, to help achieve solutions/goals previously identified. If implementation support is not provided, the client should ask the consultant for guidance as to other professionals who are in a position to provide this support.

END NOTES

1.   *Consulting News*. Nov. 1989. "How to Consult on Projects." pp. 41–44.

Appendix B

Guidelines to Selecting a Vendor

---

1. **For broad issues and solutions, bring in a vendor before too many decisions have been made.** Talk to several vendors. See what general directions they are able to suggest. If three or four good vendors look at the problem, they may be able to provide useful guidance before they are hired.

2. **Check the vendor's references.** Ask what jobs were done for each reference. If you are looking for a process vendor, a collection of references extolling the technical knowledge of the candidate is not useful. Also, ask the vendor about failures. An honest vendor will admit failures and will understand why he or she failed. Any vendor who claims never to have failed is either dishonest or inexperienced.

3. **Don't be distracted by unneeded skills.** For example, don't worry about communication skills if you are looking for a process vendor. If you are proposing a vendor to attack your resident curmudgeon, consider personality differences and choose someone who might impress the curmudgeon. Except for relevant technical issues, don't dwell on how much experience the vendor has had in your industry.

4. **On clean narrow issues for an expert vendor, push hard for the deliverables, the terms, the schedules and so on.** On process issues, too much attention to these details could be self-

defeating. With process vendors, you don't know what the solution will be and you don't know how long it will take. But you must trust the vendor's integrity and have confidence that he or she will not prolong the project to run up the bill. The process vendor should have flexible terms with no fixed guarantees. His or her charges are usually based on a daily rate. Any vendor should be able to tell you how fees are calculated and how issues such as travel time are handled. Be suspicious about guaranteed dollar savings unless the issue is extremely narrow and mechanical.

5. **Clarify which consultant will work on the actual project.** Sometimes the consultant you deal with initially will have little or no relationship with you once you sign on the dotted line. Though the consultant may not be able to tell you precisely who will be available when the time comes, he or she usually presents three or four alternatives from which your vendor will be chosen. The more flexible you are on time of performance, the greater your chance of getting a top vendor. On the other hand, if you insist on a specific person, you may not get the timetable you want.

6. **Ask how the vendor plans to involve your staff, particularly if you want your staff to become capable in this area.** The hands-off aspect should be a clear part of the discussion. Be suspicious of any vendor who is not willing to talk much about bringing your staff in; it is likely he or she is trying to sell you a "canned" solution that may not fit your organization.

Two More Ways to Judge

Every vendor should display a high listening-to-talking ratio. In listening to your exposition of the problem, the vendor is demonstrating respect for the uniqueness of your problem—which is absolutely essential for effective solutions. A talker, however brilliant the talk is, is not suddenly going to become a listener after you have hired him or her.

When the vendor does talk, he or she should give very specific examples, not generalities. The consultant may preface this by saying, "I don't know yet whether this applies to you, but when I was at company X, I did the following and I have heard about what company Y and company Z did." If the vendor demonstrates experience in attacking problems similar to yours, this is the person you want.

Conclusion

When using a vendor, it is essential that you know why you are asking the vendor to do something. Though this may seem simple, many organizations don't do this well. The vendor can be a valuable extension of your staff resources for specific tasks. Vendors are sometimes able to accomplish what you couldn't see clearly or make happen yourselves. Because of this, companies that virtually prohibit using vendors are missing an important opportunity.

But the ultimate doer in your company is you. It cannot be pushed off on a vendor to solve the problems or to do the difficult tasks that management needs to handle. So as usual in life, a balanced view is required. Use a vendor when it is clear that you need to, but do it yourself when you are certain you and your staff can take care of it.

Appendix C

Guidelines for Writing a Request for Proposal for Smart Card Applications

---

This is a format to follow when you are sending out an RFP (request for proposal) from companies who can provide you with a service or product.

June 2, 1995
XYZ Corporation
Account Manager
505 8th Avenue
New York, NY 10001

To whom it may concern:

The company will be implementing a corporate-wide **Smart Card application**. We are requesting information and a proposal regarding products and potential configurations that will satisfy our requirements.

Please review this RFP as soon as possible. Information must be submitted by _____ in order for us to complete our evaluation process. Information reaching us later will not be considered in this evaluation process.

After our evaluation of the responses to this RFP, we may request selected vendors to provide demonstrations and site visits to existing customers.

This RFP includes a **confidentiality and non-disclosure agreement. This must be filled in and returned.**

Please send your reply to the following address:

Thank you,

Company Name

Following this letter of introduction, you may want to include a table of contents, a description of the application, proposal guidelines, and a method of evaluating and selecting your vendor of choice.

REQUEST FOR PROPOSAL: SMART CARD

Company intends to award a purchase order for the requirements on which you ("Vendor") are being asked to bid. This request is not a commitment that an order is forthcoming. The company reserves the right to reject any proposal and will not compensate Vendor for costs incurred in proposal preparation. By agreeing to complete this Request for Proposal, Vendor acknowledges that all information provided to Vendor is proprietary information and Vendor agrees that it shall maintain the confidentiality of all information it receives or otherwise obtains in accordance with those terms and conditions contained.

Sample Table of Contents

Contents

(end)

INTRODUCTION TO APPLICATION (SAMPLE)

The nature of business clearly supports the development of a pre-pay Smart Card Program. The average transaction amount of $15.00 is low and many customers come into the stores once each day.

In reviewing various pre-pay instruments, it was determined that the technology developed must offer two critical capabilities: discreet customer purchase tracking and pre-paid declining balance. These requirements has led us to examine the use of smart cards instead of magnetic stripe cards.

Magnetic stripe cards can be produced inexpensively and will track customer purchasing information; however, the technology required to "credit" the card with additional value is very costly and unwieldy to install. Furthermore, magnetic stripe cards have very limited space for storing customer information and tend to wear out easily.

Smart cards initially are more expensive than magnetic stripe cards to produce. However, smart cards are reusable in that the technology for "crediting" smart cards with additional value can be installed far less expensively than the technology required for "crediting" magnetic stripe cards. Smart cards also offer broader application and greater flexibility for tracking customer information. In addition, long-term industry trends are pointing to the smart card technology (used in applications, such as the "electronic purse" being developed in the banking industry).

Through this RFP, the Company is actively seeking product and proposal information regarding the smart card applications. These applications should include functionality to issue the card, encode value and customer information on the card, read the card, record register transaction, decrease remaining balance, and re-value the card. The application will also need to track the customer information, audit sales, service customer complaints and lost card issues, and be able to accommodate frequency and/or loyalty-type programs.

1.1 Proposal Guidelines

This section is to provide you with the project team's stated objectives, a brief overview of the evaluation method and a point of contact should you have further questions.

1.1.1 Objectives

The project team's objectives are to implement the most appropriate form of smart card technology for the Company and to introduce this technology chain-wide following the successful completion and assessment of a smart card pilot.

The objectives of introducing smart card technology include the following:

- Increased customer loyalty through greater understanding of customer habits and a more personalized relationship.

- Increased loyalty through the commitment of pre-payment.

- Improved customer service through the convenience of pre-payment and shorter transaction time.

- Increased sales through increased number of transactions per customer and increased transactions per hour due to greater throughput.

1.1.2 Contacts

If you have any questions while preparing your response, you may contact the following individual: _____.

1.1.3 Evaluation and Selection Process

Please respond to this RFP using the attached forms or a document with matching sections and items. Responses that do not conform to this format will not be considered. This RFP should be returned to _____ by _____, by mail or other delivery service.

The attached forms outline our general requirements. Some requirements are listed for comparison purposes and may not be explicit requirements of the Company. Requirements are not listed in order of importance or priority. In addition to addressing the requirements, you may elect to provide a proposal for implementing your product(s) or include evaluation or demonstration products with your response.

Each proposal received will be evaluated against the following criteria:

1. Understanding business needs

2. Compatibility with business environment

3. Compatibility with technical environment

4. Compatibility with development environment

5. Compatibility with support environment

6. Timing considerations

7. Cost of system

8. Potential to improve competitive position

9. Potential to improve interaction with customers

10. Potential to improve internal operations

11. Vendor documentation, training and support

1.2 Vendor Instructions

1.2.1 How to Complete the Response

Please fill in all responses to the maximum extent possible. If you think we have omitted an important consideration, or if you feel that additional information would be helpful, please feel free to provide supplemental information. If you attach your response to a separate document, please cross-reference replies to the specific section heading and item number in this document.

1.2.2 Transmission of Completed Response

Your completed response should be received in our office by _____.

Please be sure to complete and execute the attached Non-Disclosure and Confidentiality Agreement.

Appendix D

Social and Environmental Issues

Concerns about the privacy issues in smart card applications, particularly access to personal data, have been voiced all across the world.[1]

The United States has no comprehensive, integrated structure of privacy laws and regulations. Nor is there any central authority to enforce privacy laws, regulations, or policies. Instead laws and regulations that provide privacy protections are drawn from a wide range of sources, including the U.S. Constitution, federal statutes, and regulations and codes of various industries and professions. Brief descriptions of the key issues follows.

CONSTITUTIONAL PROTECTIONS

In general, constitutional rights are good only against actions by the government. The constitutional inquiry in connection with smart card use is focused on government's use of records stored or transmitted via a smart card. If smart cards were ever to implicate informational privacy rights, one would be protected under the 1st, 4th, 5th, and 14th amendments.

First Amendment

Using the 1st amendment, for example, smart cards may contain transaction records for purchases of books, videos, or payment records of entertainment and social activities. Assuming that smart cards contain such records, 1st amendment difficulties could arise if the government seeks to monitor smart card transactions. If smart cards are incorporated into government programs, for example, to store government benefits electronically (as some states are now proposing), the cards may require interaction with government computer systems for storing benefits, monitoring activities, or controlling the use of funds.

More important, however, smart cards could become de facto tools of law enforcement, used to monitor transactions for possible gambling, tax fraud, benefits, insurance fraud, and other illegal credit card schemes. At minimum, this could hinder efforts to market smart cards for these types of applications. If these agencies gain access to the smart card data stored on the card, it could also be vulnerable to civil law suits.[2]

COMMON LAW AND PRIVACY PROTECTIONS

Privacy issues that might prove relevant to smart card applications can be categorized as follows:

Privacy

Many uses for smart cards have been suggested, and many of these suggestions raise privacy issues. In order to avoid the legal and business problems that can result from infringements to the privacy of a smart-card user's personal information, the industry needs to address privacy concerns early in the development cycle of new smart card products.

Four circumstances prevent simple generalizations about privacy law as it may apply to smart cards.

- First, privacy laws in the United States have developed sector by sector according to categories of information. For example, banking records are subject to entirely different controls and requirements from medical records, which in turn are subject to a regulatory regime distinct from that which applies to video sale or rental records.

- Second, it is always possible that new sorts of records—for example, toll-collection records or telephone records—will come under legislative scrutiny at either the state or federal level.

- Third, the rich variety of uses proposed for smart cards makes it difficult to catalog in advance each category of information that may raise concerns and all of the potential modes of privacy infringement. For example, we cannot yet identify all of the institutions, intermediaries, and agents that may have access to smart card records.

- Finally, a significant characteristic of smart cards is their potential to incorporate various functions on a single card. Unique privacy concerns could result when types of information traditionally isolated from one another—such as retail transaction data, telephone records, and travel records—are collected in the same place.

As smart card applications develop, time spent early in the process on thinking through privacy concerns will help prevent larger costs, delays, or enforcement difficulties when smart card products and services hit the market. In many cases, smart card applications could incorporate privacy safeguards such as anonymity or encryption in order to address concerns that consumers or regulators may have. If the existing privacy framework proves incompatible with certain potentially useful and valuable smart card applications, the industry may find it worthwhile to educate Congress and state legislatures as they revisit some areas of privacy law with an eye toward removing unnecessary barriers to the development of smart card technologies.

Credit Records

It is possible that card holders could carry "credit reports" about themselves on a smart card. The Federal Fair Credit Reporting Act limits the content, handling and disclosure of consumer credit reports. If smart card data becomes a source of information for credit files, it may be necessary to document the source of each collected information and determine its accuracy. If smart cards contain credit reports, will it be possible to assume that these reports are accurate? And if so, who will have access to the data?[3]

Cardholders Rights

Smart cards have data-protection privacy implications in respect of who shall have access to the personal data on them and who shall have the ability to read, add to, or alter the data.

Smart cards have many possible uses in both the public and private sectors. These include their use for payment purposes, perhaps with facilities which create an "electronic purse," for the prevention of credit card fraud, and for holding details of medical conditions and treatment.

In Canada, Tom Wright, Ontario's information and privacy commissioner has reported on the implications of the use of card technology by government and says such systems should be open and transparent to data subjects who should know their inherent rights when using the card, what information the card contains, how it will be used, and what risks that use implies.

Cardholders should have the right to:

- participate in the determination of what personal information the card contains and who has access to it

- access and correct information held about them on the card, as well as in any related database

All uses and disclosures of information on the card should be subject to the prior and informed consent of the data subject.

Where possible, individuals should be free to refuse the card without jeopardizing their access to the service involved. Similarly, holding a smart card would not confer benefits (other than perhaps enhanced service) unavailable to those who choose not to utilize a smart card, he says, adding that smart card technology should be used only by government to enhance access to government information and services, and not as an instrument of social control, for example, as a method of conducting surveillance or a means of creating computer profiles.[4]

END NOTES

1. Bercu, Steven A. July 1994. "Smart Card Privacy Issues: An Overview." Smart Card Forum. pp. 1–5.

2. Ibid.

3. Ibid.

4. Ibid.

Appendix E

Smart Card Trade Associations

SMART CARD FORUM

As evidence if the anticipated growth and interest in smart card technology in the United States, more than 170 companies, as well as the U.S. Treasury, U.S. Department of Health and Human Services, and the U.S. Department of Defense, joined forces in 1993 to create the Smart Card Forum, a consortium charged with developing business specifications and recommending standards for a North American smart card infrastructure.[1]

Initiated by Citibank, Bellcore, and the U.S. Treasury, and currently chaired by Citibank, the consortium is the largest in the world, indicating the growing interest in the United States for smart card technologies.

The Forum's members include American Express, AT&T, Bellcore, IBM, Hewlett-Packard, MCI, Microsoft, MasterCard, Visa International, numerous smart card technology vendors, and several large banks including Citibank, Chase Manhattan Bank, Chemical Bank, Bank of America, Wells Fargo Bank, NationsBank, Corestates Bank and National Westminster Bank. Merchant processors, such as FDR and Total Systems, and ATM networks, such as Infonet, STAR and Cash Station, are also members.

One of the Forum's main objectives is to foster communication that will result in North American trials of smart card-based applications.

Another objective is to define business specifications for various applications and recommend adoption of standards that will be interoperable across North America, as well as across different applications. The forum currently is reviewing the MasterCard/Visa/Europay specifications with this is mind.

Tapping the resources of a central Technology Committee, the forum's seven working groups—Financial Services, Telecommunications and Information Services, Health Care, Education, Travel and Entertainment, Government/EBT, and Transportation—meet every four to six weeks and have deliverables in the forum of white papers, research, specifications, and seminars.

Membership is open to non-U.S.-based companies, and the forum has been working with international groups with similar objectives, exchanging information as well as ideas.

CARD EUROPE

Card Europe's mission is to foster and encourage pan-European and nation-state smart card markets, promoting user confidence in smart cards and their integrity.

Card Europe is a not-for-profit organization intended to ensure that, as the smart card industry grows, the user and operator community have available the products and standards they require and a strong voice in the development of product designs and standards. Card Europe is the focal point through which many small and large companies can combine their efforts to create that strong voice.

With the break-up of the Eastern Bloc, taking into account the former Soviet Union (FSU) countries and the Central and East European countries (CEEC), there are over 40 independent countries in Europe, some in the European Union and others in different groupings. Card Europe has been set up to represent smart card users and operators in all these countries. It is the belief of Card Europe that only be achieving consensus across both industry and country borders, will we be able to achieve a truly representative set of a products and standards leading to full interoperability with a multi-service capability.

SMART CARD INDUSTRY ASSOCIATION (SCIA)

Smart Card Industry Association (SCIA) is the world's premier international trade association operated for the benefit of all participants in the development and use of advanced card technologies.

Established in 1989 to meet the need for an independent voice to speak for the various organizations involved with integrated circuit card technology, SCIA continues to grow and develop more programs to support our valued members.

SCIA's primary purpose as an association is educational in nature:

- To raise public awareness of the unique functionality of this technology

- To pursue promotional activities on behalf of the membership

- To monitor legislative activities that will impact the development of this technology

SCIA's mission is to promote the growth, expansion, and professionalism of the advanced card technologies. SCIA represents the leading manufacturers, integrators, users, consultants, and other service providers in the smart card technology industry.

END NOTES

1. Smart Card Forum. An Overview. April 1995.

Glossary of Terms

This condensed document is published with permission from the Smart Card Forum.

This document was published by the Smart Card Forum. To learn more about the Smart Card Forum's working groups and deliverables, please contact the Forum Office:

> 3030 N. Rocky Point Drive West, Suite 670
> Tampa, Florida 33607
> (813) 286-2339 • (813) 281-8752 FAX

ABS—Acrylonitrile Butadiene Styrene. Plastic material used to make many integrated circuit cards. Unlike PVC, it is formed through injection molding which allows the dimensions of the card and the hole into which the chip module is inserted to be precisely controlled.

Access Card—A machine-readable card used to achieve computer access, physical entry, or passage.

Algorithm—A set of rules specifying the procedures to perform a specific computation.

American National Standards Institute (ANSI)—The national standards setting body in the U.S.A.

ANSC—American National Standards Committee.

ANSI—American National Standards Institute.

Application—A commercial use or purpose for using a device, e.g., an integrated circuit card used for transfers, inquiries, credits, etc.

Application Specific Integrated Circuit (ASIC)—A computer chip designed with special features to satisfy particular requirements. In the integrated circuit card context, an ASIC generally refers to chips with special "cells" for functions such as security (exponentiation used in public key cryptography) or communications (radio frequency).

Authentication Routine—A process used to validate a user, card, terminal, or message contents. Also known as a handshake, the authentication uses important data to create a code that is verified in real time or batch mode.

Authorization—The approval or guarantee given by an Issuer to an Acquirer and/or Acceptor to honor a transaction.

Authorization Code—A specific value issued and stored with the transaction data to allow confirmation that a valid authorization occurred.

Automated Clearing House—An organization that handles automated payments, e.g., direct debits, standing-order payments, direct payroll deposits and other electronic credit transfers, and to consolidate provider billings for health care claims across multiple payors.

Cardholder—The person or entity with whom an account relationship (may not be cardholder, see "company card," "holder," and "user") is established and to whom a card is issued.

Card Life Cycle—The stages for a card from initial manufacturing to usage completion and destruction.

Card Read-Writer—Equipment that can electronically read the information on one or many types of cards and modify specific data fields.

Card Supplier—A manufacturer of plastic cards.

Cash Card—*See* Prepayment Card.

Cash Dispenser—A self-service unit that dispenses cash. *See also* Automated Teller Machine.

CEN—Committee for European Normalization.

Charge Card—A payment card that does not provide automatic credit beyond the invoice date (usually monthly).

Chip—A small square of thin, semiconductor material, such as silicon, that has been chemically processed to have a specific set of electrical characteristics such as circuits, storage, and/or logic elements.

Closed Prepaid System—A system where the Issuer and Acquirer of the card are the same party. The card is issued by the party that provides those services that can be accessed by the card.

Contactless Card—An integrated circuit card that enables energy to flow between the card and the interfacing device without the use of contact. Instead, induction or high-frequency transmission techniques are used.

Credit Card—A card that enables the cardholder to make transactions against a credit account established with the Issuer, whereby the Issuer has agreed to make available a specified amount of funds to the cardholder.

Credit Limit—Maximum amount that can be borrowed by a cardholder at any one time on an account.

Data Capture—The electronic recording of information for subsequent use and information processing for clearing payment transactions.

Data Encryption Algorithm—A cryptographic algorithm for encrypting data that is an ANSI standard. The algorithm is a key-driven and reversible process. Also referred to as the Data Encryption Standard (DES).

Debit Card—A card used to make transactions that are linked to the cardholder's direct deposit account.

Decryption—Converting encrypted information back into clear text.

Dedicated Network—A communications facility established for a specific purpose, such as servicing point-of-sale facilities.

Direct Debit—A pre-authorized payment. The payer gives the bank authority to debit the account in accordance with the payee's instructions. Both the date of payment and the amount may be either fixed or variable. In the U.S., the term direct debit often refers to something quite different—the use of debit cards in Electronic Funds Transfer at the Point of Sale (EFTPOS).

EEPROM—Electronically Erasable Programmable Read-Only Memory. A non-volatile memory technology where data can be electronically erased and rewritten.

EFTPOS—Electronic Funds Transfer at the Point-of-Sale. Any payment by a user at an Acceptor that is processed electronically.

Electronic Funds Transfer—A funds transfer that is sent electronically, either by telecommunication or written on magnetic media such as tape, cassette, or disk.

Electronic Purse—An application in a card where value is stored for low-dollar transactions. A card may be dedicated to the purse function or contain memory and programs for other applications.

Electronic Wallet—Generally refers to integrated circuit card or super smart card capable of executing a variety of financial transactions and identification functions. More sophisticated than an electronic purse, a wallet may include debit, credit, cash card, and other functions. Some people carry the analogy to a wallet further and envision a portable device with LCD display keyboard and reader/writer for a variety of cards. By this definition, the electronic wallet is a subset of the personal digital assistant (PDA) category of computer products.

Encryption—The use of cryptographic algorithms to encode clear text data (e.g., PINs) to ensure that the clear text data cannot be learned.

EPROM—Electronically Programmable Read-Only Memory. A non-volatile memory technology that can be written to only once before being erased using ultraviolet light, after which it may be written to again.

Global System Mobile—(GSM) A European Telecommunications Standards Institute (ETSI) standard for portable telephones that employs integrated cards for identification and security.

IC Card—*See* Integrated Circuit Card.

Integrated Circuit Card (ICC)—A card into which one or more integrated circuits are inserted. Includes both memory cards and smart cards.

International Organization for Standardization (ISO)—An international standards-setting body.

ISO 7810—identification cards—Physical characteristics. Specifies the nominal dimensions of identification cards.

ISO 781—Standards for identification cards—Recording technique. Consists of several parts specifying the location of embossing areas as well as magnetic track locations.

ISO 7812—Standards for identification cards—Identification of Issuers—Numbering system. Consists of several parts specifying a numbering system and a registration procedure for card issuer identifiers.

ISO 7813—Standards for identification cards—Financial transaction cards. Specifies the dimensions of financial cards (specific option of 7810) as well as the structure of the data stored in magnetic tracks 1 and 2.

ISO 7816—Standards for identification cards—Integrated circuit(s) cards with contacts. Consists of several parts dealing with the physical dimensions of the cards, the dimensions and the contact's location, the electronic signals and the transmission protocols, the interindustry commands and responses, a numbering system and registration procedure for application identifiers, data for interchange, and, in the future, the Advanced commands as well as the Security architecture.

ISO 9992—Standards for financial transaction cards—Messages between the integrated circuit card and the card-accepting device. Specifies the functions, messages, and data elements as well as the structures of a multi-application financial card built for interchange.

ISO 10202—Standards for financial transaction cards—Security architecture of financial transaction systems using integrated circuit cards. Consists of multiple parts dealing with the card life cycle, the transaction process, cryptographic key relationships, secure application modules, algorithms, and key management.

ISO 10536—Standards for identification cards—Contactless integrated circuit(s) cards. Consists of several parts dealing with the physical dimensions of the cards, the dimensions and location of the coupling areas, and electronic signals for closely coupled contactless cards.

Issuer—The institution identified on the card issued to the cardholder.

K—Kilo, Represents 1,024 units.

Laser Card—*See* Optical Memory Card.

Magnetic Stripe—The magnetic tape on a card that contains the data necessary to complete a transaction.

Magnetic Stripe Card—A card with one or more magnetic stripes.

Memory Card—Integrated circuit card capable of storing information but not having calculating capability, i.e., no microprocessor.

Merchant Service Charge—The fee paid by an Acceptor to an Acquirer for transactions made by a payment card.

Microcircuit Card—*See* Integrated Circuit Card.

Microprocessor—A microcomputer with all of its processing facilities on a single chip. Also called microprocessor-on-a-chip. A microprocessor is a computer processor on a chip including registers and possible cache memory. A microcomputer or microcontroller also has data and program memory on the same chip.

On-line—Direct access to computer-based data files and operations systems via computer terminals.

Open System—A card system that involves multiple issuers of cards that can be used to access services or purchase products at multiple service providers. An open system requires the processing of interchange transactions, usually by an independent "system operator."

Optical Character Recognition (OCR)—Character fonts that are machine-readable by optical techniques.

Optical Memory Card—Also known as laser cards, because a low-intensity laser is used to burn holes of several microns in diameter into a reflective material exposing a substrata of lower reflectivity.

Password Generation—A method of generating a unique one-time password for a computer user based on a challenge-response sequence between a host and a device possessed by the user, e.g., a smart card.

PCMCIA—Personal Computer Memory Card International Association. Association founded to standardize PC cards.

Personal Identification Number (PIN)—A numeric value used to identify users.

Personalization—The process of initializing a card with data that ties it uniquely to a given cardholder and account.

PIN Pad—A keypad for entering PIN values.

Point-of-Sale (POS)—The location at which payment transactions occur for the exchange of value for goods or services.

Point of Service—The time and place of the delivery of a service.

Prepaid Card or Prepayment—A card that is purchased with stored value for which the value is decremented when used.

Primary Account Number (PAN)—The number on the card used to identify the cardholder's account.

Prior Approval—The evaluation of a provider request for specific service by a medical professional to determine the medical necessity and appropriateness of the care requested for an individual.

Prior Authorization—The acceptance of financial liability for services to be rendered by a provider to an individual by the payor. This does not automatically ensure payment.

Private Key—In asymmetric cryptography, the key which is held only by the user for signing and decryption.

Published Key—In asymmetric cryptography, the key which is published by the user to others for their use in verifying signatures and encrypting messages.

Radio-Frequency ID—A class of methods for transmitting information from a card without physical contact between card and reader.

Random Access Memory (RAM)—A volatile memory used in integrated circuit cards that requires power to maintain data.

Read-Only Memory (ROM)—Non-volatile memory that is written once, usually during card production. It is used to store operating systems and algorithms employed by the microprocessor in an integrated circuit card during transactions.

RSA—A public key cryptography algorithm developed by mathematicians Rivest, Shamir, and Adelman of MIT. *See also* Public Key Cryptography and Encryption.

Standard—A voluntary agreement to a uniform and consistent methodology and/or specification to achieve a common action or result.

Stored Value Card—*See* Prepayment Card.

Super Smart Card—A card-shaped device that has an on-board keypad, LCDs, and batteries, as well as one or more integrated circuit chips capable of storing and processing data.

Telephone Card—A card issued by a telephone company for the payment of telephone calls. This card may be a prepaid card, a credit card, or one that adds the cost of the call to the standard telephone bill.

Track 1 (T1)—An ISO-defined read-only track on the magnetic stripe that has high density and may contain alphanumeric characters.

Track 2 (T2)—An ISO-defined read-only track on the magnetic stripe that has low density and may contain only numeric characters.

Track 3 (T3)—An ISO-defined track on the magnetic stripe that has high density, may contain only alphanumeric characters, and allows rewriting of certain data elements contained in the track.

Transaction—A business or payment event for the exchange of value for goods or services.

Universal Product Code (UPC)—A bar-code used for product identification. The code is sensed by laser/optical scanners (UPC).

Videotext—A remote television service operating with a telephone line-distributed bit stream that is converted to graphic display frame(s) at the TV set. Remote input is communicated through the telephone line.

Bibliography

Advanced Card and Identification Sourcebook, Warfel & Miller Inc. 1993.

Applications of Computer Card Technology, U.S. Department of Labor. 1990.

Begley, Thomas M., and David P. Boyd, "Psychological Characteristics Associated with Entrepreneurial Performance," *Journal of Business Venturing*. Vol. 2, No. 1 (Winter 1987): 79.

Block, Zenas and P.N. Subba Narishima, "Corporate Venturing: Alternatives, Obstacles Encounters, and Experience Effects," *Journal of Business Venturing*. Vol. 1. No. 2 (Spring 1986): 177.

Birley, Sue, "New Ventures and Employment Growth," Journal of Business Venturing. Vol. 2, No. 2 (Spring 1987): 155.

Bruno, Albert V., Joel K. Leidecker, and Joseph W. Harder, "Patterns of Failure among Silicon Valley High Technology Firms," in Ronstadt et al., *Frontiers of Entrepreneurship Research*. 1986.

CardTech/SurTech Conference Proceedings, CardTech/SurTech Inc. 1993.

CardTech/SurTech Conference Proceedings, CardTech/SurTech Inc. 1994.

CardTech/SurTech Conference Proceedings, CardTech/SurTech Inc. 1995.

Credit Cards: Business Implications for the 70's. Business Communications Corp. July 1973.

Crowner, Robert. Developing a Strategic Business Plan. Irwin 1994.

Dennis, Sylvia. "Europay International pushes smart card 'standard," *Newsbytes*. June 21, 1994. p. NEW0610027.

Dunkelberg,William C. and Carolyn Woo, "Survival and Failure: A Longitudinal Study," Babson Entrepreneurship Research Conference, Calgary. 1988.

Drucker, Peter F., *Innovation and Entrepreneurship*. Harper & Row. 1985.

Duchesneau, Donald A., and William B. Gartner, "A Profile of New Venture Success and Failure in an Emerging Industry,"Babson Entrepreneurial Research Conference, Calgary. 1988.

Electronic News, "MasterCard bares timeline for 'Smart Card' platform." July 25, 1994. p. 82.

Ernst and Young, *Business Planning Guide*. John Wiley & Sons. 1987.

Ernst and Young, *Guide to Raising Capital*. John Wiley & Sons. 1992.

Future of Prepayment on Cards: Market, Technologies and Opportunities. Retail Banking Research Ltd. July 1994.

Gartner, William B., "Problems in Business Startups," in Hornaday et al., *Frontiers of Entrepreneurship Research*. 1984.

Gorman, Michael, and William A. Schulman, "What do Venture Capitalists Do?" in Ronstadt et al., *Frontiers in Entrepreneurial Research*. 1986.

La Plante, Alice., "Citibank's Smart Move," *Information Week*, September 12, 1994. p. 42.

Los Angeles Times,"Tiny 'smart cards' our wallets of the future?." September 19, 1994. p. D4.

MasterCard internal document,"Chip Card—The Competitive Edge—A Background Document."

Memory Card Issues: Activities & Opportunities. Conference Proceedings. Battelle Columbus Laboratories. 1985.

Pinchot, Gifford, III, *Intrapreneuring*. New York: Harper & Row. 1985.

Porter, Michael E., *Competitive Strategy*. New York: Macmillan. 1980.

Prepayment Cards. The Electronic Purse Becomes Big Business. Peter Harrop. Financial Times Business Information. 1991.

Roberts, Edward B., "How to Succeed in a New Technology Enterprise," *Technology Review*. Vol. 73, No. 2 (December 1970): 25.

Schilit, Keith. *Business Plan and Raising Venture Capital*. Prentice Hall. 1994.

Smart Cards: New Bank Cards. By Jerome Svigals. Macmillan Publishing Company. 1993.

Tarrazo, Manual. *B12 Plan-Writing a Winning Business Plan*. Southwestern Publishing. 1994.

Timmons, Jeffrey. *New Venture Creation*. Irwin. 1990.

Vesper, Karl. *New Venture Mechanics*. Prentice Hall. 1993.

Vesper, Karl. *New Venture Strategies*. Prentice Hall. 1994.

VISA Documents—Learning change. 1995.

VISA Future and news release. 1995.

White, Richard, Jr., *The Entrepreneur's Manual*. Radnor, Pa.: Chilton. 1977.

Index